Book of the Explanation of the Symbols
Kitāb Ḥall ar-Rumūz

by

Muḥammad Ibn Umail

Psychological Commentary
by Marie-Louise von Franz

Corpus Alchemicum Arabicum

Volume I A

(CALA I A)

Edited by Theodor Abt and Wilferd Madelung

Living Human Heritage Publications, Zurich

Studies from the

Research and Training Centre
for Depth Psychology
According to C. G. Jung and Marie-Louise von Franz

Book of the Explanation of the Symbols
Kitāb Ḥall ar-Rumūz

by

Muḥammad Ibn Umail

Psychological Commentary
by Marie-Louise von Franz

Edited by Theodor Abt

LIVING HUMAN HERITAGE PUBLICATIONS, ZURICH
2006

The Arabic transcription follows the German standard
which is more precise than the English one.

First edition 2006
Living Human Heritage Publications
Münsterhof 16, 8001 Zurich, Switzerland
info@livinghumanheritage.org
www.livinghumanheritage.org

ISBN-10 3-9522608-3-5
ISBN-13 978-3-9522608-3-8
EAN 9783952260838

Layout: Ediz Çalışkan, Tuğba Ünlü and Theodor Abt

Printing and Binding:
Mas Matbaacilik A.Ş. İstanbul

Contents

Foreword by the Editor 7

Foreword by Marie-Louise von Franz 11

Part I: Introduction

1. The Religious Eros in the Arab Culture 15
2. The Loss of the Dimension of Divine Matter 29
3. The Transition of Alchemy into the Western World 31
4. A Modern View of Eros 39
5. The Life and Work of Muḥammad ibn Umail 49

Part II: Commentary on the *Ḥall ar-Rumūz*

1. General Reflections 59
2. Text and Commentary 61

Part III: Ending of Manuscript G, not written by Ibn Umail

1. Introduction by the Editor 145
2. Text and Commentary 147

Part IV: Apparatus

1. Bibliography 189
2. General Index 197
3. Glossary 239
4. Diacritical Signs 241

Foreword by the Editor

Alchemy was not just the forerunner of chemistry but also the root of modern depth psychology. It was C. G. Jung (1875–1961) who recognized in the symbolism of alchemy an expression of an inner psychic transformation which he and later psychologists had observed in their studies of dreams and fantasies. In the different descriptions of the alchemical process Jung saw a symbolic manifestation of the gradual differentiation and unification of the personality of the alchemist, something which he called the *process of individuation.* These intensive studies of alchemy gave his transpersonal psychology a foundation in history, showing that his suggested ways of attending to psychic development correspond to an experience that had been described centuries before.

To support his research in alchemy, he asked the young philologist Dr. Marie-Louise von Franz (1915-1998) to translate Latin and Greek alchemical texts that she considered important for his research. Among these texts was the *Aurora Consurgens*, an alchemical work attributed to Thomas Aquinas. Jung asked her to edit this text on the basis of the different manuscripts found in European libraries. Later, he suggested that she should write a psychological commentary of the text. Her edition and commentary appeared in 1957 in German, as Volume III of C. G. Jung's *Mysterium Coniunctionis*, which was published in 1956.

Muḥammad ibn Umail—called Senior in Latin alchemy—is by far the most frequently quoted authority in this text. The quotes come from a work that circulated in Europe under the short title *Tabula Chemica.* In the course of her work on the *Aurora Consurgens* M.-L. von Franz came across the Arabic original of the *Tabula Chemica*, called *al-Māʾ al-waraqī wa-l-arḍ an-naǧmīya* (Book of the Silvery Water and the Starry Earth). This book is an extensive commentary by Ibn Umail on his own alchemical poem, *Risālat aš-šams ilā al-hilāl* (Epistle of the Sun to the Crescent Moon). The commentary and poem were partly translated into Latin, in this way reaching Western culture. The Arabic text was edited in 1933 and published in Calcutta by M. Turāb ʿAlī, H. E. Stapleton, and M. Hidāyat Ḥusain, but only the introduction was translated into English.

Al-Mā' al-waraqī is considered to be one of the most explicit sources for the spiritual dimension of Arabic alchemy, as can be seen from the many quotes in the *Aurora Consurgens*. Ibn Umail represents the non-chemistry oriented alchemy, the reason why he has received little attention from historians of alchemy. However, he speaks in his texts—as he repeatedly emphasises—of symbols and not of specific substances. In spite of these clear statements most historians of alchemy continue to consider these symbols as cover names (*Decknamen*) for substances. The denial of the existence of symbols can be seen as reflecting a general attitude of a one-sided rational thinking, comparable to that of Sigmund Freud, who also tried to reduce the symbols of the unconscious to nothing but covers or signs of something quite defined and graspable.

In her later years Marie-Louise von Franz wanted to enlarge the base of the sources of Arabic alchemy in order better to understand the psychological insights of those introverted lovers of the soul. Because of her studies on the *Aurora Consurgens*, the texts of Muḥammad ibn Umail were of special interest to her. She encouraged me to do primary research on the texts of this author, because, until our publication of the *Ḥall ar-Rumūz* (The Explanation of the Symbols, CALA I), we had no English translation of his texts.

The basis of the following commentary of Marie-Louise von Franz on the *Ḥall ar-Rumūz* was a rough translation of one single manuscript of this text from the Āṣafīya Library in Hyderabad (India). It was realized as a first draft in 1987/88 by Salwa Fuad and the editor, two non-professionals in the field of the history of alchemy. As the health of Dr von Franz was deteriorating, she had to write her commentary on the basis of this first draft. It was, however, her wish to have the edition of this text done according to scientific standards and thus she encouraged intensive additional research.

The search for other manuscripts of the same text, the translation of other alchemical texts of Muḥammad ibn Umail as well as of Arabic alchemical manuscripts from authors quoted in the *Ḥall ar-Rumūz,* was necessary to become better acquainted with the way Ibn Umail was thinking. It allowed for a better translation, step by step. In 1994 and 1998 two further manuscripts for the *Ḥall ar-Rumūz* could be obtained. This cleared up translation problems which we had encountered in the first manuscript. The studies of the literature, and direct contacts with experts in the field further contributed to a better understanding. This led to many changes in the translation of the basic text. After the passing away of Marie-Louise von Franz in 1998 a fourth manuscript was obtained from the Soltan-Ali Soltani collection in Fars (Iran). This manuscript contained the most revealing introduction to the *Ḥall ar-Rumūz,* missing in all the other manuscripts. The collation of the four texts was kindly done by Prof. Dr Wilferd Madelung, Professor Emeritus at the University of Oxford. He also reviewed the translation of Salwa Fuad and the editor.

The result of this work is presented here. After the general introduction of Marie-Louise von Franz, presented in Part I, follows in Part II the first translation in black colour with parts to be corrected or to be omitted given in cyan blue. This was the text, available to Marie-Louise von Franz. The corrections that come from the new translation (published in CALA I) are given to the right of the original translation in green. This will allow the reader to see on what text the interpretation of M.-L. von Franz was based. Due to the insufficient translation she, for instance, could not see the symbolism of lead-copper or of the vapour and the smoke which plays such an important role for Ibn Umail. Only after further translation of texts written by Ibn Umail and of those texts that were for him a source of inspiration, did it become evident what he meant by these symbols. The fact that Marie-Louise von Franz could, in spite of this handicap and her bad health, write her commentary is quite astounding. The later research in other texts written by Ibn Umail and the translation of texts he quotes show clearly that her basic thoughts are all to the point and now allow deeper research into this field of Arabic alchemy. First results will be presented in the volume I B of the *Corpus Alchemicum Arabicum* (CALA I B). The commentary of M.-L. von Franz makes visible that the *Ḥall ar-Rumūz* is a key-text for a better understanding of the religious dimension of symbolic Arabic alchemy.

The commentary of M.-L. von Franz includes in Part III the ending of the manuscript obtained from the library of Hyderabad (Ms G) which we have hitherto not found in any other manuscript. Thus only ameliorations of the translation of this one single manuscript can be given. This Part III turned out to be a later text not written by Ibn Umail for reasons given on page 145 of this book.

The severe illness of Marie-Louise von Franz prevented her from supervising the edition of her book. Thus she handed its copyright to me, together with the request to improve the translation and edit the interpretation. In order to prevent any distortion of the meaning of her words, the language of M.-L. von Franz has been left in this edition practically unchanged. Necessary additions or remarks by the editor in the main text or in the footnotes are marked in green.

As the preparation of a proper text-edition of the *Ḥall ar-Rumūz* as well as the collection and translation of other texts of Ibn Umail and his quoted sources took its time, especially due to my other obligations in teaching and research, I agreed in 1999 that an early print of Marie-Louise von Franz's commentary could be published. It was strictly meant for private use only for those who wanted to have earlier access to her text. Monika Malamud had the kindness to take over the great work of preparing and realizing this private edition at a time when I was frequently abroad. Thinking of the reader she changed at certain places the original translation and replaced our original text by later improvements of the translation that I made accessible to her. But these changes were not available to M.-L. von Franz at the time of her interpretation. For the private edition it was meant to facilitate the reading of Ibn Umail's text, but for the present edition it is necessary to print exactly the translation which was available to Marie-Louise von Franz. Otherwise it would be not understandable why her commentary in the private edition is sometimes not congruent with the text of Ibn Umail. The strict forbidding of the right to quote from this private edition has, hopefully, prevented the proliferation of incorrect statements and/or criticism of the text of Marie-Louie von Franz.

The *Corpus Alchemicum Arabicum* has thus begun with Ibn Umail. Following as CALA II will be the *Muṣḥaf aṣ-ṣuwar* of Zosimos. A new edition of *al-Māʾ al-waraqī wa-l-arḍ an-naǧmīya*, a first edition of *ad-Durra an-naqīya* and *al-Qaṣīda al-mīmīya* all written by of Ibn Umail, and the *Mafātīḥ aṣ-ṣanʿa of Zosimos* have been prepared for publication soon.

A most cordial thank you goes to Prof. Dr Wilferd Madelung for the collation of the text and the co-edition of CALA, and to Prof. Dr Fuat Sezgin, Frankfurt, for crucial support of the series from the very beginning in 1988. Furthermore I express my gratitude, for logistical help during all these years, to the Swiss Institute for Archaeological and Architectural Research of Ancient Egypt in Cairo (Director Dr H. Jaritz, since 2003 Dr C. von Pilgrim). I also thank Monica Malamud for her support, Sabine Mayer-Patzel for patient background support, Dr Nikola Patzel for help as well as Frith Luton and Dr Peter Starr for corrections and ameliorations. Last but not least, this publication would not have become possible without the support of Mehmet Bora Akgül, Ufuk Şahin, Ediz Çalışkan, Tuğba Ünlü and Ufuk N. Şahin from MAS Matbaacılık A. Ş. in Istanbul.

An especial thank you for financial support goes to the Marie-Louise von Franz Foundation and the Foundation of the Research and Training Centre for Depth Psychology according to C. G. Jung and Marie-Louise von Franz in Zurich.

Istanbul, December 2005 Theodor Abt

Foreword by Marie-Louise von Franz

The history of this publication reads like a fiction story. When I lectured on alchemy in the late 1960s at the Jung Institute in Zurich, I expressed my anger that I could not get an answer from the Hyderabad Library (India) where Stapleton indicates that they have many manuscripts of Ibn Umail. Even C. G. Jung could not get an answer. A student, Dr Abt, picked up the thread and offered to go to Hyderabad. With the help of various personalities and thanks to remarkable synchronicities he could get hold of a crop of photocopies of these manuscripts. Then came the difficult task of translation because the translator had not only to know tenth century Arabic, but also to be familiar with alchemical thinking. Finally, Dr Abt succeeded in finding in Cairo, in the person of Mrs Salwa Fuad, an adequate translator of the language, and having himself learned Arabic, Dr Abt provided the alchemical choice of word. This enterprise grew and Dr Abt is now in the possession of a valuable collection of Arabic alchemical manuscripts, which we intend to publish. A look at their content shows that they constitute the missing link within the mystical branch of alchemy, between the Gnostic-Hermetic Greek alchemy and that of the mystical Latin alchemy in Europe. Up till today the text *De Chemia* of Senior—as Muḥammad ibn Umail was called in the Latin translation—was practically the only relevant writing concerning this period of time. The invaluable finding of Gnostic manuscripts in Nag Hammadi has opened up new vistas onto the tradition of Gnosticism and Hermetism and now a new world also opens up onto the whole of mystical alchemy in this period.

A rational scorn against this part of alchemy, which was useless for the history of chemistry, had blocked the view till today. It is C. G. Jung's unique merit to have shown the invaluable treasures of insight which lay hidden in this material. Hitherto, only some esoteric societies knew something about it, but their viewpoint was lacking a connection with the empirical reality of the psyche and was, and still is, in danger of drowning in historical associations.

The text of the *Ḥall ar-Rumūz* with my commentary is only an hors d'oeuvre for the meal to come. We decided to call the whole text-collection *Corpus Alchemicum Arabicum* (CALA).

I want to express my deepest gratitude to Professor Theodor Abt for his bold enterprise and incessant devotion to the task. My thanks also go to Mrs Salwa Fuad for deciphering the nearly unintelligible text. My greatest gratitude goes to Dr Barbara Davies who has been my right hand and who has helped me to realize this work and never forsook me during all my fits of despair. I also want to thank Dr Alfred Ribi and Dr René Malamud for valuable bibliographical suggestions.

Küsnacht, Summer 1997 Marie-Louise von Franz

Part I

Introduction

1. The Religious Eros in the Arab Culture

1 Muḥammad ibn Umail is known in Western alchemy under the Latin name Senior. Until now he has received only minor attention from historians of chemistry who found his works useful for dating the history of chemistry.[1] The content however of his writings has received very little attention because the chemists saw it as only allegorical, in other words as non-sense.[2]

2 It is the unique merit of C. G. Jung to have shown that alchemy in its origins was not only the beginning of chemistry but was also a kind of religious yoga and that we also find in it the prehistory of modern depth psychology.[3] The symbolic content of alchemy[4] originated in fantasy processes which the alchemists experienced while they were staring at the chemicals cooking in their retort. Today we recognize in these fantasies projections which have only very little to do with what we know of chemistry, but which reappear in the dreams and visions of people who turn their attention to their own unconscious. In *Psychology and Alchemy*[5] Jung has published the dreams of a modern theoretical physicist, which contain a large amount of

1 H. E. Stapleton, *Three Arabic Treatises by Muḥammad ibn Umail*, in: Memoirs of the Asiatic Society of Bengal, Vol. XII (1933) No. 1, p. 117 ff. See also F. Sezgin, *Geschichte des arabischen Schrifttums*, Vol. IV, p. 283 ff. and M. Ullmann, *Die Natur- und Geheimwissenschaften im Islam*, p. 217–220.

2 Especially Julius Ruska contributed to this prejudice in *Studien zu Muḥammad ibn Umail at-Tamīmī's Kitāb al-Māʾ al-waraqī wa'l-Arḍ an-Najmīyah*, Isis, Vol. 24 (1935–1936), p. 310 ff.

3 See C. G. Jung, *Lectures given at the ETH* and M.-L. von Franz, *Alchemy, An Introduction to the Symbolism and the Psychology,* p. 15, p. 21. (Some historians of chemistry assume a third aspect of alchemy: the philosophy of nature. See for that J. Weyer, *Einführung in die arabische Chemie und Alchemie*).

4 See C. G. Jung, *Psychology and Alchemy* [Coll. Works 12], § 342 ff.

5 Ibid. § 52 ff.

alchemical motifs. The dreamer was deeply preoccupied with the mystery of nuclear matter and his unconscious brought up as a reaction to his conscious preoccupation a wealth of archetypal images, which resemble closely those we find in old alchemical manuscripts. Therefore we can conclude that many alchemical symbols were *projections* of unconscious fantasies. By definition a projection is the perception of an inner psychic fact in an outer object. For the reader who cannot imagine how that process of projection works I recommend reading S. Mahdihassan's book *Indian Alchemy or Rasayana*.[6] The author still 'believes' in alchemy and with it that certain substances have a soul. Between the soul of the alchemists and the soul of matter there is a kind of *participation mystique* and the possibility of magic interaction. That is why the soul of incorruptible gold can impart immortality to the soul of the alchemist, or the soul of the alchemist can transform matter by finding the right creative attitude. It is only in the light of what we know today about matter that we can call Mahdihassan's assertions a projection. A great amount of alchemical symbols cannot be seen any longer in material processes but they can be found within us. *The non-chemical, symbolic content of alchemy is thus of eminent importance for the history of depth psychology.*

3 Many alchemists practised a form of meditation, which, as mentioned before, resembles the Indian yoga. It is a procedure in which the ego tries to deal with the deeper psychosomatic layers of the human psyche, which we now call the collective unconscious. Jung has independently rediscovered a similar method, which he called active imagination.[7] This is a disciplined creative use of imagination, which has nothing to do with fantasizing. One focuses on a fragment of a fantasy till it becomes completely real and then one has a confrontation with it and goes along with how it develops. Thus a consistent process is called forth which leads to the realization of the innermost kernel of the personality. Whilst the Indian and Chinese Taoist yoga localized the contents of their imagination in the sphere of the body (more accurately in the subtle body within their body), the Western alchemists saw the same processes happening in the outer chemical retort. Alchemy therefore was, as I want to repeat, *the* Western way of dealing with what we call today the collective unconscious or the objective psyche.

4 As I have tried to show elsewhere,[8] one essential root of Western alchemy is the Egyptian embalming ritual and its connections with the Isis

6 S. Mahdihassan, *Indian Alchemy or Rasayana.*

7 See C. G. Jung, *Memories, Dreams, Reflections*, chapter on «Confrontation with the Unconscious», p. 170 ff. See also C. G. Jung, *The Visions of Zosimos* [Coll. Works 13], § 86, n. 10, *Paracelsus as a Spiritual Phenomenon* [Coll. Works 13], § 201, § 208, and *The Secret of the Golden Flower* [Coll. Works 13], § 36.

8 M.-L. von Franz, *On Dreams and Death*, p. 86.

mysteries. The embalming process included a bathing of the corpse in soda-lye. The word 'natron' comes from the Egyptian word *nṯr* which means god. By soaking the corpse in god-liquid it was so to speak deified and immortalized. Step by step the corpse was transformed into a shape of 'eternal' matter. This immortalization was simultaneously a complete regeneration of the dead personality: a rebirth not out of the womb of a woman, but out of Nun, the primordial waters of the universe. After having been dissolved completely and even having partly been dissected, like Osiris, the dead person resurrects from the depth of nature. First this process of death and resurrection concerned only the renewal of the king, who represented the Sungod. But in later times this process of immortalization applied to everybody.

As far as I can judge, the archetypal motif of the immortalization of 5
the king was *the* original basic theme of Western alchemy. The second basic theme was that of the *coniunctio* and in a mystical way the two are connected in the theme of the *unio mystica* between man, God, and nature.

The most important Western author who, up till today, has allowed 6
us to understand the alchemical process as an inner mystical experience is Zosimos of Panopolis (today Akhmim in Upper Egypt). He explicitly mentions that the process must be accompanied by a specific form of meditation, which has a decisive influence on the chemical process. Zosimos belonged to the Gnostic-Hermetic sect which worshipped the God-man figure Poimandres.[9] The latter is a symbol of the divine man, the Anthropos of light, who fell into matter and has to be redeemed from there by the adept. Simultaneously, this man of light is something like the cosmic *nous*. I must refer the reader to the whole explanation which Jung devoted to this figure in his work *Psychology and Alchemy*: We find the God-man in unmistakable association with the priestly art (*hieratiche techne*). I give the relevant passages in a literal translation:[10]

7: «... If you have meditated and lived in human community, you will see that the Son of God has become all things, for the sake of devout souls: in order to draw the soul forth from the dominion of Heimarmene

9 See R. Reitzenstein, *Poimandres*; this basic work on the Anthropos Gnosis in antiquity has been disputed on many points concerning the origins of the Anthropos motif. Reitzenstein is certainly wrong in postulating an exclusive Iranian origin of the motif, but his general view of Hellenistic Gnosticism and Hermetism is in my view still valid.

10 C. G. Jung, *Psychology and Alchemy* [Coll. Works 12], § 456. Jung used the text published by M. Berthelot, *Collection des Alchemistes Grecs*, 'Sur les appareils et fourneaux. Commentaires authentiques sur la lettre Omega', III, XLIX, 4–12. See now the new edition of M. Mertens, *Les Alchemistes grecs*, IV. 1, Zosime de Panopolis (Paris, 1995). Paragraph numbers follow the new edition, p. 4 ff.

(destiny, in German: Gestirnszwang) into the [realm of the] incorporeal; behold how he has become all—God, angel, and man capable of suffering. For having power in all, he can become all as he wills; and he obeys the Father inasmuch as he penetrates all bodies and illuminates the mind of each soul, spurring it on to follow him up to the blessed region where he was before the beginning of bodily things, yearning and led by him into the light.

8: And consider the tablet which Bitos also wrote, and the thrice-great Plato and the infinitely great Hermes, saying that the first man is designated with the first hieratic word 'Thot', who is the interpreter of all things. The Chaldeans, Parthians, Medes, and Hebrews call him Adam, which is, being interpreted, virgin earth, blood-red (or bloody) earth, fiery or carnal earth. This is to be found in the libraries of the Ptolemies. They put it in every sanctuary, and especially in the Serapeum, at the time when Asenas approached the High Priest of Jerusalem, who sent Hermes, who translated the whole of the Hebrew into Greek and Egyptian.

9: So the first man is called by us Thot and by them Adam, which is a name in the language of the angels; but with reference to his body they named him symbolically after the four elements of the whole heavenly sphere. For his letter A stands for ascent [*anatole*: the East] or the air; D for descent [*dysis*: the West] [...] because it [the earth] is heavy; A for arctic [*arktos*: the North]; and M for meridian [*mesembria*: the South], the midmost of these bodies, the fire that burns in the midst of the fourth region.

10: Thus the bodily Adam according to his outward and visible form is called Thot, but the spiritual man in him has a proper name as well as the name by which he is called. His proper name as yet I know not: for Nikotheus alone knows this, and he is not to be found. But his common name is Man (*anthropos*) which is light (*phos*); wherefore it came that men are called mortals (*photes*).

11: Now when the Man of Light abode in Paradise, where blew the breath of Heimarmene, they [the elements] persuaded him, who was without evil and free from their activity, to put on the accompanying Adam wrought of the four elements of Heimarmene. And he in his innocence did not turn aside; but they boasted that he was their slave.

12: [Wherefore] Hesiod called the outer man the bond with which Zeus bound Prometheus. After this fetter Zeus sent him yet another: Pandora, whom the Hebrews call Eve. For, according to the words of the allegory, Prometheus and Epimetheus are but one man, namely soul and body. And sometimes he bears the likeness of the soul, sometimes that of the spirit, and sometimes the likeness of the flesh, because of the disobedience of Epimetheus, who heeded not the counsel of Prometheus, his own mind. For our mind says: "The Son of God, having power in all things and becoming all things as he wills, appears as he wills to each.

13: Jesus Christ made himself one with Adam and bore him up to that place where the Men of Light dwelt before." He appeared to the very feeble as a man capable of suffering and like one scourged. And after he had privily stolen away the Men of Light that were his own, he made known that in truth he did not really suffer, and that death was trampled down and cast out. And to this day and to the end of the world he is present in many places, both secretly and openly consorting with his own, counselling them secretly, yet through their own minds, to suffer confusion with their accompanying Adam that he may be beaten away from them and slain, this blind chatterer who is envious of the spiritual Man of Light. [So] they kill their Adam.

14: And these things are so until the coming of the daemon Antimimos, the jealous one, who seeks to lead them astray as before, declaring that he is the Son of God, although he is formless in both body and soul. But they, having become wiser since the true Son of God has taken possession of them, deliver up to him their own Adam to be put to death, and bring their shining spirits safely back to the place where they were before the beginning of the world. Yet before Antimimos, the jealous one, does this, he sends his forerunner from Persia, who circulates false fables and leads men astray through the power of Heimarmene. The letters of his name are nine, if you keep the diphthong, corresponding to the pattern [i.e. the nine letters] of the Heimarmene. Later, at the end of about seven periods, he will appear in his own shape.

15: And only the Hebrews and the sacred books of Hermes [tell of] these things concerning the Man of Light and his guide the Son of God, and concerning the earthly Adam and his guide Antimimos, who blasphemously calls himself the Son of God to lead men astray.

16: But the Greeks call the earthly Adam Epimetheus, who was counselled by his own mind, his brother, not to accept the gifts of Zeus. Yet, inasmuch as he erred and afterwards repented, seeking the abode of bliss, he makes everything plain and fully advises them that have spiritual hearing. But those that have only bodily hearing are slaves of Heimarmene, for they neither understand nor admit anything else.

17: And all who meet with success in the matter of colourings at the propitious moment, consider nothing but the great book about furnaces, for they do not esteem the art; nor do they understand the poet when he says: "But the gods have not given to men equally." Neither do they observe and see the manner of men's lives: how, even in the same art, men may reach the goal in different ways and practise the same art in different ways, according to their different characters and the constellations of the stars in the exercise of the same art; how one worker is inactive, another alone, one blasphemously desiring too much, another too timid and therefore without progress—this is so in all the arts—and how those who practise the same art use different implements and procedures, having also different attitudes to the spiritual conception of it and its practical realization.

18: And this is more to be considered in the sacred art than in all the other arts. … »[11]

7 In his comment to this Zosimos text, Jung stresses that this God-man figure is more Gnostic than Christian and resembles the Iranian Gayomart, but like in later Christian alchemy this God-man figure is a sort of paradigm of sublimation, i.e. of the freeing of the soul from the grip of the astrological powers. He also is identical with Adam and has a quaternarian structure like the philosophers' stone in the whole of alchemy.

8 Zosimos uses for the chemical process of transformation the word *taricheia*, which means embalming. He makes it therefore explicit that what he describes in his treatise *Peri Aretes*[12] is what happens psychologically during the embalming of the corpse of Osiris until he resurrects. In his treatise, however, Zosimos tells us what happens in the form of several dream visions. C. G. Jung has interpreted these visions extensively and has shown that they refer to an inner psychic process of transformation, which we now call the process of individuation.[13] It is a process by which one becomes aware of and learns to relate to an inner core of one's psyche, which corresponds to the God-image of all religions. This inner figure is first buried in the unconscious and only when the individual relates to it and works on it does it become a positive inner *psychopompos*. In the vision of Zosimos, human beings are tortured by a priest figure who is also himself dismembered until he becomes the 'man of gold' which is the name for the Anthropos or the inner God-man (Osiris) in every individual. It is as if during the embalming process the human side of the dead person and its divine core are simultaneously and mutually tortured in order to produce the immortal inner personality, i.e. the philosophers' stone. The embalming process, which until now we knew only from its outer manipulations,[14] is revealed by Zosimos to be simultaneously an inner process which not only takes place in the dead person but also took place within the psyche of the living alchemist when he worked on the philosophers' stone. The search for immortality is *the* central theme of alchemy, its oldest roots,

11 For further details and references see Jung's extensive notes. Ibid. § 456.

12 *Sur la Vertu*, M. Berthelot (ed.), *Alch. Grecs*, III, I.

13 C. G. Jung, *The Visions of Zosimos* [Coll. Works 13], § 85 ff.

14 See G. Roeder, *Urkunden zur Religion des Alten Aegyptens*, p. 297 ff.

but gradually the theme of love mysticism also became predominant, in the East through Tantra yoga and in the West through the symbolism by which the adept unites with his female helper. The most famous Western couple of this kind are Zosimos and Theosebeia. Ibn Umail seems to have been especially interested in the coniunctio motif. These archetypal themes of love and death were the great motivations for man to extend this search into the realm of body and matter.

In October 1938 Jung began a series of lectures at the ETH Zurich 9
on Indian yoga exercises and especially Tantra yoga texts and their parallelism in Western alchemy.[15] He was able to show that the parallelism is especially close between Tantra yoga and alchemy.[16] The parallelism is underlined by the fact that only in Western alchemy and in Tantra yoga women played a role.[17] In using a medieval Buddhist Tantra yoga text called *Shri-Chakra-Sambhara Tantra*, Jung shows step by step the parallels between this Indian form of meditation and our medieval alchemical imagery, which the latter evoked by a technique that the alchemists called *imaginatio vera*. This true imagination is not mere fantasizing, but is a true use of the imagination, which, according to the alchemist, acquires something of the way by which God imagines the world and therefore has a supernatural magic effect on matter.[18] Mircea Eliade has since then corroborated these findings of Jung.[19] He writes: «All these legends and all these references to the symbiosis tantrism-alchemy leave no doubt of the soteriological function of alchemical operations. We have here no prechemistry, no science in embryo, but a spiritual technique, which, while operating on 'matter', sought first of all to 'perfect the spirit', to bring about deliverance and autonomy. If we set aside the folklore that proliferated around the alchemists (as around all 'magicians') we shall understand the correspondence between the alchemist working on 'vulgar' metals to transmute them into 'gold' and the yogi working on himself to the end of 'extracting' from his dark, enslaved psycho-mental life the free and autonomous spirit, which shares in the same essence as gold.»[20]

15 See C. G. Jung, *Lectures given at the ETH 1938/39*, p. 11 ff.

16 C. G. Jung, Ibid., p. 107 ff., S. Mahdihassan in his *Indian Alchemy or Rasayana* completely underestimates this fact because he despises Tantra yoga as 'mere sexual gymnastics', but Tantra yoga is concerned with the mysteries of the chthonic spirit in sexuality. A good example of a Tantric text can be found in: *Das Tantra der verborgenen Vereinigung*, P. Gäng (ed.).

17 *Das Tantra der verborgenen Vereinigung*, ibid., p. 60, p. 110.

18 See C. G. Jung, *Lectures given at the ETH 1938/39*, p. 11 ff., p. 107 ff.; for the parallelism of symbols cf. ibid., p. 112 ff.

19 M. Eliade, *Yoga, Immortality and Freedom*, p. 278 ff.

20 M. Eliade, ibid., p. 281.

10 Beyond that, Jung went on to show that the alchemical symbolism contains a lot of erotic fantasies which modern man experiences no longer as a quality of matter but in the real woman. The unconscious in a man has feminine qualities, which Jung termed the anima. Jung writes: «The medieval philosophers projected the part of the psyche which we project into real women, into the *materia*. The word *materia* comes from *mater* and the feminine symbol, the anima, is first projected into the mother, from whom it can quite naturally extend into the *materia*. We see the same process in the East, for the word *māyā*, building material, is also related to *mater*. We think of *māyā* as illusion, deception, but it is also building material, illusion which becomes real. So Tantric philosophy even calls matter the distinctness of divine thought. The East starts inside and works outwards into outer reality; we begin, on the contrary, with outward reality and never ask ourselves about the inner processes from which material tangible objects spring. The alchemists insisted on the importance of matter, and they were in a certain way right in this, because the psyche *is* projected. Matter was *the* unknown thing to them so their psyche was projected into matter and they sought for it there. Affinity and sublimation, for instance, as chemical terms are concepts which express man's psychological experience. We also experience affinity and sublimation, but the latter is really more a moral concept. We understand it like that and give it that name; nothing is sublime or low in itself. We call a snake a poisonous reptile, for instance, but it does not know it is poisonous; it merely acts according to its nature. So when solid or liquid were changed into steam, into volatile substances, in the retort, the alchemists said they were sublimated, and we find the same term used now in psychology. If we regard alchemy rationally, it seems complete nonsense, but it is exceedingly meaningful psychologically, the whole riddle or secret of the human psyche is to be found in it. In turning their love and devotion to matter the alchemists returned to the mother, the first carrier of the feminine unconscious. This is why the incest motif occurs so frequently, incest between parent and child or brother and sister, this incest being really the coniunctio between the conscious and the unconscious.»[21]

11 Jung's most outstanding observation that especially Tantra yoga resembles alchemy has since been corroborated by new facts: a Zosimos text has been discovered by Fuat Sezgin which contains pictures of the coniunctio of king and queen, sun and moon.[22] The illustrations of this

21 C. G. Jung, *Lectures given at the ETH 1938/39*, p. 116 f.

22 Zosimos, *Muṣḥaf aṣ-ṣuwar*, see F. Sezgin, *Geschichte des arabischen Schrifttums*, Vol. IV, p. 75 ff. This book will be published as CALA II.

manuscript display Tantric influences. Tantra yoga thus seems to have influenced the Arabic versions of the coniunctio symbolism and has probably contributed to give it such central position in Sufi alchemy.

As Jung explained in his lectures, the coniunctio has two important 12 aspects. It is a coming to terms of the conscious with the unconscious on the one hand and the coming to terms between the two sexes on the other hand. It therefore includes recognition of the feminine element in the world and with it of matter, which is lacking in most of the other yoga systems of India as well as in official Islam and Christianity.

In Sufism however, there has been a strong awareness of the inner 13 feminine element in man. Whatever their style of love was, these Islamic mystics developed *an awareness of the anima* as being an independent inner figure in man. Some united first with her in order to then unite, transformed into a woman, with Allah. As Henry Corbin has shown, the awareness of the anima in Islam seems historically linked with the old Persian tradition of the Daēnā. The still older idea is the Persian Fravarti. This is a feminine tutelary spirit, which personifies the archetypal models of ideas, according to which the visible objects and beings were created. It is not a pure idea or allegory, but a being of subtle body reality. The Mazdean Daēnā is a more developed and individualized archetypal image of the same order. The Daēnā is more incarnated and belongs to the individual man. Corbin writes: «In fact, the incarnate Fravarti, the Angel-soul that has given up its 'celestial' condition to confront the horror of Ahrimanian humanity, is not alone: the soul in its terrestrial condition, making common cause with all the beings of light, wages at their side its 'battle for the Angel'. The 'Angel' is simultaneously its faith and its judge, its existence and its super existence, its celestial *paredros*. This fact will be revealed to the soul only *post mortem* and that is why Daēnā, the Angel of the incarnate soul (for which the Fravarti, having come 'to Earth' has chosen to answer) is also called *ravān-i rāh*, 'the soul on the path', that is, the *Anima coelestis* which the *Anima humana* meets 'on the path' to the Chinvat Bridge.»[23]

Corbin then draws from this Mazdean tradition a line to Islamic 14 Shiᶜite mysticism, especially as it was developed in Sufism by Suhrawardī and Ibn ᶜArabī. In this context the *anima coelestis* becomes also identical with Fāṭima as a personification of the 'Eternal Sophia'. Corbin acknowledges the identity of this figure with Jung's concept of the anima, to which we will return later.

This becoming conscious of the anima in Islam led, at least in men, 15 to a differentiation of the religious eros and it is *that* element, in which the

23 H. Corbin, *Spiritual Body and Celestial Earth*. From Mazdean Iran to Shiᶜite Iran, p. 41.

Islamic culture was very superior to the Western Christian world. As far as I can judge, the whole differentiation of the man's anima in the poetry of the troubadours and in the novels of courtly love has sprung into life through Islamic influence. Miguel Asin Palacios has collected a whole series of stories, which illustrate the encounter of the mystic with his anima: «A tale attributed to ʿAlī aṭ-Ṭalḥī, who lived prior to the tenth century, reads as follows: "In a dream I beheld a woman fairer than any of this world. 'Who art thou?' I asked, and she replied, 'I am a houri'. I said to her, 'Pray let me be thy husband', to which she replied, 'Ask me in marriage of my Lord and name my dowry'. I asked, 'What is thy dowry?' and she answered, 'That thou shouldst keep thy soul unspotted from the world.'"»[24] Another story, attributed to the ninth-century ascetic Aḥmad ibn Abū al-Ḥawārī, runs: «In a dream I saw a maiden of the most perfect beauty, whose countenance shone with celestial splendour. To my asking, 'Whence comes that brilliance on thy face?' she replied, 'Dost thou remember that night spent by thee in weeping (and devotion)?'. 'I remember', I answered, and she said, 'I took those tears of thine and with them anointed my face, since then it has shone in brilliance'.»[25]

16 A tale, attributed to ʿUtba al-Ġulām, certainly dates before the eleventh century: «In a dream I saw a houri of beautiful features, who said to me, 'I love thee passionately and trust thou wilt do no deed that might keep us apart'. I replied, 'Thrice have I abandoned the things of this world and hope never to regain them, so that I may be able to meet thee [in heaven]'.»[26] A tale told by ʿAbd ar-Raḥmān ibn Zaid of the eighth century, runs as follows: «A youth, moved to devotion by spiritual reading, distributes all his patrimony among the poor, keeping only enough to buy a mount and arms, with which he sets off to the holy war. Whilst on service, he fasts during the daytime and spends the nights in prayer and vigil as he guards the horses of his sleeping comrades. One day he cries out in a loud voice: 'Oh, how I long to be with the large-eyed maiden!' and to his companions he explains how in a dream his soul found itself in a lovely garden watered by a river;

24 M. Asin Palacios, *Islam and the Divine Comedy*, p. 132 f.

25 Ibid., p. 132f.

26 Miguel Asin Palacios shows in *Islam and the Divine Comedy*, p. 270, that Ibn ʿArabī only sums up—in an allegorical commentary to his love songs—a topos which appears already much earlier. Ibn ʿArabī later also used these motifs to hint at the deeper meaning of such an encounter: «One night», he (Ibn ʿArabī) says, «I was in the temple of the Kaaba, walking, as required by rite, round and round the holy dwelling. My mind felt at ease and a strange peace overcame my soul. To be alone, I went out of the temple and started to walk along the roadway. As I walked, I recited aloud some verses, when, of a sudden, I felt a hand softer than velvet touch me on the shoulder. I turned and lo! a Greek maiden stood before me. Never had I

on the bank of the river stood a group of fair maidens in rich attire, who welcomed him saying, 'This is the bridegroom of the large-eyed maiden whom we serve'. Proceeding on his way, he comes to a second river, where other maidens again welcome him. A few steps further, and he meets the heavenly maiden herself enthroned on a seat of gold within a tabernacle of pearl. When she beholds her betrothed, she wishes him joy of having come to her, but warns him that his present coming is not final. 'The spirit of life yet breathes within thee, but tonight thou shalt break thy fast in my company'.»

I am aware that for so important a theme these few allusions I have 17
quoted are completely insufficient. I only wanted to give the reader a hint to what is meant when I use the words religious eros in a modern context. Like all religious movements, Islam was confronted with the problem of love and (influenced by Hermetism and Neoplatonism) it wavered between ascetic spirituality and attempts to include the physical love into the inner experience. Most Islamic mystics adhere however to the Platonic idea that the ultimate goal of love is the experience of the divine, in their context: of Allah.[27] The Islamic alchemists had the same idea of love as the mystics but in addition to the latter they worked on their own souls (*nafs*) through their alchemical opus. In that way the element of matter and the body was more included than with the purely spiritually oriented mystics.

The above-mentioned double aspect of alchemy (chemical and reli- 18
gious) constitutes a great inner polarity. It appears clearly in the title *Ta physika kai ta mystika* (The physical and the mystical) of a text of Pseudo-Democritus at the beginning of our millenary.[28] Already then many alchemists knew, or at least had a hunch, that their symbolism contains a physical and mystical, i.e. a material and an inner psychic, meaning. This polarity continued to exist throughout the history of alchemy and plays therefore also a role in the Arabic period. It is the great merit of Henry

beheld so beautiful a countenance, nor heard so soft a voice; never had I met a woman more endearing or with speech so refined, who expressed such lofty thoughts in more subtle language. Verily she surpassed all the women of her day in delicacy of mind, in literary culture, in beauty and in learning […].» Asin Palacios further comments (ibid., p. 270): «Prefacing his [Ibn ᶜArabī's] work with the narration of this fictitious episode in his life, which he alleges led to the composition of his songs, the author proceeds to give the allegorical meaning of each verse. His beloved, he explains, is the symbol of Divine wisdom; her virgin breasts, the nectar of its teaching; the smile on her lips, its illuminations. Her eyes are the emblems of light and revelation. The mournful sighs of the lover represent the spiritual longings of the soul.»

27 See for that, A. Schimmel, *Mystical Dimensions of Islam*.

28 M. Berthelot, *Alch. Grecs*, II, I.

Corbin to have brought to light the mystical, or as he also calls it, theosophical side of Arabic alchemy.[29]

19 Whilst Paul Kraus has mainly studied the chemical aspect of the *Corpus Ǧābiricum*[30] (the main bulk of Arabic alchemical tradition before Ibn Umail), Corbin has for the first time explained a whole series of mystical Islamic concepts and their connection with Shiʿite mysticism. Our author, Muḥammad ibn Umail, who has been neglected until now by the historians, belongs definitely to the religious-mystical current of alchemy, more even than Ǧābir and in contrast to ar-Rāzī who attended more to the chemical aspect of alchemy. He belonged to the Ismāʿīlīyan Hermetic mystics of the Shiʿa. Therefore he is of essential importance, not for the history of chemistry, but for the mystical alchemy of the Arabs.

20 It is generally known that the Arabs have preserved the Hellenistic cultural values and traditions. In the realm of alchemy they also preserved and developed the chemical and the mystical aspects as well. The chemical progress they achieved has been studied, but except for Corbin's work little attention has been given to defining the Arabic contribution in the realm of mystical alchemy. If we try to circumscribe the creative contribution of Islamic alchemy, we might point out the following facts: In a first phase (seventh to eighth century) the Islamic scholars mainly translated the ancient Hermetic-Gnostic texts without 'confronting' their content with the Islamic religion. Gradually however this confrontation took place. The Arabs began to think independently and experiment themselves in the realm of alchemy. There two elements slowly came into the foreground: the effect of the *tawḥīd*, i.e. the emphasis on the monotheistic outlook. Among other consequences it had the effect that the scholars tried more and more to create a synopsis of the diverse antique traditions in order to unify their meaning.

21 In effect, they slowly discovered that the effort of mystical alchemical tradition concentrates onto *one* inner psychic experience, namely the God-image. Ibn Umail's *Ḥall ar-rumūz* (Explanation of the Symbols) presents simply an endless list of names of the stone, the water, the *prima materia* etc, suggesting that they are all aspects of the inner mystery through which the alchemist unites with the transcendent God. The second original contribution of the Islamic world to Gnostic alchemy was the addition of a passionate feeling tone. In order to express this much greater intensity of feel-

29 H. Corbin, *Creative Imagination in the Sufism of Ibn ʿArabī*; H. Corbin, *Spiritual Body and Celestial Earth.*

30 P. Kraus, *Jâbir ibn Ḥayyân – Contribution à l'Histoire des Idées Scientifiques dans l'Islam*, Mémoires de l'Institut d'Egypte, Vol. 45, Le Caire 1942, Vol. I and II.

ing the mystical alchemists recur much more to a poetic language compared with the more sober language of the antique Hermetists. This greater emphasis on feeling goes along with a greater emphasis on the coniunctio motif. The antique mystical alchemists also knew about it, but the Islamic scholars seem much more aware of the transforming effect of love on the inner psychic development of man. They stressed this point to such an extent that it became the central content of an autonomous movement within Sufism. The latter has been influenced by antique Gnostic-Hermetic alchemy, but in its highest representantives, for instance Ibn ʿArabī , alchemy is no longer an outer 'natural science', but rather a symbolic language, a symbolic metaphor, which serves to express a purely inner psychic religious experience. Some of its representantives even overemphasized the spiritual realm and radically rejected the world and the body, whilst the ancient mystical alchemists included them in their work.

2. The Loss of the Dimension of Divine Matter

The development of Arabic religiosity especially in Sufism ran, to a certain extent, parallel to Western Christianity. It became more 'philosophical' in a way resembling scholasticism and became more spiritualized and refined. The masculine element of the logos slowly prevailed over matter. The Gothic cathedrals striving to the heights can be, *mutatis mutandis*, compared with the ever higher differentiation of Sufi thought and art, but *one* element got lost in both religious cultural realms. It is a loss which we only now begin to realize: the archaic archetypal idea of animated matter. The idea of matter in itself became less and less important in the high Middle Ages, or it became more and more 'spiritualized' in the hands of the theologians and artists, and wherever it subsisted it also became the object of technology. Technology presupposes namely that matter has no 'will' of its own, that it is 'dead' and therefore can be handled by man. The medieval Arabs developed a highly differentiated technology of water systems and of astronomical and medical instruments, which partly found their way into the West.[31] 22

Out of this in Europe sprang the dazzling development of modern technology beginning in the Renaissance in which man's interest returned more to earthly things. In the Christian civilization therefore matter became interesting, even fascinating, but the medieval prejudice that she was 'inferior' and could be completely manipulated by man has persisted till today. What got lost is the domain of magic, which was and still is called by both civilizations 'heathen superstition'. In the Arabic realm this loss began when Neoplatonism began to dominate more and more over Gnostic Hermetism, for the latter, especially in its Egyptian Hellenistic Ptolemaic form, preserved old Egyptian magic elements. What in my view 23

31 For that see in general the ground-breaking work of F. Sezgin, *Geschichte des Arabischen Schrifttums*, Vol. I–XII.

marks out the Egyptian religion from other religions is its balance between masculine and feminine elements and also between spirit and matter. Also the Egyptian religion never lost a specific element of the archaic African world, namely its magic. It is not mere chance that the papyri which inform us about antique magic stem from Egyptian soil. What we scornfully call magic is, however, nothing else but a more archaic form of religion which is characterized by treating matter as containing a divine and psychic element. Magic *relates* to matter instead of only manipulating it. It tries to influence matter, not by technological means, but by psychological means. In other words, the goddess of matter has to be propitiated and devotedly worshipped. Even the stupidest magical recipe presupposes thus a 'religious' handling of the materials. It also belongs to the traditional form of magical systems, which believe that man has to put himself into the right attitude in order to be able to influence matter positively. His soul then communicates with the soul of matter. When in the seventeenth century alchemy gradually became chemistry, the idea of the psyche in matter and of an *anima mundi* became lost. But, already before this, the loss had been prepared for by the split within alchemy between the *physica et mystica*. Mystical alchemy clung more conservatively to the concept of animated matter and to the idea that one can contact the soul of matter by meditation. It also preserved many of the so-called 'occult' practices which the developing chemistry discarded more and more.

24 This whole world of mystical alchemy unexpectedly returned to our attention through C.G. Jung's discovery of the collective unconscious. He first saw it as a transpersonal psychic dimension of its own which he also called the objective psyche. But towards the end of his life, mainly by studying synchronistic phenomena, it became more and more probable for Jung that the objective psyche relates somehow to inorganic matter, as if it were so to speak its inner psychic aspect. Therefore Jung postulated an *unus mundus*, a unitary world, which when observed from outside appears as matter and when observed from inside appears as the collective unconscious.

25 These late developments, however, do not primarily concern us here. But we need to know about our author that he still seems to have lived in the Hermetic-Gnostic world where matter was alive and where inner psychological work upon oneself influenced the chemical processes. With this goes the sense that a certain feminine element, which seems lost in later texts like Ibn ʿArabī's or al-Ġazzālī's, still persists in Ibn Umail's work. He seems to have a better relationship to nature. The loving way in which he describes the snail, the frog and the ostrich are not pale metaphors, but seem to have been for him a living reality.

3. The Transition of Alchemy into the Western World

Before alchemy returned through the Arabs into the Western world it had already begun to flow into two different river beds, that of the more chemical interest and that of the more religious inner psychic interest, but they were still flowing together and were transmitted together. Not only the chemical texts but also the religious Arabic alchemy evoked a similar movement in Europe, a movement, which was much greater than most of the historians were willing to recognize until now.[32] It is as if the hatred of the Christians against Islam, the spirit of the Crusades, has persisted in the West until today. 26

A first return of Neoplatonic Hermetic alchemy happened between the late ninth to the twelfth century (mainly in Spain and in Sicily). A second return happened, as is well known, in the Renaissance. The investigations of Miguel Asin Palacios show more and more that there has been an enormous influx of Arabic culture as early as the tenth century (the time of Muḥammad ibn Umail) or even earlier in Spain. Asin Palacios writes:[33] 27

«1. Islam, after the conquest of the countries bordering on Arabia, spread rapidly throughout the north of Africa, Spain, the south of France and southern Italy, and extended its dominion over the Balearic Isles and Sicily. The effect of war in imparting to the belligerents an intimate knowledge of each other is notorious; but in times of peace, too, contact between the two civilizations of Christianity and Islam was established across their eastern and western frontiers through the medium of commerce.

From the eighth to the eleventh century an active trade was carried on between Moslem countries of the East and Russia and other countries of northern Europe. Expeditions left the Caspian regularly and, ascending

32 See for that L. Bréhier, *L'église et l'orient au moyen âge – Les Croisades*.

33 M. Asin Palacios, *Islam and the Divine Comedy*, Part IV, Chapter II: 'Communication between Islam and Christian Europe during the Middle Ages', p. 239 ff.

the Volga, reached the Gulf of Finland and so through the Baltic to Denmark, Britain, and even as far as Iceland. The quantities of Arabic coins found at various places in this extensive commercial zone bear witness to its importance. In the eleventh century trade was conducted by the easier sea route across the Mediterranean, chiefly by means of Genoese, Venetian or Moslem vessels. Large colonies of Italian traders settled in all the Moslem ports of the Mediterranean, and merchants, explorers, and adventurers sailed at will across its waters. Benjamin of Tudela has left us trustworthy evidence, in his *Itinerary* of the twelfth century, of the busy intercourse between Christians and Moslems at that time.

To the stimulus of trade must be added the impulse of the religious ideal. Pilgrimages to the Holy Land, which had been suspended owing to the early conquests of Islam, were renewed and, with the establishment under Charlemagne of the Frank Protectorate over the Christian churches of the East, were assured by conventions and assisted by the foundation of hostels and monasteries in Moslem lands. During the ninth, tenth, and the eleventh centuries the number of pilgrims grew, until some of the expeditions comprised as many as twelve thousand; these expeditions were the forerunners of the Crusades.

The influence of the Crusades in bringing Islam and Christian Europe together need hardly be insisted upon. The Christian States founded after the first Crusades may be likened to a European colony implanted in the heart of Islam, between the Euphrates and Egypt. The civil administration and the army of these States were formed on the Moslem model, and even the habits, food, and dress of the Orientals were adopted by the Frankish knights, who poured into Syria in Crusades from all parts of Europe even as far distant as Scandinavia.

The failure to destroy Islam by the sword begot in its turn the idea of the pacific conquest of souls, and led in the thirteenth century to the establishment of the Missions to Islam. The Franciscan and Dominican friars who formed this new tie of spiritual communication were obliged to make a thorough study of the language and religious literature of Islam, and to reside for many years amongst Moslems.

2. More important and more interesting, however, from our point of view than any of these general channels of communication, is the contact of the two civilizations in Sicily and Spain. Beginning in the ninth century with piratical raids upon the coasts of the Atlantic and Mediterranean, the Normans gradually formed settlements in Moslem towns of the Peninsula (such as Lisbon, Seville, Orihuela and Barbastro) and in Sicily. The latter island, indeed, which had become permeated with Islam, was conquered in the eleventh century and ruled by a dynasty of Norman Kings until the thirteenth

century. Throughout that period the Sicilian population was composed of a medley of races professing different religions and speaking several languages. The court of the Norman King, Roger II, at Palermo, was formed of both Christians and Moslems, who were equally versed in Arabic literature and Greek science. [...] But the time when Palermo most resembled a Moslem court was the first half of the thirteenth century, during the long reign of Frederick, King of Sicily and Emperor of Germany. A philosopher, free-thinker and polyglot, the Emperor, even as his predecessors had done in war and peace, surrounded himself with Moslems. They were his masters and fellow-students, his courtiers, officers and ministers; and he was accompanied by them on his travels to the Holy Land and throughout Italy. His harems, one in Sicily and the other in Italy, were under the charge of eunuchs; and even the tunic in which he was buried bore an Arabic inscription. The Popes and other Kings of Christendom raised public outcry against the scandal of the court of such an Emperor, who, though representing the highest civil authority of the Middle Ages, was Christian only in name.

This patron of literature and learning formed a unique collection of Arabic manuscripts at the University of Naples, which he founded in 1224; and he had the works of Aristotle and Averrhoës translated, and copies sent to Paris and Bologna. Not only did he gather to his court Hebrew and Moslem philosophers, astrologers and mathematicians, but he corresponded with men of learning throughout Islam.

It was at the court of Frederick that the Sicilian school of poetry, which first used the vulgar tongue and thus laid the foundations of Italian literature, arose. The Arab troubadours assembled at his court were emulated by the Christians; and the fact is significant inasmuch as it affords an instance of contact between the two literatures, Christian and Moslem.

3. Important as Norman Sicily was as a centre of Islamic culture, it is nevertheless eclipsed in this respect by mediaeval Spain. Here were to be found the same phenomena as in Sicily, but on a much larger scale and with the precedence of centuries. For Spain was the first country in Christian Europe to enter into intimate contact with Islam. [...]

The Mozarabs formed the first link between the two peoples. As early as the ninth century the Christians of Cordova had adopted the Moslem style of living, some even to the extent of keeping harems and being circumcised. Their delight in Arabic poetry and fiction, and their enthusiasm for the study of the philosophical and theological doctrines of Islam, are characteristically lamented by Alvaro of Cordova in his *Indiculus luminosus*.

The contact thus established in the early centuries of the Islamic conquest became, as may be imagined, more pronounced in the course of time. With intervals of intermittent strife, the intermingling of the two elements of the population steadily continued. And thus we find the Mozarabs of Toledo, the ancient capital of the Visigoths, using the Arabic language and characters in their public documents as late as the twelfth century, after the reconquest of the city. The suggestion that these Christians, who had become half Arabs, communicated to their brethren in the north of Spain, and even in other parts of Europe, a knowledge of Islamic culture, may, therefore, be readily accepted. The hypothesis is strengthened by the fact of the constant emigration of Mozarabs northwards from Andalusia. [...]

4. With the gradual reconquest of Spain by the armies of the Christian kings, the Mudejars, their subdued Moslem subjects, took the place of the Mozarabs in transmitting Islamic culture. The undeniable superiority of this culture commanded the respect of the Christians, and the kings were prompt to adopt the policy of attracting the Mudejar element, thereby contributing to the more rapid and easy assimilation of Moslem civilization. Further political alliances through marriage between the royal houses of Castile or Aragon and the reigning Moslem families were frequent.

Thus Alphonso VI, the conqueror of Toledo, married Zaida, the daughter of the Moorish King of Seville, and his capital resembled the seat of a Moslem court. The fashion quickly spread to private life: the Christians dressed in Moorish style, and the rising Romance language of Castile was enriched by a large number of Arabic words. In commerce, in the arts and trades, in municipal organization, as well as in agricultural pursuits, the influence of the Mudejars was predominant, and thus the way was prepared for a literary invasion that was to reach its climax at the court of Alphonso X or the Wise.

Toledo had throughout the twelfth century been an important centre for the dissemination of Arabic science and *belles-lettres* in Christian Europe. In the first half of that century, shortly after the city had been captured from the Moors, Archbishop Raymond began the translation of some of the more celebrated works of Arabic learning. Thus, the whole encyclopaedia of Aristoteles was translated from the Arabic, with the commentaries of Alkindius, Alfarabius, Avicenna, Algazel and Averrhoës; and also the master works of Euclid, Ptolemy, Galen, and Hippocrates, with the comments upon them of learned Moslems, such as Albatenius, Avicenna, Averrhoës, Rhazes and Alpetragius. Translated into the Romance language of Castile with the help of learned Mudejars and Hebrews, these works were in turn rendered into Latin by Christian doctors drawn from all parts of Christendom.»

28 I have quoted Asin Palacios to some extent and at some length because he seems to me to put the historical facts in the right perspective, but

at one special field we have to look closer: the Arabic influence, though it was strong in the scientific sphere, was even more pronounced in the realm of eros, which, as I pointed out, is also much emphasized by the Arabic alchemists. In the development of Sufism the coniunctio became nearly exclusively identical with the *unio mystica* of the initiate with God, but it generally began with the inter-human love experience which, understood in a Neoplatonic sense, slowly sublimated itself into the experience of God. When this culturally highly differentiated expression of love came to Europe, it influenced the already existing poetry and other expressions of love.

A. J. Denomy sums up: «The currents of philosophical and hetero- 29
dox mystical thought that reached the South of France from the late tenth to the early twelfth century were Neoplatonism, Albigensianism, Arabic Neoplatonism and Arabic mysticism. Neoplatonism and Albigensianism were certainly there at the time of the first troubadours; Arabic philosophy and mysticism could have been there through the channels already indicated. These were the elements that helped to fashion the mentality and shape the mind of the South of France of that age not only in the courts and at the schools, but also among the people themselves. These were the factors that, so to speak, made that age Neoplatonically minded. We do not know where the first troubadours went to school nor by whom they were trained; we do know that wherever they went and under whomever they studied, they were exposed to these influences. The very intellectual atmosphere in which they lived and moved was saturated with them. Their poetry shows that they were trained men, at least in the art of composing verse and melody.»[34] At that time some of the great philosophers, mainly Avicenna, were translated in Spain and exerted a strong influence on scholastic philosophy, especially Roger Bacon, Albert the Great and St Thomas Aquinas. B. Carra de Vaux[35] has shown impressively how much these authors have been influenced by Avicenna even to the extent of bordering on heresy. His whole theory of the love of God has mainly influenced them, and the stress which they put on the importance of the *imaginatio* in the alchemical work is also due to him. In the same period, a considerable number of alchemical treatises were also translated into Latin, among others the *al-Māʾ al-waraqī* of Muḥammad ibn Umail.[36]

34 A. J. Denomy, 'An Inquiry into the Origins of Courtly Love', *Mediaeval Studies*, Vol. VI (1944), p. 257. See also Ibn Sīnā (E. L. Fackenheim ed.), *A Treatise on Love by Ibn Sīnā*, Chapter V: 'On the Love of Those who are Noble-Minded and Young for External Beauty', in: *Mediaeval Studies*, Vol. VII (1945), p. 218 ff. For the Arabic love poetry in itself, see J.-C. Vadet, *L'ésprit courtois en orient*.

35 B. Carra de Vaux, *Notes et Textes sur L'Avicennisme Latin aux confins du XI-XIIe siècle*.

36 It was translated towards the end of the twelfth century in Spain.

30 Till today historical scholars cling to the idea that alchemy belonging to the natural sciences was transmitted with the latter to the West and constituted the beginning of Western chemistry. This is not completely true. Alchemy had a special position because, according to Avicenna, it did not belong to the ordinary natural sciences. *It was basically a kind of magic.* The underlying theory was the following: the adept submitted himself to the process of yoga meditation and of religious exercises of self-purification through which he came closer to the divinity. Now, in Islamic cosmology, the idea of Creation is different from ours. In the Judean-Christian cosmology God has created the world, but not entered it. From the Moslem point of view God has also created the world and remained completely out of it, but paradoxically at the same time works creatively in it by an activity of *creatio continua.* All miraculous events in nature are due to this activity of *creatio continua.* But even all ordinary natural processes are not solely due to a profane effect of causality, but simultaneously linked with God's creative activity.[37] When the adept, through his effort of self-purification, has come into touch with the divinity, he begins to participate in God's creativity and therefore he can work miracles. Alchemy belongs to this kind of miraculous magic. Gold for instance cannot be produced by any profane chemical techniques, but only by a miraculous effect of the sublimated soul of the adept. This Islamic viewpoint has been transmitted to Europe through Ibn Sīnā who formulated it quite clearly.[38]

31 Alchemy according to Avicenna, and in his wake according to St Albert and St Thomas, belongs to a kind of magic. It is created by the *imagination* of the artifex, which produces—helped by astrological influences—a *magical transformation* of matter. Thus alchemy was dependent on the psychological condition of the artifex. The best description is found in the treatise *De Mirabilibus Mundi* which is ascribed to Albert the Great and which I consider genuine. Albert says: «I discovered an instructive account [of magic] in Avicenna's *Liber Sextus Naturalium*, which says that a certain power to alter things indwells in the human soul and subordinates the other things to her, particularly when she is swept into a great excess of love or hate or the like. When therefore the soul of a man falls into a great excess of passion, it can be proved by experiment that it [the excess] binds things [magically] and alters them in the way it wants, and for a long time I did not believe it, but after I had read the nigromantic books and others

37 For this, see S. H. Nasr, *An Introduction to Islamic Cosmological Doctrines*, p. 9 f.

38 For details see M.-L. von Franz, *Aurora Consurgens*, p. 175ff., esp. p. 177. Ibn Sīnā now published: *Avicenna Latinus—Liber de Anima seu Sextus de Naturalibus IV–V. Edition critique de la traduction latine médiévale,* p. 64–68.

of the kind on signs and magic, I found that the emotionality of the human soul is the chief cause of all these things, whether because, on account of her emotion, she alters her bodily substance and the other things towards which she strives, or because, on account of her dignity, the other, lower things are subject to her, or because the appropriate hour or astrological situation or another power coincides with so inordinate an emotion, and we [in consequence] believe that what this power does is then done by the soul. Whoever would learn the secret of doing and undoing these things must know that everyone can influence everything magically if he falls into a great excess [...] and he must do it at that hour when the excess befalls him, and operate with the things which the soul prescribes. For the soul is then so desirous of the matter she would accomplish that of her own accord she seizes on the more significant and better astrological hour which also rules over the things suited to that matter [...] Thus it is the soul who desires a thing more intensely, who makes things more effective and more like what comes forth [...] Such is the manner of production with everything the soul intensely desires. Everything she does with that aim in view possesses motive power and efficacy for what the soul desires.»[39] It is clear from this text that basically alchemy was, for the author, produced by psychological factors.[40] Love in its initial form of desire was the main agency in this process of transformation, and linked alchemy with the whole love mysticism in Arabic religion and philosophy. It comprehended not only the higher form of love, but began in true Platonic tradition with *concupiscentia*. Even material things contain this desire towards perfection or 'form' (in the Aristotelian sense of the word) so that the whole of all existing things yearn ultimately for the unification with Allah (*ittiḥād*).[41] Thus, for instance, every metal basically wants 'to become gold' and therefore the soul of the alchemist, which has been purified by its longing for contact with God, can produce a transformation of the metals. This basic idea links alchemy with the love mysticism of that time.

In addition to Denomy's indications Paulette Duval has (in my 32
opinion successfully) proved that Spanish alchemy has influenced and penetrated into the cycle of the Grail legend.[42] I am not specialist enough to

39 A. Magnus, *De Mirabilis Mundi,* Cologne 1485, undated incunabel in the Zurich Central Library, Gal. II. App. 429/3. Some think that this treatise is genuine. Thorndike thinks that this is doubtful, and some think that it is spurious. See J. R. Partington, Albertus Magnus on Alchemy, *Ambix*, Vol. 1, 1937, p. 8.

40 See M.-L. von Franz, *Aurora Consurgens*, p. 418.

41 See *A Treatise on Love by Ibn Sīnā*, see also S. H. Nasr, *Islamic Cosmological Doctrines*, p. 53 ff.

42 P. Duval, *La pensée alchimique et le Conte du Graal*, Paris, 1979.

judge if her hypothesis that Chrétien de Troyes wrote his text for the Valois is valid, but she is certainly right that the whole world of the Grail legend is filled with a spirit of Eros which goes back to Mozarabic alchemical sources.[43]

33 Not only in the *Minnesang* and in the novels of courtly love can we trace the influence of Arabic Eros. The mystical love of God of the Sufi has also reached the Western religious mystics,[44] but the most impressive proof among others is the book by Ramon Llull called *The Book of the Lover and the Beloved*[45] written towards the end of the thirteenth century and showing clearly the influence of Ibn ᶜArabī and al-Ġazzālī.[46] The famous 'Dark Night of the Soul' of St John of the Cross and the love mysticism of Theresa of Avila may also have been influenced in the same way. Ramon Llull initiated in his time a wave of interest for Arabic literature and it is in this connection that the main work of Ibn Umail has been translated in Spain.

34 It is because Sufi alchemy touches on religious matters that in 1317 (six years before the Council of the Canonization of St Thomas) alchemy was for the first time forbidden by the Church, though it was officially only condemned in its aspect of metal forging. It is interesting to note that alchemy as metal forging was condemned, but that the Bull of Condemnation does not touch upon the religious-magical aspect of alchemy. There were rumours at that time that the Pope himself was interested in the latter aspect of alchemy, but it cannot be proved. The religious alchemists probably hid away in an imitation of the Sufi secret societies, and therefore it is difficult to trace their activities. Wherever we find documents of this religious current in Western alchemy, Ibn Umail (referred to as Senior) is one of the highest authorities.

43 Ibid, p. 182 ff.

44 See M. Asin Palacios, *Islam and the Divine Comedy*. According to Asin Palacios even Dante's *Divina Commedia* is basically structured according to Islamic traditional visions of the beyond, which may have been transmitted partly directly and partly via some Christian legendary tales. See ibid. p. 177 ff. The whole idea of Beatrice as the guide to paradise can be found in close parallels in mystical Arabic texts. See ibid, p. 11 ff.

45 R. Llull, *The Book of the Lover and the Beloved,* edited by M. D. Johnston.

46 R. Llull, *Das Buch vom Freunde und Geliebten*, E. Lorenz (ed.), p. 11 ff. See also on the influence of Ibn ᶜArabī in the edition of M. D. Johnston, p. xxii.

4. A Modern View of Eros

In the previous chapter I tried to remind the reader that the flourishing of courtly love and the whole cultural development of the domain of religious eros stems from Islamic influences and that in its centre also blossomed the alchemical symbolism. In my view this is *the* new creative dimension which the Arabs added to medieval European traditions. On this point Islam differed from Christianity, which developed more and more into a philosophical logos-religion, whilst in the Islamic mysticism the symbolism of the coniunctio prevailed. Wherever in Western alchemical texts the symbolism of the coniunctio is of central importance, as for instance in the *Aurora Consurgens*, the *Rosarium Philosophorum*, the *Splendor Solis* etc., Senior is frequently quoted. 35

As I mentioned above, the mystical masters of Islam understood alchemy as a transformative process of the alchemist's psyche. The fire which promoted this transformation was the love of God. The latter however began first very often in the form of a homosexual or heterosexual transference to a human partner. The love of one's teacher, which took on a passionate form, was often the bridge to the realization of the love of God as it is still taught in the Hindu Bhakti Yoga and in certain Sufi circles.[47] This amazingly coincides with the discoveries of modern depth psychology, which saw that no deeper change in the patient's psyche can be brought forth without love. Whilst Freud however stressed only the sexual aspect of love or the so-called transference, Jung saw its mystical implications. When asked what eros is Jung confessed at the end of his life: «In classical times, when such things were properly understood, Eros was considered a god whose divinity transcended our human limits, and who therefore could neither be comprehended nor represented in any way. I might, as many before me have attempted to do, venture an approach to this daimon, whose range of activity extends from the endless spaces of the heavens to the dark 36

47 For a modern example of how a Sufi master deals with the transference of a woman see I. Tweedie, *Daughter of Fire, A Diary of a Spiritual Training with a Sufi Master*.

abysses of hell; but I falter before the task of finding the language which might adequately express the incalculable paradoxes of love. Eros is a cosmogonos, a creator and father-mother of all higher consciousness. I sometimes feel that Paul's words—'Though I speak with the tongue of men and of angels, and have not love'—might well be the first condition of all cognition and the quintessence of divinity itself. Whatever the learned interpretation may be of the sentence 'God is love', the words affirm the *complexio oppositorum* of the Godhead. In my medical experience as well as in my own life I have again and again been faced with the mystery of love, and have never been able to explain what it is. Like Job, I had to 'lay my hand on my mouth. I have spoken once, and I will not answer' (Job 40:4 f.). Here is the greatest and smallest, the remotest and nearest, the highest and lowest, and we cannot discuss one side of it without also discussing the other. No language is adequate to this paradox. Whatever one can say, no words express the whole. To speak of partial aspects is always too much or too little, for only the whole is meaningful. Love 'bears all things' and 'endures all things' (1 Cor. 13:7). These words say all there is to be said; nothing can be added to them. For we are in the deepest sense the victims and the instruments of cosmogonic 'love'. I put the word in quotation marks to indicate that I do not use it in its connotations of desiring, preferring, favouring, wishing, and similar feelings, but as something superior to the individual, a unified and undivided whole. Being a part, man cannot grasp the whole. He is at its mercy. He may assent to it, or rebel against it; but he is always caught up by it and enclosed within it. He is dependent upon it and is sustained by it. Love is his light and his darkness, whose end he cannot see. 'Love ceases not'—whether he speaks with the 'tongues of angels' or with scientific exactitude traces the life of the cell down to its uttermost source. Man can try to name love, showering upon it all the names at his command, and still he will involve himself in endless self-deceptions. If he possesses a grain of wisdom, he will lay down his arms and name the unknown by the more unknown, *ignotum per ignotius*—that is, by the name of God. That is a confession of his subjection, his imperfection, and his dependence; but at the same time a testimony to his freedom to choose between truth and error.»[48]

37 The numinous overwhelming aspects of love—the subject of the greatest poetry of mankind—have been experienced by most people as a bridge to the experience of the divinity. It has been praised as such by St Bernard, St John of the Cross, St Francis of Assisi and an infinite number of other great religious geniuses. In the alchemical symbolism, however, the

48 C. G. Jung, *Memories, Dreams, Reflections*, p. 386 f.

alchemists remained more aware of the lower aspect of Eros, of its dangerous subhuman side, which has ruined the life of innumerable persons and has served as a bridge to their self-destruction and death. The cold reductive view of Sigmund Freud of the so-called transference-problem stresses unilaterally the childish illusionary and destructive aspect of love which, as he postulates, has to be 'sublimated', though nobody knows how to do that. Jung on the contrary realized the impossibility for man to sublimate Eros artificially. He returned to the viewpoint of the alchemist, that only nature itself can transform it. The alchemical *sublimatio* is in that sense completely different from Freud's sublimation.[49]

The medieval mystics and the mystical alchemists were, as I have 38
mentioned, strongly influenced by Neoplatonism. As a consequence, they saw ordinary human love as a pre-stage of the love of God. From a modern Jungian point of view mysticism could be interpreted as empirical research into the Godhead, the latter being seen as the unknowable inner totality of the individual. The collective unconscious can be understood as the universe seen from within and the God image, which Jung calls the self, as its *spiritus rector*, which we encounter when we turn to the inner world. In a paper called 'Adaptation, Individuation, Collectivity',[50] Jung has clarified this surprising relationship between transference and the love of God, both being part of the process of individuation. When an individual engages in this process he must separate from collectivity. He must also separate from the inner collectivity, i.e. the collective unconscious. In contrast to the rising individuality the collective unconscious produces, as a counter pole, the God concept. In order to consolidate himself, the individual now must also separate himself from the God archetype. «In consequence, he loads himself with guilt. In order to expiate this guilt he gives his love to the soul, the soul brings it before God (the polarized unconscious) and God returns a gift (productive reaction of the unconscious) which the soul offers to man, and which man gives to mankind. Or it may go another way: in order to expiate the guilt, he gives his supreme good, his love, not to the soul but to a human being, who stands for his soul, and from this human being it goes to God and through this human being it comes back to the lover, but only so long as this human being stands for his soul. Thus enriched, the lover begins to give to his soul the good he has received, and he will receive it again from God, in so far as he is destined to climb so high that he can stand in solitude before God and before

49 See L. Aurigemma, 'Il concetto di sublimazione da Freud a Jung', in: *Prospettive junghiane*, Turin, 1989.

50 C. G. Jung, *The Symbolic Life*, [Coll. Works 18/2], § 1084 ff.

mankind. Thus I, as an individual, can discharge my collective function either by giving my love to the soul and so procuring the ransom I owe to society, or, as a lover, by loving the human being through whom I receive the gift of God. But here as well there is a discord between collectivity and individuation: if a man's libido goes to the unconscious, the less it goes to a human being; if it goes to a human being, the less it goes to the unconscious. But if it goes to a human being, and it is a true love, then it is the same as if the libido went direct to the unconscious, so very much is the other person a representation of the unconscious, though only if this other person is truly loved. Only then does love give him the quality of a mediator, which otherwise and in himself he would not possess.»[51]

39 These very condensed allusions of Jung need perhaps some explanation. First he speaks of the guilt of individuation, namely that the individuating person loads him- or herself with certain guilt by separating from society outside and from the collective God concept within. Love seems to be the compensation by which the individual expiates this guilt. Now there are two possibilities for a man: either he gives his love to the soul (i.e. the anima) and the latter, being an inner image in man, passes this love gift on to God. God or the self then bestows creativity on the man (on the lover of the anima) and this creativity represents the paying back of his debt to society. (That is the path Jung has chosen. He decided to become a lover of his inner soul image, and through her, of the self in a much similar way to that of many Islamic mystics.) The second possibility is that a man loves a real woman (i.e. the carrier of the anima projection) so absolutely that he receives the reward of God through her. That is what many troubadours did. This kind of absolute love of a human being is also cultivated in the love of the guru in Eastern mysticism. It can be a life-long attachment or can change in a certain late stage into the first type of love, by the realization that the beloved is an inner soul image.

40 The love of a human being is the more frequent starting point of the process of individuation and therefore Jung has consecrated his whole book on the transference to it.[52] There Jung distinguishes four levels of love:

1. The archaic identity or *participation mystique*
2. Mutual projections
3. Human relationship
4. The eternal union through fate.

41 The first aspect that we call 'archaic identity' is the natural state in which we believe things are just as we experience them. In general we do

51 Ibid., § 1103.

52 C. G. Jung, *The Psychology of the Transference*, [Coll. Works 16], § 353 ff.

therefore not recognize archaic identity except after its disappearance, when we realize that we have projected an unconscious part of ourselves onto an object or person in the outer world. This is often an experience we call 'love at first sight'. Later one finds out, either that the first glance was the right one—many people praise themselves that their first impression never fails—or that one has been badly mistaken, that it had all been an illusion, or as we call it, a projection. Projection means that some unconscious factor is unintentionally seen in the outer world whilst it actually belongs to our own unconscious. If the novice venerates his teacher like a God it simply means that he has not yet found that divine image in himself which he thinks to perceive in his teacher, and if (more normally) a man is hopelessly fascinated by a woman or a woman by a man, this generally turns out to be the projection of the man's inner femininity (anima) or the woman's masculinity (animus) onto an outer person. The Sufi masters knew that any great illusionary passion was the unrecognized beginning of the love of God; and we today see it in a similar vein as the vehicle of the process of individuation, as behind all human love lies ultimately the fascination by the innermost divine nucleus of the psyche which Jung has called the self.

The second aspect is a phase of working out the projections. Freud 42
had already recognized the fact that the analytical situation contained a lot of projections springing from family patterns, from the transference of father and mother, brother and sister images, creating dark und unrealistic erotic attractions filled with infantile demands and prejudices. These projections also constellate parallel inner images in the partner of which he is not aware, and almost immediately the interwoven problems will thus become manifest. The act of making projections conscious is in my opinion first of all a question of moral capacity, for the worst obstacle in the way of human relationship is the power complex, the wish to conquer or possess the other person. A friendship can only develop when the demands coming from the ego have been sacrificed to a certain degree on both sides. Ego wishes always contain a secret power drive. Even wanting to help a patient is illegitimate for an analyst and contains power: «Too much helping is an encroachment upon the will of others. Your attitude ought to be that of one who offers an opportunity that can be taken or rejected. Otherwise you are most likely to get into trouble. It is so, because man is not fundamentally good, almost half of him is a devil.»[53]

From the beginning, but increasingly so with the third aspect, it 43
becomes clear that we cannot function by rules or personal feelings alone.

53 C. G. Jung, *Letters*, Vol. 1, p. 83 f.

The decisive factor is the introspective work done on oneself, how far one has come with this task. General standpoints fail because it is the unique situation in the human encounter that is at stake. In the beginning stages of love the latter is 'impure'. It needs therefore an act of discrimination, a sorting out of one's inner motivations. As Jung points out, a relationship needs love as well as understanding. The blind dynamism of love must be mastered and corrected by the psychological understanding of one's own soul, the understanding of dissentients and the capacity to differentiate human beings. Only then can a real relationship take place.

44 The four stages of the development of the feminine element in man have four aspects: the man's anima can be Eve, i.e. biological attraction, the level of *participation mystique*, then Helen who belongs to the romantic love phase and constellates the problem of projections. Then Mary who symbolizes spiritual love as for instance between St Francis and St Clare or between Theresa of Avila and St John of the Cross. Finally there is a fourth stage: Sophia. She, however, symbolizes a subtle return to the lower sphere, for, from the point of view of wisdom, less sometimes means more. In another context Jung writes: The anima represents a desire or a system of expectations, which men project on women—i.e. a system of erotic relationship. But if his (outer) expectations, like normal sensuality, financial speculations, power drive etc. interfere then everything is lost. To make one's anima conscious means to love one's partner for herself and for the sake of love. "If I follow my love, my love is fulfilled." "A man's love can only become Beatrice, the bridge leading to transformation, if he can follow his anima without any selfish goal." "And pensively I followed the path of love … ", as Dante puts it. But at the beginning it is the anima who stirs the ambition of a man. She entangles him in guilt and blame and finally leads him into a state of isolation and possession unless he becomes aware of his lust for power.[54]

45 The development of the animus in a woman is also reflected in four stages, determined by four types of inner masculinity: the animus pictured as physical force, as a man of action (for instance James Bond), as word, and finally as meaning, i.e. the wise old man. A peaceful relationship with the other sex can only be attained if all those four aspects have been made conscious in the inner world of a woman. The positive differentiated animus means introspection and truth, but truth for its own sake, without any interference coming from sensuality or lust for power. Only if love prevails—love for its own sake—can a woman fully integrate her animus. Then her animus will become a bridge leading to an awareness of the self.

54 C. G. Jung *Seminare. Kinderträume*, 1987, p. 540.

We are now coming to the fourth aspect of love which Jung called 'the eternal connection through fate'. At this level love becomes an experience of the self, inner wholeness and God, which cannot be understood intellectually but only through love. This is no longer love through transference, as Jung states, «it is no ordinary friendship or sympathy. It is more primitive, more primeval and more spiritual than anything we can describe.»[55] In this domain we are not facing a personal vis-à-vis any more: «it means many, including yourself and anybody whose heart you touch. There is no distance but immediate presence. It is an eternal secret».[56] 46

Only alchemy, Tantrism and the religious eros of Islam have extensively witnessed this fourth realm of love.[57] Jung writes, as mentioned, that this fourth aspect of love is more primitive and more spiritual than transference, friendship and sympathy in the ordinary sense of the word. This explains the incredible paradoxes used in alchemy to express the coniunctio symbolism. I would like to illustrate this fact with the dream of a young woman, which occurred during the last World War, at a time when she had decided to accept her transference. 47

I am in Munich, close to an office building in which I knew Hitler lived. To my surprise the building wasn't guarded. Curious to know I entered the building and found myself alone, facing Hitler. I'm holding a gun in my hand and realize that my chance is unique. I shoot him and run away. I throw the gun into a sewage-pipe (this is followed by a long pursuit). At last I am in a field on my way home walking towards the Swiss frontier. In front of me is a white cock with a flock of chickens. They are walking in the same direction. The cock asks me to take him and his chickens to Switzerland. I agreed but under the condition there wouldn't be any sexual contact on the way. The cock consented and a voice said: «And so they marched on like an abbot with his nuns.» As we are walking on, I see a young beautiful couple (human beings) also moving towards the border. They are wearing golden crowns on their head. It is a king and a queen. As they look alien to me I suggest they join us. They accept my offer gratefully. We manage to cross the frontier at night. The customs-officer takes us to the quarantine camp where we have to stay for four weeks. They asked that during this time all eggs laid by the chickens should go to the Swiss state.

55 C. G. Jung, *Letters*, Vol. 1, p. 298.

56 Ibid., p. 298.

57 A premonition of this experience exists often already in the first phase, which is the reason for the deep passion with which many people want to hold on to this *participation mystique* by rejecting the conflict of human reality and by refusing to accept its limitations.

48 The shooting of Hitler means destroying the power animus, which stands in the way of the individuation process. The flight to Switzerland, which is home, points to the inner place where one belongs, the country of freedom, i.e. individual consciousness. The primitive aspect of the coniunctio, as Jung describes, is represented by the cock and his hens, a picture which can also be found in alchemical symbolism. Our Arabic author, Muḥammad ibn Umail, describes how the moon talks to the sun: «O Sun, I need you as the hen needs the cock.»[58] In other texts we would have a wolf and a dog or the stag and the unicorn or other animals representing this theme. The eggs, which play a special role at the end of the dream, are a well-known picture for the prima materia of the alchemical process. This group of chickens undergoes a spiritual discipline to prevent any disturbance, which could stand in the way to inner freedom. According to Senior's quotation, the cock and his hens represent sun and moon and so does the king with his queen in the symbolism of alchemy. In this case the royal couple of the dream simply represents another aspect of the same thing. It is related to Jung's comment on this form of coniunctio, the *hierosgamos*, that it is «a union more primitive and more spiritual than anything we can describe». King and queen represent, just like the animals, something transpersonal, something belonging to a divine domain, out of our time and space. That is why the dream pictures the royal couple as being strangers in this world. They need human help to be in touch with reality. The dream points out beautifully how on the one hand the ego works as a mediator demanding a certain spiritual discipline from the animals, and on the other hand brings the royal couple a little closer to reality. Working out the problem of love between man and woman constellates unending hardships. But, as Jung mentioned, this is vitally important today not only for the individual but also for society and indeed for the moral and spiritual progress of mankind. It is a sphere visited today by the numen, where the weight of mankind's problem has settled.[59] That is the reason why the unconscious often uses impressive and important images to express the problem of love in order to show that it is something absolutely crucial. An analysand once dreamed, after she had seen the movie *Hiroshima—mon amour,* that either the couple would really come together or the atom bomb would explode.

58 Zadith Senior (Zadith ben Hamuel), *De Chemia Senioris antiquissimi philosophi libellus*, p. 8. See H. E. Stapleton, *Three Arabic Treatises on Alchemy by Muḥammad ibn Umail*, p. 148 f. See also *Theatrum Chemicum*, Vol. V, p. 194, and J. J. Mangetus, *Bibliotheca Chemica Curiosa*, Vol. II, p. 217.

59 C. G. Jung, *The Psychology of the Transference* [Coll. Works 16], § 449.

The following dream also illustrates how love plays a vital role from the point of view of the unconscious. This dream comes from a middle-aged woman. For conventional and rational reasons she had not yet been able to come to terms with a deep love she was experiencing towards a married man who also loved her. 49

I heard the mighty sound of a bronze clock—it was an exceptional sound, as I have never heard or imagined it, a sound from the beyond, of exceptional beauty, irresistible! Fascinated, I got up because somehow I had to reach the source of this sound that had to be godly. As the sound seemed holy to me, I thought it could come from a church. Immediately I found myself in a church of pure Gothic style made of white stone. I got ready to climb the tower to find the bell, the source of this rhythmical solemn sound I was hearing. Everything around me changed. The church became a vault, like the nave of a cathedral made of transparent, living orange-red material. It was bathed in a reddish light and supported by a forest of columns, which reminded me of the stalactites I had seen in some caves in Spain. For a while I saw myself, very small, standing alone in this enormous hall, surprised at the fact that I was to investigate a whole new world: It was my heart. I was standing inside my heart and I realized that this magnificent sound which I still heard was the beating of my own heart, or, that the outer sound I was hearing was one and the same as my heartbeat. They were identical and beating in the same rhythm as the heart of the world.

This dream, I believe, needs no interpretation. It speaks for itself and shows how eros and individuation are linked together. The fact that the heart beats in the same rhythm as the universe tries to bridge the existing conflict between the outer and inner world, which plays such a great role in our love relationships and has even led many religious movements to reject the outer fulfilment of love completely. But, as Jung points out, it would be just as wrong to affect a haughty 'spirituality' as a pretext for evading the deeper outer human responsibilities as it would also be wrong to drag a relationship down to a primitive atavistic level; one has to find a way between this Scylla and Charybdis. In some way, love always leads to a crucifixion, the death of the natural human being, i.e. the unconscious man.[60] Firstly every lover will infallibly run into things that thwart and cross him, sufferings, due first to one's own shadow, i.e. jealousy, the desire to possess the partner, sexual passion etc.; secondly due to the fact that the partner is generally not as one wishes him or her to be, and thirdly due to the encounter with the collective unconscious which becomes constellated by the transference and by the affects and one's personal fate. Whichever direction one 50

60 Ibid., § 470.

chooses, it will lead to the death of the ego and, if this development proceeds rightly, it will also lead to the inner birth of the self.

51 In the mystery of the coniunctio not only a man and a woman unite but also their animus and anima. In alchemy what we call now animus and anima were represented as a royal couple, and in Tantrism they were represented as Shiva and Shakti in eternal embrace. They symbolize a cosmic oneness of opposites. There are not only two egos facing each other, but 'anyone whose heart we can touch'. It is as if only one divine couple would exist in the beyond and as if our human being can only partake in their coniunctio 'as a guest at the feast' (that is how Andreae pictures it in his *Chymical Wedding*[61]).

52 The image of a divine couple in whose union we participate points to a mystery which the alchemists called *multiplicatio*: when the philosophers' stone has been produced, it multiplies itself a thousand-fold and transforms all surrounding stones and metals into gold. When this state becomes manifest in the background of a relationship, when god and goddess are present, a feeling of eternity starts to transpire, as if the earthly encounter felt now is forever eternal. Jung called it also an 'objective cognition' and therefore he writes in his *Memories*: «In general, emotional ties are very important to human beings. But they still contain projections, and it is essential to withdraw these projections in order to attain to oneself and to objectivity. Emotional relationships are relationships of desire, tainted by coercion and constraint; something is expected from the other person, and that makes him and ourselves unfree. Objective cognition lies hidden behind the attraction of the emotional relationship; it seems to be the central secret. Only through objective cognition is the real *coniunctio* possible.»[62] And elsewhere he continues: «The decisive question for man is: Is he related to something infinite or not? That is the telling question of his life. Only if we know that the thing which truly matters is the infinite can we avoid fixing our interests upon futilities, and upon all kinds of goals which are not of real importance.»[63] It is this link with the infinite, I believe, which lights up in the dream of the cosmic heart rhythm. As Jung states, the *hierosgamos* represents the mystery of mutual individuation: «Nothing is possible without love, […] for love puts one in a mood to risk everything and not to withhold important elements.»[64] This is the only way to encounter the self.

61 J. V. Andreae, *Chemical Wedding*, London 1690.

62 C. G. Jung, *Memories, Dreams, Reflections*, p. 296f.

63 Ibid. p. 325.

64 M. Serrano, *C. G. Jung and Hermann Hesse*, p. 60. An author who excellently understood Jung's *Mysterium Coniunctionis* and commented mainly on late European alchemists who put the emphasis on the love problem is J. Trinick, *The Fire-Tried Stone*, London, 1967.

5. Life and Work of Muḥammad ibn Umail

According to Stapleton, Muḥammad ibn Umail lived in the first half 53
of the tenth century. This dating is based on the fact that he mentions in his works a friend whose life we can date: Aš-Šaiḫ Abū al-Ḥusain (or Ḥasan) ibn Waṣīf. This friend was a scholastic theologian and renowned poet. He belonged to the Ismāᶜīlīyan Shiᶜite sect and died 976–977 AD in Baghdad. According to some traditions he was burnt alive as a martyr for his creed.[65] It is clear from his works that Ibn Umail too belonged to the Ismāᶜīlīyan Shiᶜa, a spiritual movement which assimilated an especially large amount of Hellenistic tradition.[66] (The Ismāᶜīlīyans believed that the seventh Imam—either Mūsā al-Kāẓim or Ismāᶜīl ibn Ǧaᶜfar or his son—went into occlusion.) They formed a semi-secret society.[67] The next person he mentions is Abū al-Ḥusain ᶜAlī ibn Aḥmad ibn ᶜUmar al-ᶜAdawī to whom he addressed some poems in his work. He is mentioned with ᶜAbd al-Qāsim ᶜAbd ar-Raḥmān who accompanied Ibn Umail into the temple known as Sidr Būṣīr. We know from this that Ibn Umail has visited Egypt. A third friend of Ibn Umail is Mahrārīs who was an alchemist and probably wrote between 875 and 980.

Fuat Sezgin thinks that Ibn Umail lived a bit earlier and that 54
Stapleton is dating him too late.[68] His main work must have been written before 920. I am inclined to follow Sezgin's hypothesis. [69] According to

65 H. E. Stapleton, *Three Arabic Treatises*, ibid., p. 123 ff.

66 Cf. G. E. von Grunebaum, *Medieval Islam – A Study in Cultural Orientation,* p. 197 f.

67 M.-L. von Franz thought that Ibn Umail lived in Baghdad, but most probably he lived in Egypt and might even have been an Egyptian. She based some reflections on Ibn Umail's life on sources that are with today's knowledge of Ibn Umail's writings no longer accurate. See for that the more recent presentation of Ibn Umail's life in CALA I, p. XII f.

68 F. Sezgin, *Geschichte des arabischen Schrifttums*, Vol. IV, p. 283 ff.

69 M.-L. von Franz wrote further: «Like Ǧābir among the early Ismāᶜīlīyan Shiᶜites Ibn Umail especially belonged to the Qarmaṭīs. This is proved by the fact that he calls the philosophers' stone Qarmaṭ.» Qarmaṭ was a misreading of al-qidmīyā in Ms G, CALA I, p. 82.4.

W. Madelung,[70] the early Ismāᶜīlīyan movement split about 899 into two branches: one branch recognized the leadership of ᶜAbdullah, the future Fatimid Caliph al-Mahdī who claimed to be the last Imam himself. The other branch, who called themselves the authentic Qarmaṭīs, consisted mostly of the communities in Iraq, Bahrein and in Iran. It seems to me that Ibn Umail belonged to the latter, who did not join the Fatimids. He therefore probably visited Egypt before the split (before 899), a fact which would support Fuat Sezgin's earlier dating of his life. We also have no trace in Ibn Umail's work of the campaign of Abū Ṭāhir into Iraq and Bahrein, which took place in 903. Therefore it is probable that Ibn Umail had written his main work earlier.[71] According to Madelung, the Qarmaṭī philosopher Muḥammad ibn Aḥmad an-Nasafī, who wrote probably around 900, introduced for the first time the Neoplatonic Ismāᶜīlīyan cosmology into the Qarmaṭic system, which largely replaced the former Gnostic-Hermetic theories. Ibn Umail is definitely more a Gnostic Hermetist than a Neoplatonist. The famous hypostases Kūnī and Qadar[72] or other such Neoplatonic 'emanations' of Allah are not mentioned. This fact too speaks for an earlier date of his life.

55 With what I call the Gnostic-Hermetic tradition we must also include the whole big stream of syncretistic magical traditions, recipes and fragments of diverse religious texts which characterize the average Hellenistic literature of the Ptolemaic period. Two strands are in my view predominant in this *massa confusa* of late antique tradition: the so-called Chaldean astrology (our author firmly believes in it) and fragmented information about Egyptian hieratic texts, mainly funeral texts. In the same current swam along the whole bulk of alchemistic literature. When the Arabs began to become interested in the cultural traditions of the conquered countries, they first translated many of those texts as loyally as possible and without many additions of their own. Slowly, however, they began a critical sifting of the texts and a confrontation of their content with the Koranic religion. The Shiᶜite habit of interpreting texts symbolically facilitated, as Madelung puts it, a kind of inter-confessionalism, and it seems to me clear that Ibn Umail had such an inter-confessional attitude because he compares, for instance, the philosophers' stone with the mosque or an Egyptian temple.

56 The Egyptian element, we must not forget, flows in two currents into the alchemical tradition. One stream comes from the origin of alchemy, the

70 W. Madelung, *Religious Trends in Early Islamic Iran*, p. 95 f.

71 See P. Kraus, *Alchemie, Ketzerei, Apokryphen im frühen Islam*, p. XI f.

72 Kuni is a personification of Allah's creative Word 'Be' and Qadar is a personification of Allah's inner decision to create.

original secret knowledge of the priests of the embalming ritual, by which the God-man Osiris was transformed into the resurrected God. This stream is visible in the Comarius text and in the works of Zosimos. A second stream contains more the beliefs which stayed alive in the realm of Islamic culture right up to the time of Ibn Umail. We must not forget that the Alexandrian school and library still existed at the beginning of the eighth century and were transferred to Antioch by the Caliph ʿUmar. As Max Meyerhof pointed out, its science had degenerated «into a more astrological and superstitious conception».[73] 130 years later the school moved to Harran. Ibn Umail was influenced by both streams. He knew Zosimos and other works of his time, but also actually explored whatever he could get hold of on the secrets of the Egyptians, i.e. contemporary popular knowledge.

The beginning influx of Neoplatonism (around 900) had the effects 57
that the magico-religious traditions became more philosophical, more systematized. A kind of religious philosophy developed and the richness of symbolic tradition shrank in favour of a logical unifying interpretation. The masculine element of logos became predominant over the richness of magical experimenting with 'mother matter'. This masculinization and spiritualization led to the blossoming of Sufi mysticism, but it also led to a loss of what I would like to call the mystic relationship to matter, which had been predominant mainly in the Egyptian part of the tradition. The Egyptians had preserved, even in their highly differentiated and spiritualized traditions, an element of primitive African magic, which struck people of late antiquity as being highly numinous or dangerous black magic. This archaic element became more and more repressed under the influence of Islamic patriarchal monotheism. This repression is already visible in Ibn Umail's work in its trend towards systematization. But otherwise, and mainly compared with later texts, Ibn Umail is still deeply immersed in this trend of Egyptian magical mystical relationship to matter. Except for stressing the oneness of the work and the oneness of its goal, he delights in a rich amplification of innumerable similes, which for him are not poetical metaphors as they were for the Sufis, but real manifestations of the mystery of creation. Alchemy was for Ibn Umail really a religion of matter, like for primitive man, the stones and metals were part of God (not only similes of God), and therefore the opus had to be performed *tam ethice quam physice*. It is difficult for modern man to find the right empathy with such an attitude and therefore it is not surprising that Ibn Umail faded away out of historiography. This was

73 M. Meyerhof, *On the Transmission of Greek and Indian Science to the Arabs*, Islamic Culture, Vol. II (1937), p. 18. But see now D. Gutas's summary of the question of the school's continuation, *Greek Thought, Arabic Culture* (1998), p. 90 ff.

due not only to the persecution of the Ismāʿīlīya and perhaps his own introverted temperament, but also to the fact that his line of interest lay in a direction which was contrary to the historical tendencies of his time. The latter at that time ran towards masculine spiritualization and, if an interest in matter remained, it was an interest to exploit matter and to handle it, not to relate to it mystically. The Arabic evolution ran in this respect parallel to the Christian one. Along with the increasing repression of the feminine aspect of matter went a sociological 'organization' of love. The spontaneous manifestations of love in their 'divine' nature were negated and even the mystics of Islam and Christianity laid the accent more on the spiritual aspect of the love of God than onto any archaic magical aspect. Vipers and scorpions, which in Ibn Umail's work symbolize the dark shadow of the God of love, are rarely mentioned in the official mystical movements in Islam and Christianity.[74] Ibn Umail on the contrary seems to know a lot about it. Only today has this problem come up again. It is C. G. Jung's great merit to have not only turned towards this problem, but to have unearthed the old alchemical traditions which now can help us to confront ourselves with this thorny problem.

58 A point which has evoked much controversial discussion is Ibn Umail's relationship to the *Turba*. Stapleton assumed that Ibn Umail quoted the *Turba*. Ruska first reversed this,[75] but changed his opinion later. In my view the problem has been settled by Martin Plessner:[76] the *Turba* is an Arabic work written before Ibn Umail, before 900 AD, and originated probably on Egyptian soil.[77] According to Plessner the *Turba* is a creative transformation of basically Greek cosmological doctrines. It pursues essentially a literary purpose (I would say the purpose of creating a survey).[78] It aims at clarifying the cosmological basis of alchemy.[79] Just about in the lifetime of Ibn Umail the Arabs began to add more and more a creative dimension of their own. The latter consists on the one hand of extending the experimental chemical basis of Greek alchemy (that is ar-Rāzī), and on the other of changing the emphasis into a description of the alchemical process as a religious love experience (that is Ibn Umail).

74 Ibn Umail refers to vipers also in his *ad-Durra an-naqīya*, and to scorpions in his *Qaṣīda Mimīya*.

75 J. Ruska, 'Studien zu Muḥammad ibn Umail', *Isis*, 24 (1935-1936), p. 337 f.

76 M. Plessner, *Vorsokratische Philosophie und Griechische Alchemie*, 1975, p. 4, p. 6 ff.

77 M. Plessner, 'The Place of the Turba Philosophorum in the Development of Alchemy', *Isis*, 45 (1954), p. 331 ff.

78 See also M. Plessner, ibid., p. 124 ff.

79 Ibid., p. 88 ff.

As mentioned before, Ibn Umail polemicizes against the con- 59
cretistic interpretation of alchemical symbols (like using hair, flesh, milk etc.). In my view this polemic has to be seen in a wider context. Already before Ibn Umail, in the Ǧābirean Corpus, we find traces of Chinese Taoist alchemy and the same is true for Ibn Umail's work. In Taoist alchemy there has always been a certain battle between alchemists who saw the work as purely spiritual and others who projected the inner process onto bodily centres and biological materials.[80] In Greek alchemy Zosimos also polemicizes against the concretistic view of alchemy, which he thinks is the work of demons. So the coexistence of an inner tension between spiritual and chemical alchemy is an ubiquitous fact and cannot be interpreted as something between Ibn Umail and ar-Rāzī. If we want to place Ibn Umail's work into its greater historical context we could say that he belongs to the late school of Ǧābir and is preparing the way for the 'Brethren of Purity' (Iḫwān aṣ-Ṣafā᾿), whose main work is generally dated around 960. About the latter Seyyed Hossein Nasr writes: «… the Ikhwan may be connected with Pythagorean-Hermetic doctrines, much of which was best known in Islam under the name of the corpus of Ǧābir ibn Ḥaiyān. Moreover, considering the extensive use made of the *Rasā᾿il* by the Ismā῾īlis during later centuries and the presence of certain basic ideas such as *ta᾿wīl* in both groups, we may loosely connect the Ikhwan with Ismā῾īlism, especially with what has been called 'Ismā῾īlī gnosis'. But it is perhaps more significant, especially with respect to their cosmological doctrines, to describe them as a Shi῾a group with Sufi tendencies whose exposition of the cosmological sciences was to influence the whole Muslim community during the later centuries. The conception of Nature held by the Ikhwan was to have almost as great an influence among the Twelve-Imam Shi῾ites as upon the Ismā῾īlīs.»[81] A secret society of a similar kind must have existed already in Ibn Umail's time; he certainly lived in complete seclusion and his writings were only circulated among his friends and pupils.

80 See C. Po-Tuang, *The Inner Teachings of Taoism*, concerning this p. xi: «There is ample evidence, however, that the supposed alchemical enterprise did involve considerable work and experimentation in chemistry and metallurgy as well as psychological development. The coexistence of material and spiritual alchemy was also paralleled in the West, and many outstanding personalities, such as Albertus Magnus, Ramon Llull and Paracelsus, are associated with alchemy in Europe.»

81 S. H. Nasr, *Islamic Cosmological Doctrines*, p. 35 f; about the relationship between Ibn Umail, ar-Rāzī and Ǧābir newly translated texts give more differentiated insights. These will be presented and discussed in one of the next volumes of CALA. The remarks of M.-L. von Franz remain here unchanged.

60 A special problem is posed by Ibn Umail's relationship to the *Corpus Ǧābiricum*. Whilst Paul Kraus places its date around 900, that is to say contemporary with Ibn Umail, Fuat Sezgin and Henry Corbin believe that Ǧābir actually wrote most of the treatises and was a disciple of Ǧaʿfar aṣ-Ṣādiq who died in 765.[82] This would make the date of the *Corpus Ǧābiricum* much earlier (and with it also the date of the Hellenistic influence received into the Islamic countries). According to Pierre Lory[83] we have no definite reason to decide between those two dates. It is not impossible that a personality by the name of Ǧābir lived at an earlier date and that some of the treatises of the Corpus date back to him. From this nucleus the Corpus has slowly evolved by a kind of process of self-amplification, so that it now consists of different layers between which Lory tries roughly to distinguish.[84] Whatever the case may be, Muḥammad ibn Umail was probably confronted with a completed Corpus in which the last layer containing Ismāʿīlīyan influence was perfected, and in a certain sense his writings strongly resemble the treatises of this last layer. We will come back to this point during the commentary.[85]

61 As far as we know only *al-Māʾ al-waraqī* was incompletely translated into Latin. There is however a question whether the *Book of the Keys* or *Book of the Greater Wisdom*[86] could be identical with the Latin *Artefius Clavis Sapientiae*. H. E. Stapleton signals that it was.[87] In the meantime G. Levi della Vida[88] discovered one Arabic manuscript of this *Clavis* in the Vatican Library, vat. ar. 1485, and signals another as being in Istanbul, Aya Sofya 2466. The latter attributes the text to Muḥammad ibn Umail who is known to have written a book with this title. Levi della

82 See P. Kraus, *Alchemie, Ketzerei, Apokryphen*, ibid., p. 61 ff.

83 Jābir ibn Ḥayyān, *Dix Traités d'Alchimie* traduits et commentés par Pierre Lory.

84 Ibid., p. 51 ff.

85 It has been postulated (mainly by J. Ruska) that the Latin Geber writings have nothing to do with Ǧābir, but this is not at all convincing. At least the *Summa Perfectionis* contains passages which are translated from the Arabic, see H. E. Stapleton, *Alchemical Equipment in the Eleventh Century*, Memoirs of the Asiatic Society of Bengal, Vol. 1 (1905), No. 1, p. 47 ff. See also W. R. Newman, *The Summa Perfectionis of Pseudo-Geber. A Critical Edition, Translation and Study*, p. 57 ff.

86 For a list of the writings of Muḥammad ibn Umail, see H. E. Stapleton, *Three Arabic Treatises*, ibid., p. 126.

87 H. E. Stapleton, *Three Arabic Treatises*, ibid., p. 126, note 2.

88 G. Levi della Vida, 'Something more about Artefius and his Clavis Sapientiae', in: *Speculum, a Journal of Medieval Studies*, Vol. 7 (1938), p. 80 ff. Cf. also G. Levi della Vida, *Ricerche sulla formazione del antico fondo dei manuscritti orientali della Biblioteca Vaticana* p. 153.

Vida thought, however, that this *Clavis* of Artefius is not the one by Ibn Umail because quotations from it in the *al-Māʾ al-waraqī* and in a work of al-Ǧildakī do not coincide with our Latin text.[89] However, the Latin text we have *is* really a translation of the Arabic work. In Latin it is printed in Mangetus's *Bibliotheca Chemica*[90] and Zetzner's *Theatrum Chemicum*.[91] So the Arabic *Key of Wisdom* is identical with the Latin Artefius treatise. The introduction to the Latin Cambridge manuscript mentions Alfonso, which means that it was translated under King Alfonso X. A manuscript-index of the Vatican Library of the sixteenth century attributes the Vatican manuscript to 'Ebn Amhel El Endelesi' (the Andalusian). On account of this, Paul Kraus doubts the attribution to Ibn Umail.[92] He thinks that Endelesi might be a corruption of al-Abuluniyāsī and considers the work as a pseudo-writing of a pupil of Apollonius of Tyana, i.e. of Bālīnās. This work was, according to Kraus, translated relatively late into Latin, about hundred years later than Bālīnās's book *On the Causes*. It is more Islamic than the former. This time that Kraus indicates fits the time of Ibn Umail. I think we cannot brush aside the fact that two Arabic manuscripts and the heading of a Latin translation attribute the treatise to Ibn Umail. However, the two other extant manuscripts which Kraus signals as existing in Cairo, the second being derived from the first, give us as the author's name Ibn Balʿawān, probably one of the disciples of Bālīnās. This could be a reconstruction derived from the text itself because the author's name had been lost. I would propose to consider the *Clavis* as belonging to the Corpus in Ibn Umail's possession, perhaps as a translation which was made under his supervision. It certainly expresses a basic view of theurgy that he shares. The Latin author's name 'Artefius' might be a corrupted 'Asclepius' or it might be a name or pseudonym of that 'noble knight' of King Alfonso who translated the treatise into Latin. He might have had a reason to hide his real name because theurgy was forbidden and persecuted by the Church. If my assumption should be right, Ibn Umail was known to our medieval world by two of his works which greatly influenced medieval Western alchemy. He was one of the hidden masters of religious alchemy in the Middle Ages.

89 This question has now been clarified by Theodor Abt who discovered in the legacy of Stapleton the photographs of the Arabic text and of a Latin manuscript from the Cambridge University Library. These historical questions have to be discussed in detail in the next publications of Ibn Umail within the framework of the CALA.

90 *Bibliotheca Chemica Curiosa*, Vol. I, p. 503–509.

91 *Theatrum Chemicum*, Vol. IV, p. 221–240.

92 P. Kraus, *Jâbir ibn Ḥayyân*, p. 298, note 91; compare this to F. Sezgin, *Geschichte des arabischen Schrifttums*, Vol. IV, p. 84 f., 90.

Part II

Commentary on the *Ḥall ar-Rumūz*

1. General Reflections

Before plunging into the text and before commenting on it, it seems necessary to warn the reader and to inform him about the method which Ibn Umail seems to follow: the author enumerates first, and also later throughout the book, a great quantitiy of symbolic alchemical terms: magnesia, sulphur, dye, water etc. He seems not to follow a line of thought or a rational argument. Only from time to time he adds an explanatory sentence or two to one of the terms. 62

The underlying thought, though not expressed in words, is that all these terms somehow point to one and the same thing: the central secret of alchemy. Like other alchemists before and innumerable authors after him, he tries to explain *ignotum per ignotius*, the unknown by something more unknown. 63

This strange method of expression which irritates the modern scientist has at last been psychologically explained by C. G. Jung, who discovered the same method when he attempted to understand the dreams of his patients. He called it the method of amplification: one assumes that every dream image points to something unknown. Then one collects all associations and parallel images around the first unknown term. The resulting cluster of images seems to point to a common denominator behind the multiple images. The actual interpretation of the dream image, which then follows, consists of an attempt to circumscribe the unknown nucleus in psychological language. This method is not linear, but *circumambulates* an essential core of meaning [of a symbol] that cannot be made completely conscious. But one can become familiarized with [a symbol by learning] what consciousness thinks otherwise. 64

To return to our author, he seems to apply a similar procedure. He seems to want to point to a mystical experience that, he assumes, is identical with what former alchemists tried to describe as their stone. He feels that he means the same as what Zosimos, Morienus, Maria etc. tried to describe. Whether it really is so we do not know and will never know, but 65 it is a striking fact that all the most obscure alchemical texts seem to converge in their meaning and in their description of the secret. The converging tendencies seem to be based psychologically on the fact that they point to one and the same archetype, namely the inner God-man, or lapis, in the alchemist's psyche. For Zosimos and other Hellenistic alchemists this Anthropos figure was Hermes Trismegistos, or the Man of Light. For the early Arabic alchemists it was the black stone inserted in the Kaaba. For the Sufi alchemist it was the purified self of the mystic and, when this mystical tradition came to Europe, the same figure was identified with the inner Christ.

66 In order not to judge or guess ahead what the author means when he accumulates symbolic terms, we will follow the Jungian method of amplification, and only in the end will we try to define what this dream-like rambling wants to express.

2. Text and Commentary

First translation, as was at the disposal of M.-L. von Franz (Numbers give page and line in CALA I, passages to be omitted or corrected are in cyan blue.)	Ameliorated translation of CALA I (green)

Text

(3.4) In the name of the merciful and compassionate God. My success comes only from God, on Him I depend and to Him I turn repentantly. Muḥammad ibn Umail said: (3.6) 67

[Text 3.6–7.1 contains the introduction that was not available to M.-L. von Franz.]

(7.1) The names of the stone of the philosophers are as follows: The first of its names	sages
is the fountains of copper and magnesia, fountains, tin, zinc, iron, […] and silver [*waraq*[93]],	lead-copper … lead … [-] … copper
and the holy thirsty earth, the white earth, the earth of the pearls, the earth of silver [*fiḍḍa*], the earth of gold, the starry earth and the snowy earth. And when they say: the filings of silver [*waraq*] and the filings of gold that is pure,	
without cheating. They mean by that their second stone, which is fountains of copper and it	debasement lead-copper. It
is their silver and there is in it what they want. Its spirit, which they extracted from the first operation of their white body. (7.8)	their body to which they return back its spirits … their first body at the beginning of the operation

93 *Waraq* is usually the Arabic word for leaf. In alchemy it stands for the silver of the sages.

Comment

68 The text does not begin conventionally with the *prima materia* but goes right to the definition of the goal. All usual introductory invocations and rhetorics are omitted.[94] This is probably the case because it is an 'Explanation of Symbols' (*Ḥall ar-rumūz*), i.e. a later commentary to Ibn Umail's former works. If we compare it with the *al-Māʾ al-waraqī*, it begins with the so-called 'second body', i.e. with an advanced stage of the preparation of the philosophers' stone. Our text first calls it «fountains of copper».[95] According to contemporary views, copper is the microcosm, i.e. man himself. Ar-Rāzī, in his *Šawāhid*, says: «Copper is like a human being. It has a Spirit, a Soul and a Body».[96] As Stapleton points out, this goes back to the book of Zosimos *On the Explanation of the Ten Preparations.*[97] There Zosimos writes: «Copper is like a human being: it has a spirit, a soul, and a body. It is necessary before everything to break up and cause to crumble the grossness of the body, and to turn it into a tincturing spirit, agreeable to everybody.»[98] According to this statement, copper is the *prima materia*.

69 But according to the *Visions of Zosimos* it is also an image for the completed philosophers' stone. Towards the end of his treatise *Peri Aretes*[99] (*On Virtue*) Zosimos writes: «In short, my friend, build a monolithic temple like the vessel, in marble, which has no beginning and no end in its construction. In its innermost centre there is a very pure spring of water, shining like the sun [...] a dragon is lying at the entrance of the temple [...] sacrifice it and use it as a step to enter the temple. There you will find what you are looking for, the priest, the man of copper, whom you may see sitting in the spring, collecting in himself all colours; do not look at him as being a man of copper: he has changed the colour of his nature: he has become a man of silver. If you want it, you will soon have a man of gold.»[100]

70 The allusion to copper as a microcosm clearly points to the fact that for the author the alchemical process takes place *within man*. The work of

94 The missing text with the introduction to the *Ḥall ar-rumūz* was found in Ms D. It comments on the attitude towards the work and on the symbolic character of the process. Either this passage got lost in Ms G or it did not seem relevant for the copyist. The Ms D was only found after M.-L. von Franz passed away.

95 The editor of the private edition, mentioned in the foreword, changed the text of von Franz from the first incorrect translation of *abār-nuḥās* as 'fountains of copper' to the later correct translation 'lead-copper'. This led to an incomprehensible inconsistency in the commentary of Marie-Louise von Franz, e.g. why does she not comment on lead?

96 H. E. Stapleton, *Three Arabic Treatises,* ibid., p. 137.

97 Copy of Ms in Cairo, fol. 5r, lines 3–11 (*Kitāb Mafātīḥ aṣ-ṣanʿa*).

98 H. E. Stapleton, *Three Arabic Treatises,* ibid., p. 137, note 1.

99 M. Berthelot, *Alch.Grecs*, III, I.

100 Ibid., p. 120.

alchemy is performed on man himself, not on his ego, but on what the old alchemist called the divine God-man or Anthropos, who is buried in the depths of the human being. In an obscure Tibetan tradition the continuity of royalty from the first recorded king onwards is somehow connected with the fact that the copper coffins of the former king are poured out onto the earth. The dead king's corpse is elevated in a high tomb and then, when the vessels of copper are poured out from above, the successor can establish himself as king. Copper seems therefore to represent the mystical *mana* of the king, which is passed on to the successor. It is his God-man quality.[101]

This view is already clearly formulated by Zosimos and also by 71
Arabic authors of the mystical branch of alchemy, for instance Morienus, who says: «This stone is that thing which more than anything else is within you, created by God, and you are its prima materia, and it is extracted from you and wherever you will be it remains inseparable from you [...] and, just as man is composed of the four elements, so is the stone, and he (the stone) comes from man and you are its prima materia, namely on account of the procedure, and it is extracted from thee, namely on account of the science. In other words the object is within you, namely in the Mercurius of the wise. You are its prima materia, it is included in you, you keep it hidden in you and it is extracted from you, as it is you who reduce it to its essence and dissolve it, because it cannot be completed without you and you cannot live without it, and thus the beginning reminds one of the end and vice versa.»[102]

This passage, which must have been known to the author, clearly 72
expresses the idea that the lapis is the inner man. Zosimos and the gnostic tradition around him taught that the divine Adam or cosmic Anthropos sank down into creation and dwells in everybody. It is therefore the task of the mortal man to redeem this cosmic inner Anthropos.[103] For our author the alchemical opus is therefore primarily an inner-psychic work which strives to redeem the inner man. This inner Anthropos was later most beautifully described by Ibn ᶜArabī (born 1165) in his famous *Meccan Revelations* (*Al-Futūḥāt al-Makkīya*): When Ibn ᶜArabī circulated around the Kaaba he found himself in a kind of vision of «the eagle stone of the Youth, zealous in devotion, of the silent speaker who neither lives nor dies,

101 J. Bacot, F.W. Thomas, Ch. Toussaint, *Documents de Touen-Houang relatifs à l'histoire du Tibet*, p. 123 ff. I owe this information to Dr Barbara Davies.

102 Rosinus ad Sarratantem Episcopum, in: *Artis Auriferae*, p. 178 ff. See also C. G. Jung, *Aion*, [Coll. Works 9/2], § 256, § 258 ff.

103 H. Corbin, *L'Homme de Lumière dans le Soufisme Iranien.*

the noncomposed, the all encompassed encompasser».[104] This divine youth is a kind of personification of the black stone, which is inserted in a corner of the Kaaba.

73 Looked at from the outside, the Kaaba is only a dead stone. The youth however is its revealed mystery, the divine Anthropos. In answering the question of Ibn ᶜArabī, asking who he was, the youth says about himself: «Behold the articulation of my nature and the order of my structure and from them thou wilt find what you are asking for. For I am no speaker and no partner in conversation. My knowledge extends only to myself and my essence extends only to myself. I am the knowledge, the known and the knower. I am the wisdom, the work of wisdom and the wise.»[105] Later he continues: «I am the garden of the ripe fruit, I am the fruit of totality, lift my veil and read what is chiselled in the lines of my existence.»[106] Fritz Meier[107] and Henry Corbin[108] rightly interpret this figure as the Alter Ego or the self of Ibn ᶜArabī, a concept which goes back to the Hellenistic *Theology of Aristotle*, a Neoplatonic work. In a later passage, Ibn ᶜArabī makes it even more clear that this mysterious youth who evokes in him passionate love is none other than the inner Godhead or the divine I, as Corbin calls it. What Ibn ᶜArabī reveals in clear words, Ibn Umail also alludes to, but he keeps it more hidden under the veil of alchemical expressions; but he is clearly concerned with this mystical figure and not with chemistry.

74 I think it is even possible that our author did not operate chemically at all, but through a kind of yoga meditation, worked directly on his endosomatic life, which was regarded at that time as being a subtle body within the body. He obviously continues the tradition of Zosimos who also used a kind of meditation or active imagination to further the alchemical process.

75 Copper is the metal of Venus, which alludes to the fact that the philosophers' stone springs from the erotic inner life of the human being. In the context of Islamic mysticism this means that the prima materia of the alchemist is his eros, which has to be sublimated into the love of God, but which is first experienced as ordinary love or as love for the imam. The 'fountains of copper' are in that sense the creative Spirit of God in the psyche of man, which induces man to search for God. Our text speaks of

104 See W. Neumann, *Der Mensch und sein Doppelgänger – Alter Ego Vorstellungen in Mesoamerika und im Sufismus des Ibn ᶜArabī*, p. 157. Translation into English by the author. Cf. also F. Meier, *The Mystery of the Kaaba*, p. 149–168.

105 W. Neumann, *Der Mensch und sein Doppelgänger*, p. 159 f.

106 Ibid., p. 161.

107 F. Meier, *The Mystery of the Kaaba*.

108 H. Corbin, *Creative Imagination in the Sufism of Ibn ᶜArabī*.

the 'fountains of copper' also as magnesia, and the latter he calls *abār nuḥās*.[109] According to Ruska, *abār nuḥās* is the Arabic translation of *molybdochalkos*, an alloy of lead and copper, which plays a role in the writings of Zosimos and Olympiodorus.[110] There it means the whole of the work.[111] The explanation is to be found in *al-Māʾ al-waraqī,* where we read: «Mariyah has called Abar Nuhas the 'Honoured Stone', and this is the completely perfect and super-perfect Abar Nuhas that imparts colour. Consequently it gives birth to the Perfect Gold, for the latter is inferior to it (the Abar Nuhas), because it (the Gold) is (only) perfect, whereas that (the Abar Nuhas) is super-perfect. Surely and undoubtedly this Abar Nuhas is (completely) perfect.»[112] In the context of Islamic mysticism something completely perfect can only be Allah Himself. Thus the philosophers' stone is the identity of the perfected man with God. The living impulse, the flow of love towards God, is the real philosophers' stone.

[After the magnesia, which is not commented on,] the third desig- 76
nation of the stone is the tin, the zinc, the iron and the silver,[113] a variation of the many famous *tetrasomias*, the quaternarian components of the stone, like the four directions of the compass, the four elements, the four basic principles of matter, the four letters of Adam, etc. This leads to the enumeration of the silvery earth and its many variations. 'Fountains of copper' designate more the dynamic, active aspect of the stone; the many earths, the receptive, passive aspect. They symbolize the subtle body-soul of the alchemist when it has been completely sublimated by the process and is ready for the union with God. Henry Corbin has shown that many Islamic mystics practiced a kind of active imagination by which a new earth was created that lies in between the sphere of material reality and the Platonic realm of ideas.

Through his active imagination the alchemist came in contact with 77
an inner subtle body reality, which is a whole cosmos in itself. This earth *hūrqalyā* is the purified soul (*nafs*) and the purified world soul in its material-nonmaterial aspect (*Suhrawardī*).[114] These 'white earths' (the *terra*

109 This is an unfortunate misunderstanding as *abār nuḥās* means lead-copper, a symbol that was first translated as 'fountains of copper'.

110 J. Ruska, *Arabische Alchemisten*, p. 21; H. E. Stapleton, *Three Arabic Treatises,* ibid., p. 153, note 8. The symbol lead-copper will be amplified in CALA I B.

111 M. Berthelot, *Alch. Grecs*, III, XXVIII. 2.

112 J. Ruska, *Arabische Alchemisten*, p. 21, p. 25. H. E. Stapleton, *Three Arabic Treatises*, p. 130.

113 These are the four metals given in the Ms G, whereas in the Mss A, B, and D we find copper instead of zinc.

114 Cf. H. Corbin, *Spiritual Body and Celestial Earth*, p. 84 ff.

alba foliata of the Latins) are also called by the author 'ashes' or 'ash of ashes', which is the 'crown of victory'.[115] As Stapleton points out, this phrase is of Alexandrian origin. Elsewhere in *al-Māʾ al-waraqī* it is quoted as a saying of Theodorus: «Take one part of those ashes and keep it with you for it is the crown of victory».[116] The ashes are produced through a process which the Latins called *contritio*. This word reveals the psychological meaning. It is a 'pulverization', a reduction to 'dust and ashes' through repentance. Through the tears of remorse, depression and suffering, the adept is reduced to ashes and thus becomes purified, spiritualized, and open to the reception of the divine spirit. The 'crown of victory' comes into existence by the annihilation of the ego. Then, as *al-Māʾ al-waraqī* says: «The lower body rejoices in the heavenly nature because it is of the same form and it is produced from it.»[117] This union takes place between the subtle bodies.

Text

78 (7.9) And when the stone becomes white, they named it the flower of the salt. And it grows to a part of the ancient and glorious philosophers. And the explanation of the ancient is the body of the land. That is before it becomes black for the second time, after which comes the whiteness, after which comes the redness. And it is the filings of silver [*waraq*], the filings of burnt copper, ashes, dust, the slave and the student. It is the thing which is dyed and the dyer, the one who catches and the one who controls, the one who completes.[118] (9.1)

The envious ones of the sages named it zinc ore and earthen zinc ore. … zinc ore is the white body

holder, the regulator and the clinger. And it is the oxymel.[119]

Comment

79 This is a continuation of the description of the white earth, which is clear by itself. Only a few expressions need an explanation. The 'flower of salt' is a new word for the goal of the work. It reminds one of the 'golden

115 *al-Māʾ al-waraqī*, in: H. E. Stapleton, *Three Arabic Treatises*, ibid., p. 162.

116 Ibid., p. 137, note 1.

117 Ibid., p. 137.

118 *Akšmīl* was intially read as being related to *akmala*, 'to complete'.

119 Oxymel stems from Greek *oxymeli*, being a mixture of vinegar and honey.

flower' of Chinese alchemy. As Jung has shown, salt in alchemy is a symbol of love, the wisdom of achieved and differentiated eros.[120]

The slave is known as the *servus fugitivus* of the Latins and he is 80
Hermes. But a new expression is introduced by the word 'student', which clearly expresses that the adept himself is meant. The dyed one and the dyer are the lover of God and God Himself. The one who catches, who controls and who completes is the sheikh or the imam and thus again ultimately God Himself.

In this beginning of the text the author obviously presupposes that 81
the reader knows his other works and knows the symbolism of alchemy. For such a reader he becomes quite explicit: the philosophers' stone is nothing other than the unification of man with God, a unification which takes place in the psychic subtle body or sublimated soul of the mystic.

Text

(9.1) The explanation of the 'moderator': that is when the stone became moderate in its mixture so that it becomes neither hot nor cold, neither moist nor dry.	and the explanation of the oxymel is the moderator. That	82
And it is named būrnaṭīs when it became white, and	pyrite	
with ten colours, and the ten things are the	[-]	
magnesia. [...] the body and the water [...]	And when ... became red	
after the dye, they named it the golden flower. (9.7)	flower of gold	

Comment

This allusion of the text to the stone being balanced links the 83
author's teaching directly with the Ǧābirean Corpus. As Paul Kraus has proved, the teaching of the balance (*mīzān*) is of central importance to Ǧābir, and Kraus even sees in it the beginning of quantitative chemistry.[121] The latter seems to me doubtful, but we certainly have here the archetype which lies behind quantitative chemistry, consisting in the idea that anything of more lasting consistency in this world, be it psychic or material, is held together by a certain *homeostasis* or balance of energy. According to Ǧābir, this balance is the soul of each object and its very essence. It is expressed in numbers. In this first allusion our text only hints at the four basic qualities of matter: hot, cold, dry and wet.

120 C. G. Jung, *Mysterium Coniunctionis*, [Coll. Works. 14], Chapter *Sal*, III. 5, § 234 ff.

121 Cf. P. Kraus, *Jâbir ibn Ḥayyân*, ibid., Chapter: La théorie de la balance, p. 187 ff.

84 The name *būrnaṭīs* is unknown to me,[122] but it is clearly a designation of the prima materia or the stone, because it is identified with magnesia. The text gives it the attribute of ten colours or ten things. As Stapleton points out, *al-Māʾ al-waraqī* alludes to the tetractys of the Pythagoreans in the following words: «Then they say four, which (then) becomes (with the previous six) outwards ten, but in its hidden meaning it is (still only) four. This number completes the magnesia, which is *abār nuḥās*, which is composed of four. The ten are four, and from the ten proceed four, and from the four proceed ten. Consequently these (four) are the four natures, earth, air, water and fire: and all created beings come into existence from them. Understand this!»[123]

85 This points to the completion of a cosmic totality in which all basic qualities are united by the soul and the tincture. The result our text calls a 'golden flower'. This is an important name because it might point to Chinese influence. In Taoist alchemy the goal of the inner process is most frequently described as a golden flower. This image reappears in Buddhism, but the idea in itself also existed before this in antique Hellenistic alchemy.[124] In the *Book of Sophé* we read: «The science and the wisdom of the best rule over both [the Hebrews and the Egyptians], they came from ancient tradition and their generation is without a king, autonomous, immaterial; it [wisdom] seeks nothing in the material, corruptible bodies, it operates without suffering their influence, being held together by prayer and divine grace. The symbol of alchemy is derived from the creation. [It is the alchemists] who save and purify the divine soul, which is fettered in the elements, and above all which separates the divine spirit, which is lost in the flesh. Just as there exists a sun, a flower of the fire, a heavenly sun, the right eye of the cosmos; in the same way the copper, when it becomes a flower through the purification, becomes an earthly soul, which is the king on earth like the sun is the king of heaven.»[125]

86 This text, which is also attributed to Zosimos, renders the same Gnostic views, namely that the World Soul, the Wisdom of God, has to be liberated from matter into which she has been lost. This liberated divine soul appears as a sunlike golden flower. This text suffices as a source for

122 *Būrnaṭīs* = pyrite, a sulfide of iron and copper, stems from Greek *pyrites,* being firestone. The main source for obtaining copper is copper-pyrites ($CuFeS_2$), thus it is related to copper.

123 H. E. Stapleton, *Three Arabic Treatises,* ibid., p. 19, lines 2–4. This has been discussed more in detail by J. Ruska, *Turba philosophorum,* p. 297 ff. on the basis of an Arabic text of the *Turba*, found by P. Kraus in Paris (Ms 5099, fol. 223v).

124 See *The Secret of the Golden Flower*, translated and explained by Richard Wilhelm.

125 See M. Berthelot, *Alch. Grecs*, III, XLII. Rendered in English according to the translation of Ch.-E. Ruelle.

Ibn Umail, but his designation of the goal might also have been influenced by Taoist yoga, which calls the result of the opus a golden flower. Perhaps the two sources came together in early Arabic alchemy.

Psychologically, the symbol of the flower, in contrast to human or animal symbolism, points to a spirituality which is far removed from ego consciousness. A flower does not move, but wherever fate places it, it quietly grows according to its own inner laws. As a symbol it is the birthplace of the inner realization of the divinity, as the Eastern symbol of the lotus proves. In Jungian terms it symbolizes the self, that is, the slow gradual realization of a divine cosmic centre in the unconscious psyche of the individual. 87

Text

(9.8) In the whiteness they named it the 'white lead' and the 'lead enlightened by a luminous white'. And it is called *qašhaš* with the letter *qāf*. More often it is used with the letter *bā'* for its strong whiteness and the *baṭbarīš* and the *nasṭarīṭ*. All of that is because of its strong whiteness and the corporeal *ḫaršaqlā*. All these are the names at the time of its second whiteness, after which comes the purpleness. They name this whiteness the one that produces oxidation [rust][127] and the making of the rust, and the rust is making red. (9.14) 88

lead *ibšimīš*. And it can be named *ibšimīṯ* and it is named *ifšimīš* with the [letter] *fā'*.

alabaster

chrysocolla[126]

the rusting

Comment

I have not been able to find out what the words *qašhaš* and *ḫaršaqlā* mean, but they are clearly other names for the white earth, i.e. for the lapis in the state of the albedo.[128] 89

126 A greenish-blue mineral consisting of hydrated copper silicate; used in ancient times for soldering gold.

127 Oxidation or rust is the name for the Greek *iosis*, which is the last completed stage of the lapis (Comarius).

128 On the basis of a wrong reading (*fā'* and *qāf* differ in Arabic just by a point), M.-L. von Franz commented: «The letter *qāf* might hint at the world mountain *Qāf*, or at the *Qā'im*, the hidden lost Imam who will appear at the end of the world.»

Text

90 (11.1) And they name it the source of	mother
colours, the source of tinctures, the	mother of dyes, the mother of
source of the gold, the mother of tinc-	gold, the mother of the natures,
tures, the mother of Gods and the uncov-	the mother of gods, the glue …
erer and the origin of the tinctures. And	dyes
the origin for every dye and the sea of the	
two vapours and the sea of wisdom, […]	the sea of the sages,
and the alabaster stone and the anderani-	the marbly stone, the rock-salt,
salt and the salt of houses [common salt]	
without which nothing tastes good nor	
becomes valid. And they name it a frog,	
because it is from the water, and because	
of its changing colours, and submersion	way of existing
back in the water, from which it origi-	
nates and with it it regulates [its life].	which it gets operated
(11.8)	

Comment

91 Most of the names which are mentioned here are understandable without comment. They describe the lapis in its final stage of the *rubedo*, which is a more active state of the lapis than the *albedo*. It is the source and origin of all colours, in other words the active principle of all life. Only the image of the frog is more unusual. The Latins knew later the synonym of *bufo noster* (our toad) as a synonym of the prima materia. It is probable that with our text we have to look at the Egyptian symbolism of the frog. The old Egyptians knew a birth goddess Heket who had the shape of a frog. She sits at the head of the mummy and there she has the meaning of resurrection and rebirth.[129] Even in Coptic times there existed little oil lamps with the image of Heket and the inscription: *anastasis* (resurrection).[130] In Hellenistic-Egyptian papyri we have a picture of a frog sitting in a lotus.[131] The frog replaces the more usual Horus child sitting in the lotus. This proves that the frog was Horus, the reborn sungod. In my opinion that is where the frog symbol came into alchemy.

92 In Antiquity it was believed that the frog would come to life without biological sexual processes but through *generatio aequivoca*, primary

129 See H. Bonnet, *Reallexikon der Aegyptischen Religionsgeschichte*, p. 284 f., s.v. Heket.

130 See E. A. W. Budge, *The Mummy*, p. 266. I owe this to the kindness of Dr Barbara Davies.

131 See Th. Hopfner, *Griechisch-Aegyptischer Offenbarungszauber*, Vol. 1, p. 132.

generation. That is probably what made him a symbol of resurrection, because the old Egyptians believed that the dead were dissolved into the original ocean Nun and then came to life directly out of it again.

According to the oldest alchemical tradition the lapis is actually the 93
resurrection body, which can be discovered and completed already in a lifetime through the opus. The text *Comarius to Cleopatra*,[132] which belongs to the first century, gives a complete testimony for this fact. It describes the alchemical work as a mystery of the death and resurrection of man and, in my opinion, draws this from Gnostic Egyptian sources. This has survived unaltered in Islamic mysticism until today.[133]

In general Hellenistic views, the frog belongs to Dionysos. Its limbs, 94
blood and bones were used for love charms. Interpreted in modern language, it therefore also symbolizes the creative spontaneous upsurge of erotic impulses and their overwhelming 'divine' nature. Referring to the famous fairy tale of the frog prince, Jung points out that the frog contains the superior or divine man within a humble husk. He says: «When the frog appears in dreams or visions or fairy tales, it means man under his chthonic aspect, his 'nothing but' aspect. Our consciousness of what man is, of being human, is the frog; it means man looked at as a mere biological being. But that is only the outer shell of something very much more beautiful and perfect inside, the shell that will be broken through and cast off, either by death, when the beautiful superior man is liberated, or by the intervention of the mystical ritual in initiation.»[134] Alchemy has been understood since Zosimos as such a mystical ritual that liberates the divine man.

Text

(11.8) And they name it [...] the snail of the mountains and the chameleon when it becomes coloured by the soakings to which it is exposed, one colour after the other, at the time of the making red. And [they name it] with many colours and the peacock, because of its multitude of colours and [they name it] the aṭlaisūs, whose explanation is the multi-coloured. (11.13)	the snails of the sea, ... etesian[135] stone	95

132 M. Berthelot, *Alch. Grecs*, IV. XX.

133 See H. Corbin, *Spiritual Body and Celestial Earth.*

134 C. G. Jung, *Visions, Notes of the Seminar given in 1930–1934*, Vol. 1, p. 544.

135 Etesian means annual, from Greek *etesios* = annual.

Comment

96 The snail can be explained by the *al-Māʾ al-waraqī,* which runs: «In the same way they compared the silvery water to the water of the snail and they have three reasons for their comparison: first the snail is circular and round like a pearl. Therefore Hermes said in one of his epistles regarding the marriage of the male with the female and her sisters: "marry him with four wives." Afterwards he said: "If you do not know them, then they are from a moist beautifully round pearl." The sage [Hermes] compared their water to the moist pearl [...] The second reason for this comparison of it to the water of the snail is that when the snail creeps on the mountain it leaves along its way from its moisture a thin white gleaming moisture with a bright radiance that shines in the sun. And they compare their water [with the water of the snail] because of the whiteness of their pure silvery water, its radiance and its sparkling. [...] The third reason for their comparing it with the water of the snail is that the snail comes out from its dry hard body and drags along its hard body wherever it creeps. Then it returns and enters it, disappearing in it. Thus it cannot be seen. The outer appearance of the snail is a dry white stone while in its interior there is a moist, white, moving spirit. And the body of the sages is dry, having soul, spirit, life and the ability to grow. [...] its solid dry stony body is that which is visible and in its inside there is a moving spirit, created from it and by it. Thus all of this is created from water and in the water. [...] This is the stone about which Democritus said: "A stone and not a stone." And it is the stone, which the sage Āras compared to the eagle-stone because the eagle-stone *(ḥağar al-ʿuqāb)* is a well-known stone and that stone has in its inside a stone that is moving. He meant by that the rising water and the ashes that come out of ashes.»[136]

97 The last sentences of this quotation are revealing in their explicitness: the snail is the philosophers' stone and is an image for the wise man, i.e. the master or the sheikh. More than the Greek alchemists, the Arabs seem to have openly expressed the fact that the opus is a 'chemical' simile for an inner development in man himself, a process carried along by the divine power of love, which is a dynamic manifestation of God Himself. The 'fourfold marriage' mentioned in the text alludes again to the quaternarian structure of the inner self. The house of the snail is a spiral, which in general mythology carries the meaning of development and resurrection

136 H. E. Stapleton, *Three Arabic Treatises,* ibid., p. 47. An unnoticed *ʿain* (ʿ) in the word *al-ʿuqāb* led to the following commentary of M.-L. von Franz: In spite of the different spelling, the word *qāb* might be an allusion to the black stone which is inserted in the corner of the Kaaba. For Ibn ʿArabī this smaller stone meant the innermost symbolic essence of the 'dead' outer Kaaba.

as well as concentration onto the centre. In certain African tribes the spiral symbolizes the creative vibration which emanates from the highest Godhead; and in most mythologies the journey of the dead takes on a spiral form. The latter was also the case in Egypt,[137] which must have been known to our author. The Arabic word *ṭāfa,* which is the term for circumambulation of the Kaaba, has actually the meaning «to walk around, to circle».[138] The centre of the spiral is the Godhead in man, which is in touch (but not identical) with God Himself. Thus the snail symbolizes psychologically that inner process which Jung called individuation. The snail, according to Chevalier, is a lunar symbol because it shows and hides its horns[139] and because of its moist nature. It is an alchemical symbol also in Latin alchemy.[140]

The name of 'chameleon' for the stone is immediately understandable 98
because of its capability to change colours. In the stage after the nigredo, a phase comes in the opus in which the prima materia displays many colours in changing varieties. It is the so-called *cauda pavonis*, and we will find that our text mentions the peacock a little later. Psychologically, it announces the return of inner life after a death state in the nigredo.

In the language of the later mystic Nasafī (thirteenth century), the 99
many colours represent the different psychological impulses in situations that tear the ego of the adept into different directions: love, anger, greed etc. A whole 'variability' assaults him. But when he has reached his goal this variability is replaced by a 'colourless' constancy.[141]

If we stop a minute to reflect on what our text is aiming at, it 100
becomes clear that it tries to give a sort of catalogue of all the symbolic names of the philosophers' stone, making it clear that the *mille nomina* all point to the same mystery. He does not comment on chemical procedures but tries to unify what he has already written elsewhere by giving a key to the different names of the stone.

Text

(11.13) And they name it the son of the 101
year because it is born every year and it
takes a colour every two months from one changes

137 *Dictionnaire des Symboles*, eds J. Chevalier and A. Gheerbrant, p. 334, s.v. Escargot.

138 See F. Meier, *The Mystery of the Kaaba*, p. 164, note 41.

139 *Dictionnaire des Symboles*, ibid., p. 334.

140 For instance in: Lambsprinck, 'De lapide philosophico', *Musaeum Hermeticum*, p. 355.

141 See F. Meier, *The Problem of Nature in the Esoteric Monism of Islam*, p. 149–203.

colour to another colour in the course of every degree of the operation. And they named it a thing because everything they need in their work is in it and from it and by it and for it. Everything is in it itself. And it doesn't need anything else from anything else and nothing that is not from it enters in it. That is because, if something foreign would enter into it, this would corrupt it and paralyze it and it would take away its strength and its activity. (13.3)

everything

All of that is in it and from it and by it only because

Comment

102 The name 'son of the year' refers to the stone's Greek name *lithos etesios* in Greek alchemy. Its meaning is probably that it condenses in itself all the qualities of the astrological months, the course of the sun through the zodiac. The stone is not only the completeness of nature, but also the completeness of time. That nothing outer should be added to the opus is a well-known adage which needs no comment. Individuation means, by definition, uniqueness which is free from outer and collective influences.

Text

103 (13.3) And they named it a staff because the staff of Moses had a spirit in it and it became a dragon that swallowed all that was thrown to it. Likewise their stone is a spirit that swallows all of the nourishment and absorbtion of colours which are given to it. (13.6)

staff of Moses

soakings

Comment

104 Moses and Joseph were considered by the Arabs as alchemists (Moses appears already as an alchemical author in Greek alchemy).[142] Both learnt the art during the stay of the Israelites in Egypt. The staff miracle of Moses demonstrates the transformation of inorganic matter into a living thing, which is the main endeavour of alchemy, the snake being *the* well-

142 P. Kraus, *Jâbir ibn Ḥayyân,* ibid., p. 34.

known symbol of Mercurius. The snake that originated from the staff of Moses conquered the many snakes which plagued the children of Israel. It condensed the dissociated many-foldedness into a oneness, just as according to Ibn Umail the philosophers' stone condenses the many colours into one. In psychological terms individuation unifies the formerly dissociated personality into an inner oneness.

Text

(13.7) And it is the dragon and from it		105
comes the head of the dragon that is its		
water, which goes out from it and with it		
and in it. And it is the residue and the fiery	its sediment and the sun	
body. And it is the moon, the two years	the furnace	
and the white sulphur, the red sulphur and		
the sulphurs. (13.10)	[-]	

Comment

The dragon appears at the entrance of the monolithic temple in the Zosimos visions. It is a variation of the ouroboros, the head end of the snake representing the part which is nobler than the tail end. For the author, all of that is his divine water, the unitary basic substance of the opus. This unitary substance contains a latent duality which the author mentions in the following lines as the two years, the two sulphurs, etc., and as the moon, which consists of light and darkness. These are clearly allusions to the dualities mentioned in the *al-Māʾ al-waraqī*: the two birds, the two rays of the sun, and a whole other 'Two in One'. 106

Text

(13.10) They name the red *kibrīt* with all	and the red sulphur. They	107
of these different sulphurs. And it is	name it with all of this when	
white, and it is the ferment of the water,	it is white,	
the ferment of silver, the ferment of gold,		
and acid ferment, and the bread, and	lime	
human excrement, and dung and the		
white wood when it is desiccated and	firewood	
dry. And it is the source of life and who		
has drunk from it never gets thirsty		
again. And it is the source of life and the	eye of the animal	
mountain of the sources, because from it		

comes out their divine, silvery, pure water and life-giving to its earth and everything on it. (13.16)

which revives their

Comment

108 Here the text alludes to the *al-Māʾ al-waraqī*, the silvery water, which is the basic substance of alchemy, the *hydor theion* of the Greeks and the *aqua permanens* of the Latins. It is not ordinary water but a mystical substance, the basis of all existence. In the context of Arabic mysticism it means the living connection of man with the creative manifestations of the Godhead. In our modern terms it would mean the psychic aliveness and healing effect which comes from the contact with the unconscious and the self.

Text

109 (13.17) And it is the copper and the *qinbāl*

cinnabar and in every cooking it takes a colour from the red [colours], until three soakings, three cookings and three successive uprisings are completed for it. Thus it becomes a red cinnabar. And at this time it is named cinnabar.

and they also named it the wool and the wood of the wool. And they named it the iron when the female pointed to it, and it resisted the fire like the resistance of the iron because the iron doesn't dissolve in the fire like other things and it doesn't escape from the fire. (15.7)

They
firewood
entered in

Comment

110 This text needs no comment as it contains only general alchemical adages. The lapis *qui resistit ignem* is naturally in this context the permanent inner resurrection body which suffers no decay.

Text

111 (15.7) And they named it brain. Marqūnis named it the brain of the ghoul, because

the idea [opinion] is imprisoned in the	thinking is concealed
brain and like that one of the qualities	the dye of their stone is concealed
of their stone is that they [the philosophers] hide themselves in its inside, just	
as the idea is hidden in the brain and	thinking is concealed
doesn't appear, and what appears from	
the idea are only its results. (15.11)	thinking

Comment

The source for identifying the lapis with the brain is probably the trea- 112
tise of *Platonic Tetralogies*, a work which also influenced Ǧābir. C. G. Jung gives in *Psychology and Alchemy* a detailed comment on its Latin version, the *Liber Platonis Quartorum*.[143] This book of Pseudo-Plato recommends the use of the occiput as the vessel of transformation, because it is the container of thought and intellect. The brain is the seat of the divine part in man. By mere analogy the alchemists produced the lapis out of matter by simultaneously trying to reach the highest culmination of consciousness. That the brain of the cosmic man is the *prima materia* of the universe is already the teaching of the Gnostic Ophites.[144] According to them, the divine basic matter of the universe is the Ouroboros snake. This snake is like the river which originates in the garden of Eden and spreads out in four directions. It is the divine Logos. Eden is the brain of the Anthropos, the heavenly spheres are its membranes which wrap it up. The four rivers of Eden are the eyesight, the hearing, the breathing and the mouth etc. Our text (quoting Marqūnis) especially mentions that the brain of a ghoul is needed, not that of a human being. A ghoul is a desert demon of a varying shape, a dangerous power which can cause possession. This refers to the well-known motif that, at its beginning stages, the stone can appear as a dangerous enemy of the alchemist. The *Liber Platonis Quartorum* warns: « … At a certain hour during the preparation certain kinds of spirits will oppose the work and at another time this opposition will not be present.»[145] Jung writes: «In the Arabic *Book of Ostanes* there is a description of the arcane substance, or the water, in its various forms, first white, then black, then red, and finally a combustible liquid or a fire which is struck from certain stones in Persia. The text continues: "It is a tree that grows on the tops of the mountains, a young man born in Egypt, a prince from Andalusia who desires the torment of the seekers. He has slain their leaders. […] The sages are powerless to oppose him. I can see no weapon against him save resig-

143 C. G. Jung, *Psychology and Alchemy*, [Coll. Works 12], § 366 ff.

144 H. Leisegang, *Die Gnosis*, p. 141.

145 *Theatrum Chemicum*, Vol. V, p. 126.

nation, no charger but knowledge, no buckler but understanding. If the seeker finds himself before him with these weapons, and slays him, he [the prince] will come to life again after his death, will lose all power against him [the seeker], and will give the seeker the highest power, so that he will arrive at his desired goal."»[146]

113 The water, the tree, the young Egyptian, and the Andalusian prince all refer to the stone. Water, tree, and man appear here as its synonyms. The prince is an important symbol that needs a little elucidation, for it seems to echo an archetypal motif that is already found in the Gilgamesh epic. Enkidu, the chthonic man and shadow of Gilgamesh, is created by the gods at the behest of the insulted Ishtar, so that he may kill the hero. In the same way the prince 'desires the torment of the seekers'. He is their enemy and 'has slain their leaders', that is, the masters and authorities of the art. This motif of the hostile stone is formulated in the *Allegoriae Sapientum* as follows: «Unless thy stone shall be an enemy, thou will not attain to thy desire.»[147] «The clearest of all», Jung stresses, «is Olympiodorus [sixth century]: "And all the while the demon Ophiuchos instills negligence impeding our intentions; everywhere he creeps about, within and without, causing oversights, fear, and unpreparedness, and at other times he seeks by harassment and injuries to make us abandon the work."»[148] Olympiodorus also points out that lead is possessed by a demon which drives man mad.[149] C. G. Jung devotes a whole chapter to this dangerous demonic aspect of the stone, which symbolizes not only physical dangers of explosions and poisoning, but also mental dangers of going mad. As long as ego consciousness has not the right attitude towards the self or is too naively unprepared to understand what the self wants, the self (stone) assumes a dangerous aspect and can even cause a psychotic explosion.

Text

114 (15.11) They also named it the skull vessel, the alembic (*qarʿa*), [...], the temple and the congregational mosque because it gathers all

146 C. G. Jung, 'The Philosophical Tree', in: *Alchemical Studies* [Coll. Works 13], § 424. The *Book of Ostanes* is found in M. Berthelot, *La Chimie du Moyen-âge,* Vol. III, p. 117.

147 *Theatrum Chemicum*, Vol. V, p. 59.

148 C. G. Jung, 'The Philosophical Tree', in: *Alchemical Studies* [Coll. Works 13], § 430 where he quotes from: *Sur l'Art Sacré*, in: M. Berthelot, *Alch. Grecs*, II. IV, 28.

149 Ibid., Vol. III, II. IV.43, p. 104 ff.

persons of knowledge among the people and thus the *qarʿa* [skull] has collected in it the mixture which is their stone, which is the fountains of copper, which is the magnesia that is the temple.	of our science and likewise the vessel collected in it the mixture, in which they have all that is in it, and therefore they named this mixture—which is their stone, lead-copper and magnesia—the temple.
And they named it the congregational mosque because it collects whatever they need from the moist, dry, hot, cold things, the spirits, souls, ashes, material things and the *ḥāʾir*, and dyes. Thus, it is the all and from it is all [...]. (17.4)	bodies ferments and in it is all

Comment

The word *qarʿa* [now translated as vessel] can mean gourd, pump- 115
kin, skull, but in this connection, where the author spoke of the brain, it primarily means the skull, which Plato already in the *Timaeus* compared with the firmament. In Greek alchemy it was a symbol of the alchemical vessel and simultaneously (because of its round form) a symbol of the stone. Most remarkably Muḥammad ibn Umail identifies it here with an Egyptian temple. But it is not surprising if we remember that Zosimos already described the lapis as a temple that consists of white marble.

We also know from Ibn Umail's *al-Māʾ al-waraqī* that for him the 116
temple is the place where he discovered the mystery of alchemy written on a tablet in the hand of a Hermes statue. The temple is therefore like the skull, the container of the Hermetic mystery. In many Egyptian temples the images on the walls mostly represent, as in the royal tombs, the resurrection mystery of the king: his corpse on the embalming table, the different phases of the *taricheia* (mummification), and finally the erecting of a statue or the pillar *djed* as a symbol of the completed resurrection. As I have pointed out in my book *On Dreams and Death*,[150] this resurrection mystery also underlies the oldest Greek alchemical texts. Knowing or not knowing that Greek alchemy originates from the Egyptian death and rebirth mystery, the Arabs projected the idea of that mystery back into the pyramids and temples. Helmuth Jacobsohn has already pointed out that the alchemical lapis has an older parallel in the so-called *bnbn* stone, which forms the point of the Egyptian obelisk and has the shape of a pyramid.[151] It is placed

150 M.-L. von Franz, On *Dreams and Death,* p. 125.

151 H. Jacobsohn, *Das göttliche Wort und der göttliche Stein*, p. 217 ff.

so that the first ray of the rising sun illumines it. Such *bnbn* stones were also placed in the tombs of the dead. The word is also related to the *bn.w*-bird, the phoenix, which symbolizes resurrection. Thus the identification of the Arabs of the lapis with a pyramidal stone has deep archetypal roots.

117 In Ismāʿīlīyan Gnosis temple means quite generally the resurrection body, into which the dead were allowed to move when going into paradise. In accordance with Greek alchemy (Comarius) the philosophers' stone is identical with the resurrection body. But the temple as a symbol for the stone could also be replaced by the image of the mosque. The mosque is for the Islamic believer the place where he recollects himself and purifies himself through ablution, a place of spiritual rebirth. Our text stresses that the mosque collects the person's knowledge just as the skull collects the ingredients of the philosophers' stone. Being the seat of consciousness, the skull congeals so to speak the scattered psychic factors into a unified personality.

Text

118 (17.4) And they also named it everything, and all of
these are from the unknown known one, and they well-known
named it also the midwife at the time of the distilla- receiver
tion and the descending of the water to the meeting to it, for the reunion
place of the spirits. (17.7)

Comment

119 The philosophers' stone is here characterized as an instrument (midwife) of its own birth because in all mystical journeys it is the self itself which induces and leads the finding of the self. In the soul of the mystic it acts like a midwife[152] towards its own birth.

Text

120 (17.8) Muḥammad ibn Umail, may God have mercy on
him, said: «The extraction of such meanings and their
precise expressions from their books is extremely difficult for people. But who is able to uncover the secrets
of people who have died and passed away with their
secrets hidden in their perished consciousness and bygone consciences

152 The word *midwife* was an incorrect reading. The soul of the mystic would be a receiver for the divine water.

in their decayed hearts, except the one whose mind God opens and whom He supports with His spirit?» (17.13)

Comment

This is obviously a gloss which slipped into the text. 121

Text

(17.13) And they named their stone—which is the magnesia—gold and said: «Make […] a dyeing poison.» They also said: «Whoever is able to turn gold into a dyeing poison has found the true way. And whoever is not able to make poison is without any use.» (19.2) 122	the gold into And whoever found the true way found it. And whoever is unable to turn it into a killing poison is nowhere

Comment

Already in the text of Comarius[153] the result of the whole process is 123 an all-permeating poison which 'kills the body'.[154] Probably this refers to the fact that the achievement of individuation, the realization of the self, ultimately coincides with death. This reminds one of the Hindu belief that death is Maha-samadhi, the ultimate enlightenment.

Text

(19.2) And they also said about this magnesia: «O all 124 of you seekers of this science, if you want to cure your souls from the disease of poverty and from all seductions and sorrows, then dye the gold into red. For if you dye it red it will hold the dye and it will be dyed, the exalted God willing.» (19.6)

Comment

Dyeing the gold red is already in the Comarius text the fourth and 125 final stage of the opus. From what the text said before, it is a psychologi-

153 M. Berthelot, *Alch. Grecs*, IV. XX, 17.

154 *Pharmakon phoneuton*

cal transformation through which the adept overcomes poverty, wrong desires, errors and worries. Thus the rubedo, which is here described, means clearly a psychological achievement which comes forth with the help of Allah.

Text

126 (19.6) Concerning this, H̱ālid ibn Yazīd said: «The ancient philosophers in all periods of time got tired to dye gold except from the gold.» He meant by that verse the gold of the philosophers, which is their magnesia. But the people imagined that it is the gold which is in their hands. Therefore they ruined it with different kinds of operations and they became tired and did not succeed. (19.12)

philosophers who passed away … failed to dye gold unless it was gold
sages

Comment

127 The text quoting H̱ālid ibn Yazīd clearly points out that gold is the beginning and the end, which would be chemically meaningless. But psychologically it makes sense, the self being the basis and the goal of the individuation process.

Text

128 (19.12) In another place he [H̱ālid ibn Yazīd] said: «Make the gold white.» And they also said: «Turn the gold into silver [*waraq*].» By that they meant the making white of this magnesia, when the blackness appeared on it during the operation. Thus these statements […] prove the rightness of the philosophers saying to you first that the philosophers name their white stone when its whiteness is completed into gold. As they say: «Dye the gold red.» And as they say while it is in its blackness: […], till it becomes the colour of silver, because they named their magnesia, during the state of blackness and in the state of whiteness, gold. Under that blackness there are strongest dyes about which only the exalted God knows.

they
of the sages
my saying to you
sages
becomes extreme,
«Turn the gold into silver». That means you must turn the stone white and remove its blackness
powers and

The philosophers were unable to know that. sages
(21.10)

Comment

This rather confused text seems to say that it is always the same substance, the gold, which undergoes the different stages of colour, the blackness (*nigredo*), the whiteness (*albedo*) which is called magnesia or *waraq*, and finally the redness (*rubedo*). *Waraq* therefore is not the metal silver, which is different from gold, but a stage of gold itself, its feminine receptive aspect. What Ibn Umail says about the blackness is interesting: it contains the strongest dyes. We know that in the *nigredo* the demonic forces appear which, under the veil of depression, hide the intensity and power of passion of love in its elementary form, and that is the real secret of Allah! 129

Text

(21.10) Therefore […] the more you soak the stone, the more dye you get from it. And that rises in rank and this increase continues forever without end. (21.12)	they said that By that it	130

Comment

The secret of Allah is the love He instils in the searcher, and that love keeps on growing, and the more you saturate it, the more it grows. 131

Text

(21.12) And it is a great secret from the secrets of the exalted God, especially in the stone which appears from him by the operation. It has been hidden from all the people because they [the philosophers] recommend to each other not to put it in a book. And they deferred its matter to the exalted God so that He gives it to whom He wants and withholds it from whom He wants. The dye is in their water, and what is dyed is in their earth. And by it [the water] appear its traces and its dyes. Thus, the water dyes the earth and the earth likewise dyes the water … (23.4)	. It is a characteristic that God put in this stone, which appears from it sages [-] [-] flowers	132

Comment

133 The water is the creative emanation of God and the earth is the receptive purified psyche of the adept, which dye each other in the coniunctio.

Text

134 (23.4) … with its colours and its sulphurs, which are in it [the earth], and it [the earth] retains the dye and does not let it escape [the dye] while the water disappears at the time of its drying. During that the philosophers did what they called the whitening of the gold and the reddening of the gold. Otherwise there is no benefit for them. What wisdom could obligate them to turn that into silver, which has more in it than the value of the silver? (23.10)

This is the explanation of what the sages meant by their statement: «Make the gold white and make the gold red.»

value

Comment

135 Through the colours and the sulphurs the earth gets impregnated with the qualities of the Godhead, and, even if the influence of the Godhead recedes, these 'dyes' remain in the psyche of the adept.

Text

136 (23.10) But by that they rather meant what I explained to you about the whitening of the black body in order that its colour turns into a colour like the silver after it was black. Then it turns into red with the rest of the water, which is set aside for the reddening, which they named the dyes and the flowers of grapes in order that it turns into gold, that means that the sulphur becomes a dyer. (23.15)

manifestation of the herbs

it

dyeing elixir

Comment

137 This complicated passage tries to explain how the basic material changes within itself and that the *agens* and *patiens* are of the same nature. The material turns *within itself* from *nigredo* to *albedo* and to *rubedo*. Interesting is the name of the dye which brings forth the *rubedo*: «flowers

of grapes». That harks back to Greek alchemy where we meet the expression «grapes of Hermes». The *rubedo* has thus to do with wine, with an ecstatic drunkenness of a religious nature—a drunkenness which is well known in Persian mysticism. In the *rubedo* the sulphur becomes active and becomes the dyer. Throughout these last passages it becomes clear that the author adheres to the Ǧābirean doctrine that the whole of mineral nature consists of sulphur and mercury. Sulphur is the name for the male active principle through which God manifests the mineral world. Mercury (sometimes also called the white sulphur) is the feminine, passive, receptive principle. This teaching of Ǧābir was also carried on (after Ibn Umail), for instance by the Brethren of Purity and Ibn Sīnā. Sulphur and mercury, or the red and white sulphur, are cosmic principles, not material substances. They could be compared with the Chinese Yang and Yin principle. Today we can no longer adhere to the sulphur-mercury doctrine as far as chemistry is concerned, but it is still valid in the realm of depth psychology. As Jung has shown in *Mysterium Coniunctionis*, in his chapter on sulphur,[155] the latter means 'Getriebenheit' (motive factor in consciousness or compulsion), the less spiritual aspect of the *prima materia*. This element returns in the *rubedo* in a spiritualized form.

Text

(23.15) When many people heard the 138
mentioning of gold and the statement of
the philosophers: «make the gold red» and sages
«dye the gold», they took the gold of the
people and sought from it what is not in it.
Therefore it didn't give them a dye,
because it is [already] perfect in its dye
and its richness. It does not give colour, it is self-sufficient with it
nor does it accept a dye since the dyeing is
for the spirits, not for the bodies. (25.4)

Comment

The *aurum vulgi* is not fitting for the process because it cannot 139
develop. The *aurum non vulgi* is the compulsion of the psyche, an imperfection which by its very nature can undergo transformation.

155 C.G. Jung, *Mysterium Coniunctionis* [Coll. Works 14], § 151.

Text

140 (25.5) But in fact by the statement of the	
sages: «Bodies are [produced] by bodies»,	get dyed
they only meant by the bodies the six	
dyeing saturations which are the water,	soakings for dyeing from
with which they make red, because they	
were bodies, which the philosophers made	sages
from a subtle spirit. Then they turned	returned
them by the dissolution and the regulation	operation
into dyeing souls and fiery spirits with	
which they have dyed their single body,	
which comes from their work in the last	first operation
regulation. Therefore they said: «Bodies	
are dyed by bodies.» And they also named	
their stone, which is the body, bodies,	
with what entered in it from its sisters.	because of its many sisters
Then it is one body and in number it is	that entered into it. Thus it is
one. (25.14)	a body and what concerns the
	number it is bodies.

Comment

141

The procedure is to separate a part of the material from the main body of the stone and to saturate the latter with it later. The separated materials are the 'wives' or 'sisters' of the main material. Psychologically, in a man's psyche, it is the making conscious of the anima. He first has to isolate and personify the anima in imagination and separate her so to speak from his own personality. Sometimes this is a whole group of *animae* (wives and sisters). In the *rubedo* however, a reunion with the anima takes place, and with it a return to the activities of life on a higher level of consciousness. The returning anima dyes the whitened material, that is, she bestows the colours of life on the adept who, in the *albedo*, had become completely detached from life. The final sentence however stresses that this is all only one body, namely the inner personality of the adept.

142 What is bewildering is that the author sometimes calls the sublimated material soul or spirit, and sometimes body. Obviously it is both or neither, in other words it is something real within the 'reality' of the psyche.

Text

(25.14) While it is in the dissolution, afterwards it is a spirit because it was a corporeal spirit, a truth resistant to the fire and it took on the colour and great powers. Thus it became a great matter. When it gets burnt for a second time with water	And in the dissolution after solidification it is a spirit because it was a corporeal spirit, so that it resisted	143
and gets decomposed, it became a spiritual body. Thus the spiritual [...] spirits enter into it [the body] because it became subtle and similar to them and belongs to them. And it has a soul and a spirit similar to what is in that water. But both are not operated. Then the soul and the spirit	turns again into fiery	
which are in the dyer meet the soul and the spirit which are in the second body.	dyeing water,	
Therefore the philosophers said: «The	sage	
close one [...].» (27.6)	met the close one [the beloved met the beloved, only in Ms D]	

Comment

This passage is, in spite of its complications, understandable if we keep in mind that the author is groping to describe something which is neither spirit nor body, but something in between which is both and neither. As Jung explained in his Lectures on Alchemy at the ETH, there is a sphere where the deeper layers of the unconscious psyche, which we call the collective unconscious, gradually merge with the sympathetic nervous system and the matter of the body.[156] But the body is ultimately a little speck of cosmic matter. At the base of our being we are carbon, iron, magnesium, copper etc. Thus we possess an inner psychic connection with inorganic matter and through this an unconscious knowledge of it. By their meditation the alchemists tried to reach that knowledge. 144

The sentence «the close one met the close one» refers to the *unio mystica* of two friends: the divine spirit and the purified soul of the alchemist. In this union the gap between God and man, spirit and matter, creator and creature is bridged. 145

156 C. G. Jung, *Lectures given at the ETH Zürich*, p. 67 f., p. 177 f.

Text

146 (27.7) And he also said: «Nature enjoys nature, and	
nature is attracted to nature, and nature conquers	holds on
nature», and «being enjoys being and the being	
clings to being». (27.9)	

Comment

147 This is a description of the coniunctio and of the love experience as a partly personal and partly impersonal coming together of the opposites in a transpersonal medium.

Text

148 (27.9) By all of this they [the sages] meant	
the insemination of the soul and spirit,	union
which are in the body, with the soul and	
spirit coming out in the divine water from	
the first body, which is the fountains of	complete lead-copper
perfect copper. Thus when these regulated	the perfectly operated [and
soul and spirit entered into the second	thus refined]
body, the whole became one perfect thing,	
beyond perfection. (29.2)	

Comment

149 This is a description of the resurrection or second coniunctio when the sublimated soul returns to the body. The mediating element is now mentioned: the divine water, which is also the fountains of copper, the prima materia. In an Islamic context the divine water seems to mean the creative loving emanation of Allah, the primary impulse of love in God towards man. After the alchemical operation this love becomes perfect.

Text

150 (29.2) Then the dye gushes forth from it,	
which makes imperfect things perfect.	
Then the [...] gold comes from it.	perfect
Thus I have explained [...] the meaning of	to you
their statement «the close one met its	

close one», and their statement «nature conquers nature» and «being holds being». The soul which is in the second body held on to the soul which is in the divine water. And each of the two became joyful to meet the other one. (29.9)

Comment

The triumphant bliss of the reunion of soul and body in resurrection 151
is already described by the Comarius text.[157] It is a mystical wedding of soul and body, and simultaneously of man and God.

Text

(29.9) Therefore the body survived and revived 152
lived the eternal life. Thus the meaning in their statement «nature is for nature» and «being is for being» is the same and brooks no disagreement. And therefore Maria the Hebrew put forth this statement and said: «We are the people of one city and each of us recognizes the language of the others. Therefore who is not from our city and doesn't know our language must not enter into our work.» (29.14)

Comment

In the coniunctio the body acquires immortality, but one must 153
remember that it is not the gross body but the sublimated second body of the alchemists. The quotation of Maria the Prophetess alludes to the temple and to the mosque, which were mentioned before. They represented in the former quotation a spiritual community of those who have the secret knowledge and this is repeated here: only the alchemist who has gone through the inner experience of the opus understands the language of the alchemistic texts. In European alchemy this idea corresponds to the idea of an *ecclesia spiritualis*, an invisible community of all those who have become more conscious.

157 M. Berthelot, *Alch. Grecs*, IV. XX.

Text

154 (29.15) They also named their stone the red nūrīṭīs, the iron, the reddish sweet and the reddish copper. All of these are from the names of the magnesia. (31.1)

pyrite … reddened
reddened … [-]

Comment

155 The wrong writing of būrītis (= pyrite) as nūrīṭīs in Ms G led to this commentary: Nūrīṭīs comes probably from the Arabic word *nūr*, which means light. The lapis is the red stone of light.

Text

156 (31.1) And the glass and the bottle and it was named like that because of its whiteness and because it does not accept any dirt nor a thing that is not from it, like the pure body of glass. But it accepts the dyes […]. And they named the magnesia, which is a stone, with the names of their divine water and they named the divine water with the names of their dry body, which is the fountains of copper. It is also the magnesia because it is from one thing, […] in order to confuse whoever hears it. But it is not obscure for the one who knows the water and the body. (31.9)

[They also call it] … a piece of glass
in the same way as the glass accepts all the dyes … their
lead-copper
I mean from one water,

Comment

157 First of all the whole text describes the basic separation of the body from a liquid or sublimated other part, which is called spirit or soul, but now, in this passage, Ibn Umail identifies the two: the divine water is the body *and* the soul. If we want to understand this through an example we can turn to Mahdihassan's 'explanations' of Indian alchemy: minerals and crystals are living entities because they grow, they have a soul in contrast for instance to rust which is dead. Now «a self-growing entity becomes reproductive when it is made up of two opposites»,[158] and «a fertilized egg is bi-elemental incorporating two centres of potential

158 S. Mahdihassan, *Indian Alchemy or Rasayana*, p. 33 f.

growth».[159] Certain Hindu alchemists thought that plants had a more spiritual soul, metals more corporeal souls. Therefore, if you mixed for instance copper with a certain plant juice, the latter absorbed its corporeal soul. Then you throw the mortal body of the copper away and reincorporate the soul in a more lasting body, for instance, in the corporeal soul of gold. Now this product has acquired 'eternal life' and can therefore also impart eternal life to somebody who eats it. It has become an elixir of immortality.

It seems to me that Ibn Umail's description of the philosophers' stone comes very close to these Hindu views, only that he gave them an Islamic meaning. For him, this coniunctio is the resurrection, which is the union with the Beloved, i.e. Allah. In this union is the true remedy of immortality for the alchemist. 158

Text

(31.10) Among the names with which they alluded to the magnesia is the grapes of coffee beans, and they squeeze their water out of it. And they named it [the magnesia] the Book [Koran] and all what had happened in it. And they named it arsenic and zandarīǧ. (31.13)	a bunch of grapes because … a Book [*muṣḥaf*], and all that flows out of it, books	159

Comment

Here suddenly the author reveals to us what his divine water is, namely the *aqua doctrinae* of the Koran, which is vivifying like coffee [the new translation has 'bunch of grapes'] and nourishes the spirit. The Shiʿite symbolic interpretation of the Koran is the true water of life. It is called arsenic because it is masculine, i.e. an active spirit. 160

Text

(31.13) And they named it, when it became solid and dry, mercury, white sulphur, whitened sulphur, and the white arsenic. 161

159 Ibid., p. 37.

[…] the firmness of all the parts which are in it and with it and from it comes the firmness of […] and the quicksilver […], because it is the origin of everything for them, as the poison of magnesia is everything. (33.1)

They named it also a mortar, and all parts, which are in it and with it and from it mortars. And they named the mercury everything … they have. Likewise they named the magnesia everything

Comment

162 When the mystical teaching of the Koran consolidates in the psyche of the adept it becomes the 'magnesia', a white entity, or the philosophers' stone in the *albedo*. It is called poison because it penetrates every other thing.

Text

163 (33.1) And they named the mercury Hermes the stone, the skilful teacher, because he operates their stone, which they named everything. And they named it also the male which they have, which is the fiery stone, the teacher, because he teaches the natures, I mean the spirits, fighting against the fire and to be patient with him [the teacher] against it. (33.6)

sage

it

Comment

164 The philosophers' stone is also Hermes the wise teacher. In the Islamic context it is the sheikh who carries temporarily the projection of the inner self of the adept. This teacher figure (in the alchemical context, Hermes) is in the texts of other Islamic mystics the archangel Gabriel. He symbolizes the spiritual inner Anthropos in the mystic, his own future inner self who guides him on the spiritual journey.[160] At the beginning stages of the inner journey this inner figure is seen in the beloved, the teacher, who domesticates the fiery spirits of the adepts, in other words, he teaches the adept to be patient and stand the fire of passion.

160 H. Corbin, *Spititual Body and Celestial Earth*, p. 86.

Text

(33.6) This is the meaning of the statement of Ḫālid ibn Yazīd, who said: «They said: "No human being can know them [the spirits] without a human teacher."» By that he means that nothing of the work could come into existence except from the male and the female. Therefore they symbolize it by the cock and the hen. (33.10) 165

Comment

The love relationship of the teacher and the adept is only foreground, the true union is between the male and the female. Either Allah is the female beloved and the adept is the lover, or the soul of the adept is the female and God is the lover. And both are one. This attraction to each other is described as a longing of the hen for the cock, a famous simile, which comes from Ibn Umail's *Love letter of the sun to the waxing moon.*[161] This saying has always, again and again, been quoted in Latin alchemical texts and stresses that the animal nature of love is included in this highest coniunctio. The continuation of the text will show that the author interprets the soul of the alchemists as the female who unites with the male Allah. 166

Text

(33.10) They also named the male the		167
aḍrīs, the *dārṣīnī* and the red yellow saffron for its redness. And they named the	reddish, the cinnamon, the saffron and the blond	
female for its coldness and whiteness the camphor, the flower and the magnesia.		
And they named it [the female] magnet	. And they named the magnesia	
because it attracts the iron so that it [the iron] clings to it. And they named it [the female] also the vessel because it is a	the magnesia	
body. And the body is the vessel for the soul.		
And they named it [the female] the furnace	the magnesia	

161 *Risālat aš-šams ila al-hilāl,* in: H. E. Stapleton, *Three Arabic Treatises*, ibid., p. 148. See also *Theatrum Chemicum*, Vol. V, p. 194, and J. J. Mangetus, *Bibliotheca Chemica Curiosa*, Vol. II, p. 217.

and the congregational mosque, because it gathers everything of them in it and for it.	they have in it and to it.
And they named it the city and they named it 'all birds'... (33.19)	the meeting place of the birds

Comment

168 The names for the female part, the soul of the mystic, are more numerous than the names of the male part. It is a vessel or 'body' for the divine spirit, a city or mosque in which the soul is 'collected', and it is called 'all birds'. The latter name reminds one at once of Farīd ad-Dīn ᶜAṭṭār's *Conference of the Birds*.[162] ᶜAṭṭār was born in 1120 AD. Is the name 'all birds' a later interpolation or have we here a source of ᶜAṭṭār? I must leave this question for specialists to solve.

Text

169 (35.1) ... and the seat of the spirits and the *ḫilfa*, and the linen rag. (35.1)	dwelling place [--]

Comment

170 The word for seat means a fixed place in which obviously the roaming spirits are assembled in a state of fixation, and the linen rag has, as we will see, a similar meaning. This is a most moving thought: the soul of man is the point of *fixatio* for the divine spirit. It is where Allah becomes 'real' and finds His resting place. In a most hidden way the mystic alchemist expresses a fact, which, as Jung has shown, is a general idea in alchemy, namely that man is the redeemer of God. Jung writes: «For the alchemist the one primarily in need of redemption is not man, but the deity, who is lost and sleeping in matter. Only as a secondary consideration does he hope that some benefit may accrue to himself from the transformed substance as the panacea, the *medicina catholica*, just as it may to the imperfect bodies, the base or 'sick' metals, etc. His attention is not directed to his own salvation through God's grace but to the liberation of God from the darkness of matter. By applying himself to this miraculous work he benefits from its salutary effect, but only incidentally. He may approach the work as one in need of salvation, but he knows that his salvation depends on the success of the work, on whether he can free the divine soul. To this end he needs meditation, fasting, and prayer.»[163]

162 Farīd ad-Dīn ᶜAṭṭār, *The Conference of the Birds* (*Manṭiq aṭ-Ṭair*).

163 C. G. Jung, *Psychology and Alchemy* [Coll. Works 12], § 420.

According to the alchemical context, the linen rag is used to mop the upper part of the retort. It absorbs the overflow. Psychologically this means that the effervescence of love, its sublimated part, is absorbed into the linen rag. That latter therefore is a parallel to the white purified earth into which the sublimated soul returns. As A. J. Festugière has pointed out, the cosmology of the *Kore Kosmou* in the *Corpus Hermeticum* contains alchemical images.[164] In it the souls are created from the foam which appears on top of the cosmic mixture. In the same way the alchemists considered the effervescence of matter as representing the soul of matter. It was also called a spermatic liquid (*aphrospermatismos*). It was considered white and brilliant like the moon. It was identified with the 'divine water'.[165] In Tantra yoga the last was also identified with the sperma, but here in Ibn Umail the source is probably the *Kore Kosmou*, and the foam represents the psychic material, which rises from the depth of the retort and is absorbed by a linen rag with which the adept wipes the retort. 171

Text

(35.1) Therefore, when they say: «Wipe the vessel with a pure linen rag from its sides in order to remove what has risen up of the medicine to the sides of the vessel» they meant that the pot is wiped with the medicine, which comes from the bottom of the vessel, which did not rise to pick up what ascended from it [the medicine] because of the live coal of the fire, which is adhering to the sides of the pot. Thus when it gets wiped with the body, which they alluded to without mentioning it by naming it a linen rag, for it to adhere to the medicine which has risen up and has fallen down. Thus it returned to the medicine which is at the bottom of the vessel. This is the explanation of their statement: «Wipe the pot with a linen rag.» 172
Therefore their statement: «Wipe the vessel»

heat
thus it stuck
it clings to whatever has risen up from the medicine. And whatever falls back returns

164 A. J. Festugière, *Hermétisme et Mystique Païenne*, p. 230 ff.
165 Ibid., p. 233 ff.

is correct, without any symbolic meaning, but their statement «with a linen rag» is a riddle as they alluded with it to the body. (35.13)

Comment

173 This complicated explanation alludes to the fact that the medicine (the natural love impulse) is sublimated by cooking, but when it returns back downwards, it returns and at the same time does not return to the same body. It returns to a transformed body or a symbolic body.

Text

174 (35.14) They also named the magnesia the body and also the two sulphurs. And they named the lower one 'froth of the moon'. And they named it [the magnesia] claudianus and that is when it turned white like marble. (37.2)

sulphuric body

sediment 'foam

Comment

175 The 'froth of the moon' is the Greek *aphroselinon*. The whole complication of this part of the text springs from the fact that the author tries to describe with his 'second body' (rag, magnesia, lower sulphur, etc.) what Jung called the reality of the psyche, which has a physical and non-physical consistency. Henry Corbin called it *la dimension imaginale*. In this dimension there is no longer a difference between spirit and matter.

Text

176 (37.2) These names belong to different languages of the people of every period, and they also named it [the magnesia] nature [temperament, character]. When the body became red they named it the burnt copper. And they named it [the magnesia] in the state of blackness the black *naṭrīs*, and when it became red they named it the red *naṭrīs*.

are in different languages in accordance with the language of the people of all times. They

alabaster

alabaster

And when they mentioned the white *naṭrīs*, then they distinguished between it and the black one. And so when they say the red *naṭrīs*, then they distinguished between it and the white one. (37.9)

alabaster

alabaster

Comment

Here the text becomes explicit that the prima materia is the inner 177
nature (temperament, character) of man himself. All the different names for the prima materia mean the same, and the different colours mean 'the moods' of the same thing.

Text

(37.9) Marqūnis named it the ostrich, 178
which swallows embers and red burning iron and sheds both of them as flowing water. Likewise their female stone swallows their fiery body, then it gets dissolved by the rotting and it [the fiery body] comes out from her inside as flowing dissolved water. In the same way every female is compared to their stone for a meaning which is no jest. And as among them it is both a bird and not a bird because it has been proved that the ostrich is also considered to be a bird in spite of the fact that it cannot fly. (39.2)

because the ostrich

Therefore, everything about their stone is made similar to something

it [the female stone] is from a flying water, which cannot fly because it became fixed, likewise

Comment

The simile of the ostrich which swallows fiery coals and iron without 179
killing itself and then sheds them as the water of life reminds one of the vision of Zosimos in which Ion, the priest on the altar, representing the prima materia, swallows himself in great agony and later reappears as the golden man in a spring of water. The legendary capacity of the ostrich to swallow hot stones, hot coals or glowing iron is already testified in Graeco-Roman tradition. We find it in Aristotle, Pliny,[166] Aelian, Valerius Maximus[167] and

[166] C. Plinius Secundus the Elder, *Historiae Naturalis* Lib. XXVII, Vol. X, § 2.

[167] Valerius Maximus, *Factorum et Dictorum Memorabilium*, Libri I-IV.

the Physiologus,[168] but I have not been able to trace the motif that the ostrich spills out these hard materials again in the form of fresh water. It seems possible that this part of the motif is an original invention of our author. Naturally, the ostrich is more legendary in North African countries, where it seems to have played the role of a sacred bird. In the ancient Egyptian symbolism the ostrich is associated with the goddess Ma'at, the goddess of cosmic order, balance and justice. Ma'at wears an ostrich feather on her head. The eggs are probably associated with resurrection symbolism.[169] The African nation of the Dogons associates the ostrich with water, as does surprisingly enough Ibn Umail. The association of the latter leads naturally to the 'silvery water', which for him represents the mystery of the divine presence in matter. Our author was most probably acquainted with the famous scholar an-Naẓẓām[170] (he wrote from 835–845) who tried to verify the legendary digestive powers of the ostrich by experimenting.[171] As Rudi Paret has rightly stressed, an-Naẓẓām's experiment had not the same meaning as would a modern experiment. An-Naẓẓām wanted to penetrate under the surface of coarse material events into the more hidden aspects of matter.[172] In my view, he tried to reach the mysterious divine self-manifestation of God, which is present in all created things. One could compare this endeavour with the researches of our scholastic theologians into the mystery of transubstantiation, but, with us, God was only present in the consecrated Host, whilst for the Arabic scientist a trace of God was present in all things.[173] (This was however not pantheism because God was simultaneously completely separated from His creation.) If an-Naẓẓām and his famous pupil al-Ǧāḥiẓ[174] (780–868) did not go as far as that (which I do not know), Ibn Umail certainly did: his mystical *hydor theion* is a cover word for the divine presence in the cosmos. This detail allows us some far-reaching conclusions: our author seems to have been conscious that he was searching for the traces of God's presence, and only that, in matter. It is a shift of emphasis from the material to the divine, from chemistry to mysticism. This shift is obviously due to the *tawḥīd*, the passionate confession of the Oneness of existence. Our text stands at the very point in history

168 *Physiologus* (Codex parisianum graecus), 1140 A.

169 See E. A. W. Budge, *The Mummy*, p. 338.

170 See for that F. Sezgin, *Geschichte des arabischen Schrifttums*, III, p. 360 f.

171 See R. Paret, 'an-Naẓẓām als Experimentator' in: *Der Islam*, Vol. XXV (1939), p. 228–233.

172 Ibid., p 233.

173 See O. Pretzl, 'Die frühislamische Atomlehre', in: *Der Islam*, Vol. XIX (1931), p. 124.

174 See F. Sezgin, *Geschichte des arabischen Schrifttums*, Vol. III, p. 368 ff.

when Sufism began to develop out of alchemy. In Sufism the work of transformation was more and more achieved on the inner-psychic condition of the adept. What we now call chemical research was more and more abandoned. If we look at the ostrich legend from the standpoint of modern depth psychology, its meaning is profound: if we can 'swallow' the inordinate fiery passions and aggressions which come up from the depths, instead of letting them explode outside, they get transformed into a source of creative spiritual life.

Text

(39.2) When they say *naṭrīs* and do not mention alabaster 180
white or red or black and kept silent, they mean by that no other than the white one. And they named it moulds, a stone with three angles, the mountain of lead, the triangular stone, the square stone, a round stone, the litharge and the eagle stone which is a stone in whose inside there is another stone which is moving. (39.8)

Comment

Naṭrīs is obviously a secret name which means the same as magne- 181
sia, the subtle resurrection body, within which the opposites of soul and body have become one. The text calls it a mould, a passive empty shape, which is open to the influence of God. That the stone is triangular, quadrangular and round refers to the famous alchemical problem of the three and the four. The eagle stone we have already met and explained above on page 72.

Text

(39.8) Their stone is like that, as when the male 182
unites with the female and is entering into her, he becomes concealed in her because of her prevailing victory over his red colour with her white colour. Thus it [the red] cannot be seen. They also named the male the dog and the female the bitch, and they named the fiery body the lion, and they named the magnesia the immaculate virgin … (39.12)

Comment

183 The philosophers' stone is nothing else but the coniunctio itself. The male disappearing in the woman alludes to the *Visio Arislei*, where Gabricus disappears and is dissolved in the body of Beja.[175] The dog disappearing in the bitch and the lion in the immaculate virgin are parallel images.

184 The dog mating with the bitch goes back to Ḫālid ibn Yazīd's *Book of Secrets*. The Latin translation runs: «Hermes said: "My son, take a Corascene dog and an Armenian bitch, join them together and they will beget a dog of celestial hue, and if ever he is thirsty, give him sea water to drink: for he will guard your friend, and he will guard you from your enemy, and he will help you wherever you may be, always being with you, in this world and in the next." And by dog and bitch Hermes meant things which preserve bodies from burning and from the heat of the fire.»[176] Jung has extensively interpreted the role of the dog in alchemical symbolism. The dog appears mainly associated with the lunar feminine principle in its positive aspect. The blue dog of Ḫālid represents the spiritual aspect of Eros, but in other texts he has also a dark side, causing madness and hydrophobia when he represents uncontrolled sensual appetites and states of madness and possession.

185 The lion who disappears into the immaculate virgin refers to the «lion hunt of Marqūnis», which is described in Ibn Umail's *al-Māʾ al-waraqī*.[177] The text describes the following procedure: first it is emphasized that Marqūnis is a symbol. He explains to his mother how he hunts the lion. He does not kill him, but he watches where he goes and there digs out a trap with a glass cover (meaning the retort). Then he attracts the lion with a stone and this stone, which the lion loves, is a woman, and the lion disappears in her. After a while he puts a paw out which the mother cuts up. After a few days another paw comes out and so on. Then the head and the four paws are bound together and are cooked in water which is extracted from the heart of statues and then they are returned to the body of the lion. In this parable the lion is a parallel of Gabricus, the latter meaning sulphur (Arabic: *al-kibrīt*). Thus the lion is an image for the red sulphur, which is the masculine fiery active aspect of the prima materia. Sulphur was in

175 See J. Ruska, *Turba Philosophorum*, p. 323 ff.

176 Calidis Liber Secretorum, *Artis Auriferae*, vol. I, p. 340 f., quoted from C. G. Jung, *Mysterium Coniunctionis* [Coll. Works 14], § 174.

177 See H. E. Stapleton, *Three Arabic Treatises,* ibid., p. 32.11 ff.; the text of M.-L. von Franz is adapted to the Arabic text. See also C. G. Jung, *Mysterium Coniunctionis* [Coll. Works 14], §§ 386, 409 f.

Greek called *to theion*, the divine substance, a connotation which is present here. In later Arabic mysticism (Sufism) red sulphur is a constant cover word for the elixir. As such, it is the goal of the inner work and also its initial incentive, the burning love of God.[178] Jung concludes on the meaning of sulphur that «it represents the active substance of the sun, or, in psychological language, the *motive factor in the consciousness*: on the one hand the will, which can best be regarded as a dynamism subordinated to consciousness, and on the other hand compulsion, an involuntary motivation or impulse ranging from mere interest to possession proper. The unconscious dynamism would correspond to sulphur, for compulsion is the great mystery of human life. It is the thwarting of our conscious will and of our reason by an inflammable element within us, appearing now as a consuming fire and now as life-giving warmth.»[179]

In contrast to the alchemical red sulphur there is also the white sub- 186
stance magnesia, virgin, mother, which causes the albedo to prevail. The latter represents psychologically a state of detachment from the world, a passive feminine attitude towards life, and—in a man's psychology—a predominance of the feminine element, of the anima.

In the lion hunt, the lion mates with his own mother. The alchemical 187
coniunctio is generally an incest. Jung writes about this: «One has the impression that this 'sacral' act, of whose incestuous nature the alchemists were by no means unconscious, was not so much banished by them into the *cucurbita* or glass-house, but was taking place in it all the time. Whoever wished to commit this act in its true sense would therefore have to get outside himself as if into an external glass-house, a round *cucurbita* which represented the microcosmic space of the psyche. A little reason would teach us that we do not need to get 'outside ourselves' but merely a little deeper *into* ourselves to experience the reality of incest and much else besides, since in each of us slumbers the 'beastlike' primitive … ».[180] The incest takes place in the retort. Jung interprets this as being symbolic for the fact that it takes place outside the ego. Today we would say that it takes place in the objective psyche. By realizing that the lion and his mother are not himself, the alchemist was able to let the coniunctio happen without disturbing it. The first incest as a union is always followed in alchemy by the catastrophe of the nigredo.

178 See C. Addas, *Ibn ʿArabī ou la quête du soufre rouge*, Paris, 1989.

179 C. G. Jung, *Mysterium Coniunctionis* [Coll. Works 14], Chapter 'Sulphur', § 151.

180 Ibid., § 410.

Text

188 (39.13) … [and they named it] the noble body, the master of bodies, the beloved body and the alkali. While it is in the state of blackness [they named it] the coal of the mountain … (41.2)

honoured
body of the beloved

Comment

189 The nigredo corresponds to a state of deepest depression, also of confusion and disorientation. It is called the honoured body because in a depresssion one is de-pressed down into one's body, one touches the deepest just-so-ness of reality. Coal (carbon) is the basic material of our physical body, the prima materia of our own being. The text continues to quote other black materials, which have all the same meaning:

Text

190 (41.2) … and the kohl[181] and the land of Ethiopia, plus everything black in the world, and with everything white when it becomes white, and with everything red when it becomes red. (41.5)

earth

Comment

191 This passage is only important in that it shows that the author knew that the many different colours and names of the secret substance mean all one and the same thing. The colours only allude to different phases and moods of the inner work.

Text

192 (41.5) And [they named it] the mountain of lead and the tree from which whoever eats never gets hungry anymore. And [they named it] the mixing and the compounding and the solid, coagulated water and the powerful lion and the holy water which prevents the fugitive slave from escaping and the horse which doesn't run [away] as long as it lives. (41.9)

mixture, the compound, the composition, the solid composed water, the violent lion,

181 Kohl [Latin: *collyrium*] is that black substance which oriental women put around their eyes.

Comment

These latter alchemical images refer to the end stage of the work when that changeable, dangerous and fugitive inner nature (which we call today the unconscious) has been consolidated into something constant, reliable and a source of inner life. 193

Text

(41.9) And [they named it] the widow and the green chrysolite, which does not accept the dyes, and the strong bull, which has six horns. They meant by the six horns the six parts that are rising up on the surface of the water. And [they named it also] the eggs, the egg shells, the free bull … (41.12) talc 194

Comment

The widow is an important alchemical symbol. It refers originally to Isis who is the great teacher and the prima materia of the process itself. Isis is vicious and murderous, but also a healer. She collects the dismembered Osiris. Jung writes:[182] «As such she personifies that arcane substance, be it dew[183] or the *aqua permanens*,[184] which unites the hostile elements into one.» This synthesis is described in the myth of Isis, «who collected the scattered limbs of his body and bathed them with her tears and laid them in a secret grave beneath the bank of the Nile». The cognomen of Isis was the Black One. Apuleius stresses the blackness of her robe (*palla nigerrima*: robe of deepest black), and since ancient times she was reputed to possess the elixir of life as well as being adept in sundry magical arts. She was also called the Old One, and she was rated a pupil of Hermes, or even his daughter. She appears as a teacher of alchemy in the treatise *Isis, the Prophetess to her Son Horus*. She is mentioned in the role of a whore in Epiphanius, 195

182 C. G. Jung, *Mysterium Coniunctionis* [Coll. Works 14], § 14. For further details and references see Jung's notes 69–101.

183 Ibid., note 83: 'I am Isis who is called dew', in: K. Preisendanz, *Papyri Graecae Magicae – Die griechischen Zauberpapyri*, Vol. II, p. 74.

184 Ibid., note 84: Synonymous with *aqua vitae*. The relation of the 'soul-comforting' water of the Nile to Isis is indicated on a bas-relief (illustrated in R. Eisler, *Weltenmantel und Himmelszelt*, vol. I, p. 70) in the Vatican of a priestess of Isis bearing the *situla* (water-vessel). The two great parallels are the cup of water in the Early Christian communion, and the water-vessel of Amitabha. For the Christian cup of water see C. G. Jung, 'Transformation Symbolism in the Mass' [Coll. Works 11], § 296 ff.; for the holy water in the worship of Amitabha, see Hastings, *Encyclopaedia*, I, p. 386 b, s.v. Amitayus.

where she is said to have prostituted herself in Tyre. She signifies, according to Firmicus Maternus, earth, and was equated with Sophia. She is *murionumos* (thousand-named), the vessel and the matter of good and evil. She is the moon. An inscription invokes her as «the One, who art All». She is named *soteira*, the *redemptrix*. In Athenagoras she is «the nature of the Aeon, whence all things grew and by which all things are».

196 The name 'widow' for Isis refers to a specific stage of her life: when the sungod Re has died and become Osiris in the underworld, she steps into action. She gathers the limbs of Osiris, elicits his semen from him, conceives Horus and gives birth to the new sungod. Psychologically it refers to the stage when the masculine spiritual principle of consciousness has died, and the feminine principle of nature and the unconscious takes over and rules over a mysterious process of spiritual transformation and resurrection. The result is the birth of Horus, a new saviour figure.

197 As Jung points out, Mani took on the title «Son of the Widow» and the Manichaeans were called «Children of the Widow».[185] Later, the freemasons have called themselves [also] the «Children of the Widow». In alchemy, the widow is a designation of the prima materia. «For this there are synonyms such as *mater*, *matrix*, Venus, *regina*, *femina*, *virgo*, *puella praenans*, "virgin in the centre of the earth", Luna, *meretrix* (whore), *vetula* (old woman), more specifically *vetula extenuata* (enfeebled, exhausted), Mater Alchimia, […] and finally *virago* [man-woman]. All these synonyms allude to the virginal or maternal quality of the prima materia, which exists without a man and yet is the 'matter of all things'. Above all, the prima materia is the mother of the lapis, the *filius philosophorum*.»[186]

198 The next name that our text uses for the secret of alchemy is «the green chrysolite which does not accept the dyes». Green is in Islamic alchemy the symbol for the stage of perfection. The mystic Nağm ad-Dīn Kubrā calls it the *Visio Smaragdina*. It indicates the moment when the mystic begins to elevate himself above the world of matter and attains a purely spiritual existence. The green colour is a sign of the life of the heart,[187] the last curtain which veils the divinity. Behind it dwells Allah. The inner figure of the spiritual guide, Ḫiḍr, is also called 'The Green One'. In Christian tradition the colour green belongs to the Holy Ghost, and the Western alchemists speak of the *benedicta viriditas* as a sign of life returning after inner death.[188]

185 C. G. Jung, *Mysterium Coniunctionis* [Coll. Works 14], § 14.

186 Ibid. § 14.

187 See H. Corbin, *L'Homme de Lumière*, ibid., p. 95 ff.

188 See C. G. Jung, *Psychology and Religion* [Coll. Works 11], § 118 and § 151; see also *Mysterium Coniunctionis* [Coll. Works 14], § 137.

199 The next symbol which our text mentions is «the bull with six horns».[189] Ibn Umail explains the six horns as «the six parts, which are rising upon the surface of the water». There is an Islamic tradition that the earth is the horn of a bull which is drowned under the sea. Six horns would refer to a six-fold process of raising the solid matter over the water, which is mentioned elsewhere in our text. In the Graeco-Egyptian zodiac the sign of Taurus is represented by a bull which carries the sun in conjunction with the moon on its back.[190] For an alchemist that would mean that the coniunctio takes place in the exalted erotic atmosphere of springtime where the life powers in plants and animals reach their highest effectiveness. This idea continued to be expressed in Western Latin alchemy.

200 The last symbol which the text mentions is the egg in its shell, a well-known symbol of the cosmic prima materia, which in our text probably refers to the *Turba philosophorum*.[191]

Text

201

(41.13) … and the laughing youth. They mixed the names of the male with the names of the female, and the names of the female with the names of the male because they named each one of them with the names of the other.	
It was said among the names of their land and their sky and it is the body, which we named, and the names of the water, which I am going to mention. They named their	And we distinguish between the names of their earth
water four bodies, […] fountains of copper and magnesia. (43.1)	six bodies, lead-copper

189 The commentary of M.-L. von Franz also includes a text on 'the free bull', a word that has to be read as talc. She commented (shortened quote): This symbol is not known to me in Greek alchemy; probably it is of Persian Mithraic origin, where the slaughtered bull of Mithras represents the origin of all new life. […] The free bull symbolizes psychologically that the creative principle in matter should be allowed to exercise its generative power without the conscious control of man. Alchemy is understood in Islam as an achievement of God's creativeness in matter. The adept must not interfere with it, but must allow God's creativity in matter to roam about freely within himself.

190 E. A. W. Budge, *Amulets and Superstitions,* p. 410.

191 See J. Ruska, *Turba*, ibid., Sermo IV, p. 112; translation ibid. p. 177.

Comment

202 The names of the female principle can be summed up as earth, and those of the male principle as sky. Then the author goes on to mention names for the water. There is not much to comment on as the text is clear in itself. It is, however, remarkable how the author mostly gives such long lists of names and very little context. His intention seems to be to stress the Oneness of the secret of alchemy. It is the *one* God Allah, and Allah alone. Here we have the very beginning of Sufi mysticism, which branched out from the alchemical tradition. The chemical aspect of the operation begins to get lost in favour of a unitary concentration on the Godhead.

Text

203 (43.1) I have already explained that the six bodies and the seven bodies are the divine water. Thus their statement about the fugitive bodies means their divided water because they were bodies which were dissolved and rose up. Thus they rose up as spirits, and then it is the liable one and the needed body and it is the ferment of the gold, … (43.5)

became … the one that things cling to and the body is the one that clings

Comment

204 After his list of names of the prima materia the author begins to comment on the operation. The first step is to make the spirits rise up. That is the process of sublimation. Psychologically, this is done by applying a symbolic understanding of what one had considered before to be material reality. In the beginning of a modern Jungian analysis this is the first turning point: to teach the patient to understand all that has happened to him in a symbolic way and by that as an inner psychic process. Then 'the water', the vivifying effect of the unconscious, begins to flow. Our text calls this «the ferment of the gold» because with this step an inner fermentation of the personality begins, or a cooking process through which the individual is matured.

Text

205 (43.5) and the flower of the gold, the glue of gold, the […] gold and the mercury of cinnabar.

aqzal

The cinnabar is the compound and the mercury which is rarely found, and the red compound [...] and the red sulphur, or vinegar mixed with honey. [By that] they meant the spirit and the soul [being] carried in the beginnings of its affair. (43.10)

the sulphur

red sulphur [masc.], the sulphur [fem.] ... and

water. [They also named it] milk of a woman.

Comment

All these new names also refer to the beginning of the cooking. 206
Cinnabar, quicksilver sulphide, is like the «red compound,» or, more frequently in other texts, the «red sulphur». It refers to the beginning of the love of God, which very often begins with a falling in love with another person or with a transference onto the sheikh. This falling in love is, as the text says, the spirit or soul of the beginner's work. Modern psychology rediscovered this in the phenomenon of the transference. Without this fire of love an inner transformation of the personality is not possible. In Islamic tradition (following Neoplatonism) this love for a person is really the beginning of the love of God, though the beginner might not recognize it.

Text

(43.10) And it is the milk of the bitch, 207
the virtue of the immaculate slave, milk of the she-asses, milk of a male calf, milk of the female calf, milk of a pregnant animal, and with milks of [...], milk of all animals, milk of the dragon, the milk of asses, milk of the goat, the milk of every living tree, and the water of the tree of love. Every body is their water. And likewise they named their body [with the name of] every body, and a sea having waves, and stones, and seven idols. The water is the ferment of the body and the body is the ferment of the water and each one of them is a ferment to its companion, that means it improves its companion. Then they became one single dyeing dye. (45.8)

milk of an immaculate virgin

[-] ... euphorbia plants

tree having milk

, hence

Comment

208 The word 'milk' refers, in the mystical language of late antiquity, to the religious instruction which the beginner receives. In Hellenistic antiquity milk and honey were looked upon as stimulating and inspiring, much the same as wine. In a magic papyrus we read: «Drink milk and honey before sunrise, and in thy heart there will be something divine.» Milk also stood for spiritual teaching in the Christian world: «... as newborn babies desire the sincere milk of the word (*logikon*), that ye may grow thereby: if so be that ye have tasted that the Lord is gracious.» (1. Peter 2.2). And: «... ye have need that one teach you again which be the first principles of the oracles of God; and are become such as have need of milk, and not of strong meat. For everyone that useth milk is unskilful in the word of the righteousness; for he is a babe» (Hebrews 5.12).[192] St. Paul described himself and his followers as «children» in Christ (*pais Theou*), and Clement of Alexandria even calls the Christians directly *galaktophagoi* (milk-drinkers). Milk stands for an emanation of the Deity. In the so-called *Odes of Solomon* we read: «A cup of milk was offered to me; and I drank it in the sweetness of the delight of the Lord. The Son is the cup, and He who was milked is the Father; and the Holy Spirit milked Him; because his breasts were full, and it did not seem good to Him that His milk should be spilt for nought; and the Holy Spirit opened his bosom and mingled the milk from the two breasts of the Father; and gave the mixture to the world,[193] without its knowing it; and they who received it are in the perfection of the right hand[194].»[195] As Reitzenstein doubtless rightly interprets it, the drink of milk denoted the beginning; and the draught of wine, on the other hand, the complete fulfilment of man's divinity.[196]

209 In complete accordance with these general antique views, milk was also in alchemy a maternal spiritual substance with which the *filius philosophorum* was nourished after his birth. It represents the aspect of the stone or elixir in its spiritually nourishing function. The Egyptian alchemist ᶜIzz ad-Dīn Aidamir ibn ᶜAlī al-Ǧildakī (died 743/1342) mentions a text in which Cleopatra instructs the pupils.[197] The same text is mentioned by Hasan

192 See also 1. Cor. 3.2.

193 Literally: aeons.

194 Literally: on the right hand in the pleroma.

195 *The Odes of Solomon*, ed. by J.H. Bernard, in: *Texts and Studies*, contribution to Biblical and patristic literature, Vol. VIII, no. 3, Ode XIX.

196 R. Reitzenstein, *Die Hellenistischen Mysterienreligionen*, p. 330.

197 See M. Ullmann, 'Kleopatra in einer arabischen Disputation', in: *Wiener Zeitschrift für die Kunde des Morgenlandes*, Vol. 63/64 (1972), p. 163.

Aga Sirdar (seventeenth century) as a teaching of Maria.[198] In it we read: «24. The Queen asked: "Why is the stone called milk?" They answered: "Because he is white. And when he is cooked, he coagulates like milk. And just as the milk is a nourishment of every child and animal, so is our water the nourishment of the body." […] 29. She asked: "Why is the stone called milk of the tree?" They answered: "Because the milk of the tree is hidden in the tree so that one cannot see it. In the same way the water is hidden in their stone." […] 32. Then she asked: "Why is the stone called 'milk of a woman who gave birth to a boy'?" They explained: "Because he is the nourishment of the male body to whom his mother gave birth." 33. She asked: "And why is he called 'the milk of a bitch'?" They answered: "Because it nourishes many puppies in spite of its small amount, in the same way a small amount of our water nourishes a great amount of bodies."» Like the queen in this text, the author shows that milk is one of the many cover words for the divine water. In the expression «milk of a male (animal)» the author understands the milk symbolically. Similarly, in the *al-Māʾ al-waraqī*, Ibn Umail makes it clear that the alchemical 'water' is not H_2O but a mystical liquid which is contained in all natural liquids, in other words it is for him the creative essence of Allah in nature. It is also the tree of love. This expression we find also in the *Conference of the Birds* of Farīd ad-Dīn ʿAṭṭār, meaning the inner growth of the love of God in the psyche of the adept.[199]

Text

(45.8) [And they named it] the herbs, the water of copper and the flowers of gold. They also named it the speech and the mouth because of its coming out from the mouth of the alembic […]. (45.11) 210

in the same way as speech comes out from the mouths of people

Comment

Allah has given to everything in nature its 'speech' by which it manifests itself and manifests God at the same time. According to our author, alchemy is bringing out into manifestation the secret speech of nature. By cooking the elements in the retort they begin to speak out what they really are, namely a manifestation of God's creative power. 211

198 Ibid. p. 164 ff.

199 Farīd ad-Dīn ʿAṭṭār, ibid., p. 50.

Text

212 (45.10) Maria the philosopher named it a king who	sage
comes out of the earth and descends down from the sky	
and he is the one who is born about whom Marqūnis	the new born one
said: «It is conceived in the bottom of the pot and it	vessel
is born in its head.» (45.14)	at his top

Comment

213 The philosophers' son, which is also the lapis, is here described as coming from below and above, from earth and sky, the bottom and head of the retort. This reminds one of how the *filius philosophorum* is described in the *Tabula Smaragdina.* There too he collects in himself the powers of above and below.[200]

Text

214 (45.14) He means the dye that is […],	the soul
which they named the *ḫaršaqlā* and the	chrysocolla[201] and the honey.
temple and he says about this water that it	And about this water Hermes
is Hermes, who rises up to the sky where	said: «It rises up to heaven
he absorbs the lights from above and then	where it acquires
he descends down to the earth, having in	
him the power of the above and the below.	.»
Thus he gives power to the below because	it is given mastery over the
he has in him the light of the lights.	above and the below
Therefore the darkness flees from him.	
That is as Maria said: «He is a king com-	
ing out from the earth and coming down	
from the sky.» Then she said: «The earth	
with its moisture accepts him [the king].»	
And the explanation of her saying «The	
earth accepts him with its moisture», she	
meant with the earth, the second body to	
which is returned the spirit and the soul	they return
extracted from the first body. (47.9)	

200 J. Ruska, *Tabula Smaragdina*, p. 158 ff., where Ruska gives the Arabic original together with the German translation.

201 As the translators did not know the meaning of *ḥaršaqlā* at the time of their first translation, M.-L. von Franz could not extract any meaning from that symbol. It means chrysocolla and it will be amplified in the forthcoming commentary on this text, CALA I B.

Comment

This is still a clear paraphrase of the *Tabula Smaragdina*. 215

Text

(47.9) And by the second body, which she named «the earth that accepts him [the king] with its moisture», she meant the [...] soul and the spirit, which are the moisture which are unregulated in it [the earth]. It is that, about which we have said before: «The close one meets its close one, and nature enjoys nature, and being attracts being.»	unoperated [-] holds on to	216
All their speech has different examples and similes, but the meaning which they want to point out with that is a single one with no disagreement. They only differ in the names and in the descriptions [...], because in their body there is a soul [in the same way] as in their water there is the soul of their first stone in the moist cold spirit ... (49.4)	and in the images coming forth in	

Comment

Here our author really gives us the «Solution of the Enigmas» [this title of the Book, *Ḥall ar-rumūz,* was later translated more accurately as «Explanation of the Symbols»]. The coniunctio and the king, who is born in it, are the union of the alchemist's purified soul with God, and the king is the actual self-manifestation of God in the alchemical process. Here we can see how the *tawḥīd* changes in a subtle way the Hellenistic tradition of alchemy. It reinterprets it in a creative new way and reformulates it in a new mystical way in which the emphasis lies on the explicit *unio mystica* with God. 217

Text

(49.4) ... which is the tamarisk with the soul that rises up with it and in it, and it is the sulphur and the arsenic which they say makes them rise up while they are in the tamarisk. And thus Ars,[202]	vapour. And the soul is coming forth [about] which they say: «Make them [sulphur and arsenic] rise up in the vapour.»	218

202 Ars (Āres or Āras) al-Ḥakīm was an influential alchemist who has, however, up to now not been clearly identified. See F. Sezgin, *Geschichte des arabischen Schrifttums* IV, p. 68 f. and M. Ullmann, *Natur- und Geheimwissenschaften*, p. 183 and p. 190.

the philosopher, said: «Every moisture that is rising upwards is a tamarisk.» […] (49.9)	sage
	vapour. And the soul that is rising up with it and in it is the sulphur and the arsenic, about which they say: «Raise both of them in the vapour.»[203]

Comment

219 The word *āṯāl* was first wrongly translated as tamarisk. It is, however, the well-known word for vapour. M.-L. von Franz interpreted this passage on the basis of the word 'tamarisk': The tamarisk is here the name for the vapour in the retort (Ruska therefore translates it as 'vapour') but it is the vapour rising like a growing plant. According to Egyptian tradition the coffin of Osiris was made of a tamarisk trunk and was generally depicted as a trunk with a *bn.w* bird, a phoenix, sitting on it.[204] The tamarisk therefore represents the vessel in which the mysterious resurrection of Osiris takes place. The phoenix represents the volatile substance of his resurrected body. It is what carries the dead king in his intermediary state before his resurrection, just as the vapour in the retort carries the sublimated soul of the lapis before its definite birth.

Text

220 (49.9) And they named it eagle and the shining lightning and the glistening light. And they named it the word and they meant by the word the utterance of the exalted God when he says to things: *Kun!* (Arabic = Be!) then it becomes […].	brilliant between the letter *kāf* and the letter *nūn* and after the letter *kāf* and before the letter *nūn*
And they named their water […] the word, because it is going through the things they have and because of its perfect speed in how it works. (49.15)	[= spirit] of its effectiveness in quickness of its perfect working

203 (49.8–9) is missing in Mss, A, B, G.

204 See E. A. W. Budge, *From Fetish to God*, p. 99.

Comment

It is now explicit what our author understands by the water: it is the 221
creative power of God and God's self-manifestation in all things. Seyyed Hossein Nasr writes: «The *Rasāʾil* emphasize that the relation of God to the world is not just that of a mason to a house or of an author to a book: "The world in relation to Allah is like the word in relation to him who speaks it, like light, or heat, or numbers to the lantern, Sun, hearth or the number One. The word, light, heat and number exist by their respective sources, but without the sources could neither exist nor persist in being. The existence of the world is thus determined by that of Allah … ." The use of numerical or light symbolism does not prevent the Ikhwan from emphasizing the absolute transcendence (*tanzīh*) of God with respect to the world. Yet, they know also that His Qualities are "lines drawn by the fiat of effusion in the Book of the Universe like verses engraved in souls and in matter". […] Also contrary to the Peripatetics and certain other Greek schools and their followers in the Muslim world, the influence of God in the Universe is not limited to the heavens nor bound by the 'position' of God as the 'Prime Mover'. The Ikhwan envisage a Universe whose anatomy is based upon an ontological and not just a logical hierarchy. One of the Ikhwan tells us: "I have heard that some foolish men suppose that the favours of God Most High do not pass the lunar sphere. Were they to attentively regard and reflect upon the circumstances of all existing things, they would learn that His goodness and loving kindness comprehends all—small and great." In this Universe of purpose where "God, Most High, has created nothing in vain" there are correspondences and analogies, descents and ascents of souls, differentiation and integration, all knit into a harmonious pattern, which is very far from a 'rationalistic castle'. It is rather the 'cosmic cathedral' in which the unity of Nature, the interrelatedness of all things with each other and the ontological dependence of the whole of creation upon the Creator, is brought into focus.»[205]

Text

(49.15) And the ẖaršaqlā is the meat and it is the food and the flower of the copper	chrysocolla	222
and it is the thing which holds everything together. And they named it the head, and	that grasps all things … it [water = spirit]	
the head is not complete without its body. And its lower parts that are the two legs.	the sediment is	

205 S. H. Nasr, *Islamic Cosmological Doctrines*, p. 54 f.

[They named the water] the water of the arsenic, the water of the sulphur, and fresh oil and tar, because it came out of a dry body, the flying eagle, the falling eagle and the [...] oil and the balsam tree and the oil of the balsam tree, [...] and a herb having seven leaves, and by that they meant the seven parts [...] coming out from it. (51.4)

moist pitch
fresh olive
the oleander and leaves of oleander,
of the water

Comment

223 Like in his *al-Māʾ al-waraqī* the author shows that he practically understands all liquids as different aspects of the divine water, as the divine influence of Allah. The seven leaves are an allusion to the seven metals (which are born from the seven planets), which are all different aspects of the same basic substance.

Text

224 (51.5) [They further named it] gums and all types of gum. They named the parts of their water, which regulate their stone, the physicians, because they [the parts of the water] treat it [the stone]. Because they regulate it and take away its disease and darkness, which are in it and they give it life after death and they transform it [the stone] from one thing to another, and from one nature to another nature, and from weakness to strength. They named these parts of the water also the philosophers, and every part from it they named a philosopher. And in the same way they named their stone the philosophers' egg. They meant that it is from these things [waters], which they named philosophers. And they did not want to say that it is the philosophers' egg of the people. (51.14)

operate
cure it [the stone], since they
operate on it
sages
sage
sages'
sages
mean
egg of the sages

Comment

Our author here stresses first the healing aspect of the divine water. Then he continues to explain that the seven waters are also the teaching of different philosophers (possibly the seven Imams of the Shiᶜa). What they produce is not the ordinary philosophers' egg of the popular alchemists, but the lapis in the specific mystical sense of the Ismāᶜīlīya. 225

Text

(51.14) This is the explanation of their		226
saying the philosophers' egg. It is like	egg of the sages	
their naming the male a cock and the		
female a hen. And they named it froth of	it [the water]	
bubbles and froth and dense gold.	butter … coarse grease	
Maria the sage named it, I mean their water,		
calcified mercury, […] fat of eggs […] and	bat dung, fat of castor beans,	
	… water of eggs,	
every fat, bitterness, and the brain, the soul,		
the blood, the nature, the air, the fire, the	dye	
seven crowns for the seven parts […].	of the water	
(53.5)		

Comment

This should be understandable by itself: all these substances are secret names for God's working in the soul of the mystic. 227

Text

(53.5) And [they named it] the water of		228
the Nile, the rain, the reviving abundant		
rain, and the water of a rain-cloud,		
because they named their copper—I mean		
their stone—a rain-cloud. And when the		
bodies became mercury they named it	them	
the water of the sulphur because sulphur	sulphur	
holds the sulphur, and it is the holding of		
the water […]. And they are both the spir-	by the water	
it and the soul when they get mixed		
together and become ripe by the rising up.		
And when the water became clarified		

from [...] filth and became white they	its
named it white lead. And when they regu-	operate
lated it [the water] until it becomes pure,	
they named it pure water and a moist	
tamarisk and a dry tamarisk. (53.14)	vapour ... vapour

Comment

229 In these many names for the transformation substance there is a constant wavering between stressing its oneness and alluding to its secret doubleness: two sulphurs, arsenic and sulphur, cock and hen, dry body and moisture, fire and water, etc. This probably alludes to the problem which all these mystics felt: does the adept in his ultimate union with God become completely one with Him, or does there remain in the coniunctio an ultimate slight separateness, because a complete union, like for instance Ḥallāǧ postulated, was considered heresy?[206] The author seems to understand it as a paradox: a two-oneness or both in one.

Text

230 (53.14) By the moist one they meant the spirit in	
which they have raised up the spirit of the stone,	
which is its soul. By the dry one they meant the soul	
because the soul is the moisture of the dry bodies.	
They referred it [by that] to its origin, which is the	related it
dry body. (55.2)	

Comment

231 Here we still have a description of a two-oneness: water and dryness are spirit and soul. The water within the *unio mystica* is a self-manifestation of Allah, the soul which stems from the dry body is the psyche of the mystic. It comes from the sterile material world that has been 'vapourized' so that it becomes more or less identical with the divine spirit. If we understand the text in this way, the next part also becomes clear.

Text

232 (55.2) And they named the water, with which and	
in which they have raised up, and with which they	cause to rise [the soul]

206 Abū al-Muġīṯ al-Ḥusain al-Ḥallāǧ (died 922), a mystic executed in Baghdad. He expressed his union with God in the controversial words 'I am the Truth' (*anā al-Ḥaqq*).

had dissolved it from their body, a moist	
tamarisk, referring it to its origin, which is	vapour, relating
the water. They named the soul the smoke	
and the sediment, referring to its dry ori-	relating it
gin, because smoke comes from dry logs.	firewood
And they named the spirit in which they	
have raised up, the moist vapour, ascrib-	relating it [the spirit] to its ori-
ing it to the moisture and to the water.	gin, which is
And the vapour comes from the water,	moist vapour
and the soul is the smoke […].	because it came out from the dry body. And therefore they said: «The vapour and the smoke.»
And they named it [the soul] the two	both of them
vapours. And likewise they named their stone the sea of the two vapours. And they named this soul the red sulphur, the	
arsenic, the zandarīğ, […] the ammonia,	every sulphur that rises up in
the mercury in the	the vapour of the people, and other salts, and the ammonias. Thus this is their statement: «Raise up the sulphur, the arsenic,
tamarisk, and the tamarisk is in fact the	vapour» … vapours
water of the philosophers, … (57.1)	spiritual water of the sages

Comment

The two vapours (in Greek: *aithalai*) occur in Greek alchemy in the 233
sayings of Maria Prophetissa. She teaches the union of the two vapours as being the essence of the alchemical process.[207] What Maria Prophetissa meant is difficult to reconstruct because the tradition is too fragmentary, but our author certainly interprets it as the union of the sublimated soul of the adept with the divine spirit, who condenses in order to come down into the human soul.

The following text stays as it is, in spite of the fact that it is based on the wrong translation of *āṯāl* as tamarisk. The basic psychological meaning of the text of M.-L. von Franz, however, fits well in the whole flow of her thoughts.

207 See for that the picture of Maria pointing to the union of the two vapours reproduced in C.G. Jung, *Psychology and Alchemy* [Coll. Works 12], p. 160, fig. 78.

234 When the two spirits are united they form the tamarisk. The name of the latter got lost in Western alchemy and was replaced by the expression: the tree of the philosophers. C. G. Jung has extensively commented on the tree symbolism in alchemy and I refer to his paper 'The Philosophical Tree'.[208] From this it becomes clear that the tree represents the life process of man, his inner growth towards consciousness, his going through death, rebirth and resurrection, and by that acquiring wisdom and the gnosis of God. Jung sums up: «Like the vision of Zarathustra, the dream of Nebuchadnezzar, and the report of Bardesanes (AD 154–222) on the god of the Indians, the old Rabbinic idea that the tree of paradise was a man exemplifies man's relationship to the philosophical tree. According to ancient tradition, men came from trees or plants. The tree is, as it were, an intermediate form of man, since on the one hand it springs from the Primordial Man and on the other hand it grows into a man. Naturally the patristic conception of Christ as a tree or vine exerted a very great influence. […] In so far as the tree symbolizes the opus and the transformation process *tam ethice quam physice* (both morally and physically), it also signifies the life process in general. Its identity with Mercurius, the *spiritus vegetativus*, confirms this view. Since the opus is a life, death, and rebirth mystery, the tree as well acquires this significance, and in addition the quality of wisdom, as we have seen from the view of the Barbeliots reported in Irenaeus: "From man (= Anthropos) and gnosis is born the tree, which they also call gnosis." In the Gnosis of Justin, the angel Baruch, named the "wood of life", is the angel of revelation, just as the sun-and-moon tree in the Romance of Alexander foretells the future. However, the cosmic associations of the tree as world-tree and world-axis take second place among the alchemists, as well as in modern fantasies, because both are more concerned with the individuation process, which is no longer projected into the cosmos.»[209]

235 The continuation of Ibn Umail's text describes now the result of the union of the vapours; in other words, the following text enumerates a long list of names for the philosophers' stone.

Text

236 (57.1) … by which they meant the body. And they destroyed it, and by that they extracted its soul and raised the two [body and soul] up in one place.	made rotten took it out

[208] C. G. Jung, *Alchemical Studies* [Coll. Works 13], p. 251 ff, § 304–482.
[209] Ibid. § 458 f.

This is what Ars said to the king about this	Ares
soul: «If you don't raise it from its	do not extract
tamarisk it will not give you mercury	sediments[210], you will not have
from cinnabar.» This spirit, which is the	
dyeing water for the soul, dyed with it. At	is [also] dyed by
that time it becomes one dye. And they	
named it […] fiery poison, and it is the	fire, dyeing poison and
flying eagle, and it is the pure eagle, the	[-]
benefit which has many names, and the	
fiery water, and the fiery one is the ashes	
of ashes which are its soul and its spirit	
that are extracted from it [the body]. And	
it is the moon. Therefore they named their	
water spittle of the moon, froth of the	
river, froth of every moist. And they	and dry
named it the dry, and the froth of the sea.	… foam
And the dung of every young animal, and	animal
the dung of a dog, and the moisture of a	
gall bladder of every beast, … (57.11)	

Comment

Most of the names have occured already in the text, the only new terms are the dung and gall of several animals. This has become a famous adage in Western alchemy: the stone *in sterquilinio invenitur* (is found in the dungheap). In the absolutely unreflected natural products of fantasy we now find the process of individuation again in the most despised corner of the psyche. 237

Text

238

(57.12) … and purer than the fire and the	
magnet and the cloud. They explained it	
with everything they were able to. [And	
they named it] the glue of Ašqūniyā, the	gum
murderess of her husband […]. And they	and the torturer of her husband
named it Asṭānis and they named their	Ostanes
earth Maria and they named it Rūsam and	Zosimos
their earth Atūtāsiya and Alexander and	Theosobeia
their earth Ṯāḏāb of Ḫarīṭis […]. (59.3)	and … and their earth Biyā

210 Ms G has vapour while Mss A, B, D have sediment.

Comment

239 Not all the names can be explained here, but Atūtāsiya means probably Theosobeia. What is striking is the fact that the mystical substance is identified with famous male or female personalities. This shows clearly that the philosophers' stone was understood as the result of developing one's own unique personality.

Text

240 (59.3) And their earth is the oriental youth, and their earth is the Western slave girl […]. And [they named it] the mercury of the East … (59.5)	[they named it] and the laughing slave girl

Comment

241 Henry Corbin has so brilliantly commented on the oriental youth and the Orient that we can refer to his work. The oriental youth is the inner soul guide who appears to the adept from the Orient, from the place where the inner illumination comes.[211]

Text

242 (59.5) … and their earth is the mercury of the West. [And they named it] the sharp sword […] and the effective poison. And	which is the killing poison
[they named it] the ploughing youth[212] and their earth Hānā and it is the black andrāhūs whose explanation is the multi-	androdamas
coloured. And it is the aṭlasūs, which also	etesian stone
means the multi-coloured, and the peacock because of its multitude of colours. And the andarlīūs is the pure water of the	androdamas
sulphur, … (59.10)	

Comment

243 Here the text seems to contradict the lines before. The stone is the western country instead of the Orient; it is the poison instead of illumination; it is the sword instead of the helper. This is, however, no contradiction, but an allusion to the dark side of the stone: it brings the darkening or

211 H. Corbin, *Spiritual Body and Celestial Earth,* p. 118 ff.

212 I have not found any parallels to this motif. It might allude to the stellar constellation of the Arator.

the sunset to the former ego of the adept; it kills and poisons his whole former worldly being before the new light can appear.

Text

(59.11) … and it is the truth. And the ten names are the nine parts of the water, which are divided into nine cookings, and every cooking is for a planet, seven for the seven planets and two for the head and for	gum 244
the tail. And some of the people related to the body named them the seven days and the nine months and the nine letters. And	envious ones nine
they named them regulations just as some of them said in the feebleness and at the end of the work that is after the entering of the ninth month. […]	operations about the purpleness … [-] : «And that .» By that is meant its completion after the ninth soaking.
And the ninth month is the period of days for the first work, till the end of the distillation. This is another aspect for them in this meaning.	number
The tenth, which is the completion of the ten, is the body about which they said: «The one prevails over the ten and the ten prevails over the one.» And the meaning of the prevailing over it [the ten over the one] is that they dissolve it; and its prevailing over them [the one over the ten] is because it thickens and dries them up. (61.13)	first body

Comment

The number symbolism in this part of the text reoccurs everywhere 245
in the Ǧābirean school. Our text tries to harmonize the number seven of the planets with the number nine, the nine months of pregnancy, and the number ten as the symbol of completion. In a yet unpublished Arabic text we have the image of nine scorpions.[213] They are explained as the nine

213 To be found in the *K. Mirʾāt al-ʿaǧāʾib* of Abū ʿAbdullah Muḥammad ibn al-Muḫtār. See M. Ullmann, *Natur- und Geheimwissenschaften*, p. 245.

distillations and here in our text these nine distillations are brought into connection with the seven planets. The underlying meaning is that the philosophers' stone emerges from a temporal process, during which the many components of the human personality (represented by the seven planets) are united into one being. After nine distillations the coagulation takes place, as the last line of the text says. The fluctuations subside and the personality 'solidifies' into something immutable and eternal.

Text

246 (61.14) And they named their water saffron of the iron, sperm, verdigris, white lead, water of the lead, Egyptian alum and the	
water of the sulfate of iron. And	vitriol
Hermes the philosopher named it	sage
the philosophers' soap. He meant	soap of wisdom
by that the soul and the water […]	with which the soul gets dyed, and the
which washes the blackness. And	blackness gets washed
the water is the spirit in which	
there is the soul, […]	. And therefore the sages said: «The water and the fire are sufficient for your work.» By the fire they meant the soul and by the water they meant the spirit, in which there is the soul, and
both of them are sufficient for our	your
work. He meant by these that both	[-]
of them make the blackness disappear and both of them make appear the whiteness. Thus these	
two are the water and the fire, […]	which the sages meant. Thus by this fire
by which they wash with the spir-	I mean the soul,
it, and by which they burn the body till it becomes white. That is the meaning of their saying: «By water it gets burnt and by fire it gets washed.» So know the water and the fire with which they burn and with which they wash. Both of them are those which they meant by the water and the fire. (63.13)	

Comment

Soap and ashes, water and fire, are all cleansing elements. And as it 247
is said later they are also the philosophers' stone. Water and fire are secretly identical. They represent psychologically the fire of emotion and the penetrating quality of self-reflection or of understanding, which are needed to 'cleanse' the inner personality from the shadowy elements. But it is not the ego that can do this work of purification; it needs the secret working of the self. In other words it is an act of the grace of God if one wakes up and can see one's shadow.

Text

(63.13) And they named it a	248
horn of a goat, with all the	
alums, with every salt, the [...]	bitterness of the
salt, the crown, the crown of	oxymel
the victory, [...] the crown of	and the crown of the king. And they
everything, and everything is	named it ashes extracted from the ashes,
their stone. About these ashes	
the philosopher said: «When	sage
you take the crown of my	from my leg[214]
Saturn put it on my head, and	
do not bring the ignorant close	
to me when my crown is on my	». By his statement «on my head», he
head.» He meant that you dissolve these ashes in the water	
by turning them to it [the	returning
water], because the water is the head, and the remaining sediment in the bottom of the vessel is the Saturn. (65.7)	leg

Comment

There is here, in the text, an uncertainty concerning the words 249
'Saturn' and 'foot', but they really mean the same: the lowest residue of the bottom of the soul. This lowest element is made the highest and becomes the crown of victory. Again and again, it is only when we bend down to realize our lowest shadow motives that we can win the realization of the self.

214 The Arabic for 'leg' and 'Saturn' differ by a dot that, if misplaced, can turn *riǧl* to *zuḥal*.

Text

250 (65.8) And they named their water a green woodpecker, and it is a […] bird which is	multi-coloured
found in the harbours and in countries having much rain, and it is a multi-coloured bird, and it is of ill omen. And it is the urine of boys, the blood of gazelles,	[-]
the urine of young boys […], the urine of asses, the urine of the bitch. They compare it with urine for its coming down from	newborns, the urine of cows
[a thing like] the urethra […]. (67.3)	of the alembic because they said about their water: «Raise it with the one having an urethra.»[215]

Comment

251 The urine (*urina puerorum*) is a known, important alchemical symbol. Beside its interest in chemical constituents, it had magic, i.e. psychological qualities: it represented the completely innocent, spontaneous expression of one's being. *«Hier stehe ich, ich kann nicht anders, Gott helfe mir. Amen.»* («Here I stand, I can do no other, so help me God, Amen.»)[216]

Text

252 (67.3) And they named it the […] sun, the saliva of the dragon, the poison of the viper, the air, the spirit of the air, and the woman scaring the enemy. They meant by that the blackness and they named it the	saliva of the
water of the female as ten zodiac signs, and they carried out in them the nine soakings. Thus they made them as houses for the seven planets. By that they meant the body and the seven soakings. Thus they named the nine soakings with the names	twelve

215 This passage (67.2–67.3) is not found in the manuscript with which Marie-Louise von Franz worked.

216 German exclamation of the reformer Martin Luther.

of the seven planets, and the son of the year having the yellow reddishness, and the son of the six bodies, which are the six parts isolated from the water for the	
reddening. And [...] the water of the	they named their water
sky, the dissolving air, the airy water, the	the solution of the wind
pinkish watery milk, ... (69.1)	rose water

Comment

This part of the text returns to the symbolism of the seven planets 253
and to the zodiacal symbolism because the lapis (called the son of the year, in Greek alchemy the *lithos etesios*) arises out of the circulation of the *prima materia* through the twelve houses of the zodiac. The astrological horoscope in those days was understood as a chart of the total personality and its fate. By 'cleansing' and integrating its different aspects the personality becomes whole and that is the lapis.

Text

(69.1) ... the fiery sword, the golden rust,	rust of gold 254
and the būrnaṭīs whose explanation is the	pyrite
sulphury water [...] and the second	. And it is the first pyrite,
būrnaṭīs is the sediment and the master of	pyrite
the waters. Maria the philosopher named	sage
it the fleece of wool and the woollen	
dress. [...]	She also said: «Put the fleece of wool in the woollen bag.»
And she said: «Dye the fleece of wool.» They named the water the wool and they	
named the body the wood of the wool	firewood
and the picture of the water for the reason	. [They named] the wool
that the wool accepts the dyes, and it rises upon the body, and from the body it came out. (69.8)	

Comment

This is an (hitherto to my knowledge unknown) alchemical expla- 255
nation of the raw woollen dress of the Sufi. As is known, the Sufi wore simple dresses of fleece, not bleached and not coloured. Our text gives a

most surprising explanation: by wearing this dress the Sufi novice identifies himself with the prima materia of the lapis. He has shed and avoided all 'dyes' of the world. Later, when he has reached certain degrees of inner illumination he will (as Corbin has shown[217]) wear different colours that indicate the inner degree of development which he has reached.

Text

256 (69.8) And it is the fur of rabbits because   they named it
fur and wool rise from the body upon the
surface of the body, just as their water
rises up from their body. Thus it is also
like the feather and the hair in their rising
up from the body over the body.
Therefore she compared it with both of   it is compared
them. (71.3)

Comment

257 Our author now interprets how he sees the wool. It is like a fluffy emanation of the animal body, like the vapour which arises over a liquid, and is therefore a symbol for the subtle body. Not-dyed wool is thus a symbol of the purity of the soul of the Sufi adept.

Text

258 (71.3) In another meaning Maria named
it the talcous kohl and the burnt copper
rising in the vapour. The burning is the   from
dissolution with the water. It is also the
urine of a wild ass, […] the milk of the   goat, the milk of a goat,
sheep, the water of the ashes, sour vinegar, the water of lemon, the acid of lemon
and with every beverage. (71.7)

Comment

259 All these different liquids and juices are various aspects of the divine water. They are the different facets of the creative self-manifestation of Allah in all things. His presence speaks in every substance a different language, but basically they are all one.

217 H. Corbin, *L'Homme de Lumière,* p. 117 f.

Text

(71.8) And when the stone became alive 260
its spirit became cold and they dispersed by the soakings, they named it the human being of the philosophers, whom they put to death, and they seized his spirit and they restored it to him. Thus they revived him to the eternal life with the natural regulation by which they put him to death and revived him. It is said he died and then came back to life. (71.12)

by returning its spirits back to it and it turned purple
sages
operation

Comment

The important motif in this part of the text is the analogy between 261
the stone and the human being. It is as if the adept were approaching the realization that it is he, himself, who is cooking in the retort, but it is not his ego. It is his totality, the cosmic man within him. Probably the text is a direct allusion to Zosimos, where the cosmic man is slaughtered and the golden head is separated from the white body. Ibn Umail understands it as a separation of the masculine spiritual and the feminine earthy aspect of the *prima materia*. In modern language this would describe the beginning of the analytical treatment, in which discernment between consciousness (the head) and the unconscious (the body) takes place.

Text

(71.13) They named the colours that 262
appeared from it people and children. Therefore they said: «Our children. That means we have given birth to them and we have made them appear.» And they named the male the cinnamon, the saffron, the red-yellow and the red-brown, and they named the female the camphor. Both of them are having a burning effect, [...] even though they differ and their temperaments are different in the heat and coolness and in the moisture and dryness ... (73.5)

him [the human being of the sages]
because
natures

Comment

263 Here the prima materia on which the adept works produces children, i.e. secondary effects. And with them rises a certain duality of male/female and hot/cold qualities. In order that the original oneness can become conscious it has to be differentiated into its opposite qualities, but the *sous-entendu* remains, namely that it is one.

Text

264 (73.5) … their effect is one, namely to cause burning. And the cinnamon is hot burning, while camphor is cold burning. Thus both of them are burning.	
Therefore the philosophers did not give a	sages
name to any of their things, nor compare them with anything, unless it has an aspect which requires the contemplation of the observer and his thinking it over. (73.10)	

Comment

265 Here our author tries to justify why the alchemists use so many names for what seems to be one and the same thing: each name characterizes another nuance of the opus or of the stone. Looked at from a psychological standpoint this makes complete sense. Seen psychologically, unconscious contents can never unequivocally be defined by the conscious mind. As Jung has shown, we can only 'circumambulate' unconscious symbols, in an endless process of approximation.

Text

266 (73.10) Thus the strength was their mind	minds of the people
[of the philosophers], which outbalances	sages
the mountains. Therefore they didn't	imagination
coin the proverbs or the descriptions	examples
except in order to point by them to their hidden stone. And they did not coin them for fun nor for amusement.	

For that the water of the philosophers is	Likewise … sages
hot and cold but the effect of them both is	
one, which is that both burn the second	
body, which both of them cool and make	operate
subtle, and remove its roughness and	
density and render it spiritual and subtle	
like them. At that time the soul and the	
spirit accept to enter permanently into it	are pleased
and to stay in it, because both of them	
rendered it [the body] spiritual like the	the second body
two of them. (75.6)	

Comment

The idea which is expressed in this part of the text is as follows: 267
through the death of the prima materia a separation of the soul or spirit from the body or matter takes place. Then the latter is treated with many processes of subtilization until it loses its material coarseness and becomes as spirit-like or soul-like as the spirit itself. Then the two substances, which have become completely similar, can reunite. Together they form the resurrection body. This process is identically described by the Latin author Petrus Bonus.[218]

Text

(75.6) They [also] named their water a subtle snail,	snail, broth	268
flower of the salt, water of snow, water of lime, gall		
bladder of the whale, the pupil of the moon and the		
heart of the sun. And Arsalāūs said about this water	Archelaos	
that is raised in the vessels, about which they said:		
«May his spirit be sanctified», and they named it the	its soul	
holy water: … (75.10)		

Comment

Now our text assembles names for the philosophers' stone which 269
characterize a more advanced state of its completion. The snail and the flower we have met before. Water from the snow alludes to the albedo and so does the water of calcification. The gall bladder alludes to the bitterness of the divine water, its psychological quality of inexorable self-criticism. The heart of the sun and the pupil of the moon characterize the stone as the

218 See also the Comarius text in M. Berthelot, *Alch. Grecs*, IV. XX.

union of these two luminaries. The pupil is the Kore, a symbol of the *anima mundi*. The result of the coniunctio the author then calls 'holy water'. He means by that the Greek and the Egyptian 'divine water'.

Text

270 (75.10) … «O, all you seekers of this science, understand and beware of the multitude of things. In this science, raised in the vessels, I didn't find anybody among the philosophers who named it with only one name. Every one of them named it according to an increasing known thing and his knowledge, and to what his intelligence guided him to in the discussion for you knowing it.» And they named it, accordingly, copper and body of magnesia and mercury. And they named this water the holder of the fugitives and the holder of every dye. And it is the key which opens the doors of wisdom. And it is that about which Amūris said: «It is a closed one whose doors don't get opened without it.» And it is the staff of Moses … (77.7)

About … water
sages
the extent of his view
preventing
Homer [Amūras] … lock
, and the

Comment

271 Seen from a chemical standpoint, the symbol of the key refers to the quality that certain chemical substances have, that they can catalyze further chemical processes. Seen from a psychological angle, the key is the right way to see things. Actually we can only open the closed door of the unconscious with its own wisdom. For instance, we cannot understand a dream without the inspiration of the unconscious. Alchemy was for the adept the key to his own personality which led him to the illumination of knowing himself.

Text

272 (77.7) … and the dragon, which can hear and has feathers. And they [also] named it mild coppery water, and they named it four heroes and the six parts of it are […].

has nine heads
milky
rotls … six rotls

This is what they named [...] the salt, the	the water,
alum, the water of the glue, the fat and the	gum
natron. These six names are the six parts	
with which they dye [...].	and raise the three

These are the exact names which I extract-	some of what
ed from the names of the ashes of the	
philosophers which are extracted from the	sages
ashes: [...] dust, sediment, dung of birds,	ashes, ... dung
dung of cattle, human excrement, salt,	[-]
alum [ammonium sulfate], garbage, [...]	sand, gypsum,
salt of the houses, salt of *qilī*, the face of	potash [*qalī*]
the old one, and the ferment, and the fer-	woman
ment of ferment, ... (79.5)	

Comment

The substances mentioned here mostly have a corrosive quality. 273
They attack or affect other substances. Seen from that angle they 'impress' them. In other words they contain *mana*, psychological effectiveness. This corresponds to our modern experience. If we cannot find what 'impresses' the patient, there is no psychological healing, i.e. no transformation. Self-criticism is of no use except when it really hurts. So the analyst has to find those critical words which do not destroy the patient, but which do destroy his or her unconsciousness. This has a cleansing effect on the psyche. The continuation of the text mentions different kinds of lime. Lime still has a corrosive effect, but also shows its result because it is white.

Text

(79.5) ... and the lime of [...] and the	skulls 274
lime of bones and the lime of eggs and	
the lime of wool and the lime of marble	
[...] and the lime of the sun and the	and the lime of the moon
lime of Jupiter and the lime of Saturn	
and the lime of hair and the [...] and	litharge
with every fiery soul hidden in it, they	lime in which something fiery
being resistant to the fire.	is concealed
Marqūnis named it the liver of the earth	
[...].	and he named it earth of gold,
	earth of silver and earth of

Ars named it the controller Hermes.	pearls, and he named it Hermes, the controller of the spirits
And it is the rennet, the sponge, the glass, the talc, the earth of the pearl, the earth of	[- -]
the silver [*fiḍḍa*], the earth of silver [*waraq*], the earth of the gold, the earth of the nutrition, the mother of colours,	metals
[…] the mother of boys, and it is the holy symbols in the pilgrimage,	the mother of dyes [and in one copy the idols], the mother of boys,
the mother of gods, … (81.2)	

Comment

275 The different white substances (lime, marble, silver etc.) point to the secret substance when it has reached the stage of albedo. Then it shows the characteristics of a feminine divinity, the Mother of God, Sophia, Fāṭima, etc. It is receptive and has reached a stage of purity and sublimation in which it can receive the divine influence. The feminine principle is 'that which makes something real', the mystery which bestows material reality upon the spirit. It 'dominates' in all times when the spirit has died in its old form and needs rebirth. The text therefore continues:

Text

276 (81.2) … the dead king in his tomb, the dry	solid
water, the air, the water with eternal air, the incarnate stranger,	[- -] the strange bodily air, the eternal water
and with every permanent [indissolvable] […] *andarānī* salt	salt, and rock-salt
and others, and the warp in the tissue	welder
and the welding, the bones of the elephant, the white […], the elephant, the […], the diver,	whitened litharge, the shackle,
the controller, the seeker, the falling eagle,	the holder, the clasper
the earth of Ethiopia, the earth of Egypt, the shell of the snail, the white and the yellow marcasite, the white sulphur which neither escapes nor burns.	burns nor gets burned
And it is the marinal white zinc, the vapour of the earth, the moon of the earth, the mother of the two vapours, the fragrance of the earth-sea, the	seas … sea[219]

219 Some changed meanings of words within this page 83 of CALA I are due to differences between Ms G and the other Mss now available.

body of the eyes, the body of magnesia, the kohl, the eagle's stone, a circle, a spear, the thirsty holy land, […] the crown of victory, the crown of everything, the fiery body, the qadmīṯā and it is the female, which has been sucked that is longing for its water. And [they named it] with the name of every female and with all the names of magnesia that have been given before, … (83.6)

sources
calf
chameleon … the skin,

earthen zinc ore, which is the dried up earth

thing [reading in Mss A, B] that have been given before, like magnesia

Comment

277 The enormous wealth of the names for the feminine aspect of the godhead reveals that *this* is the important central idea of alchemy. In contrast to the patriarchal veneration of the spirit, alchemy emphasizes the importance of the body, of matter and of the Mother of God. This is the godhead of the coming age in our time. Our culture has been ruled by the masculine dynamism of the spirit. Now we will have to obey and submit ourselves to mother nature if we want to escape an imminent global catastrophe. Alchemy has been preparing this kind of feminine attitude in the underground for a long time.

278 Ibn Umail seems to have been one of those mystics who stepped out of the masculine active spiritual life of their time and who has in solitude given birth to the philosophers' stone, a new image of the incarnation of the godhead. The following part of the text imperceptibly glides from a praise of the feminine Goddess over into the praise of the *lapis philosophorum*:

Text

279 (83.7) … the ashes of fats, the ashes of *sindiyān* trees, the tower, the monster [?], the *ḫaršaqlā*, the stranger, the nature, the being, the bubbles, the tail of the dragon, the white wood, the solid poison, the spiritual body, and the cloud […].

holm oak[220] … furnace
chrysocolla

firewood
the store-houses and the raincloud. And the raincloud is the cloud and the rainclouds are the rainy clouds, carrying the water

220 Holm oak = *Quercus ilex*, an evergreen oak.

And they named it with all the names of	
magnesia because he is its son, and from	her
it he came out and became incarnate and	her
resisted the fire. And it is the brother of	he
the soul to which the magnesia has given	whom
birth [as well]. (85.3)	[-]

Comment

280 The stranger or the 'soul' are names for what Henry Corbin calls *le double*, amplifying it with Gnostic motifs like the «Man of Light», the «Light of Muḥammed», the «Perfect Man» within. He is the personification of what Jung calls the self, the inner totality and also the *imago Dei*. In contrast to the gods of the theologians, who project Him into some metaphysical realm, this god-experience of the alchemist is a palpable reality which everybody experiences in his own psyche.

281 Again, in a gliding way, the text passes over to the praise of this inner perfect man as being insolubly together with his bride the soul, an image of eternal coniunctio.

Text

282 (85.4) And she rose up into the air. And	He said: «This is the brother
this brother said: «I cannot do anything	who said
except with my sister, and my sister can-	
not do anything without me. And I with	
my sister, we cannot do anything except	
with our brother.» He meant that he can-	mother
not do anything except with his sister, and	
his sister is the high heavenly soul that	upper
cannot do anything without him, because	
he is the controller who condenses her,	ties
and when he holds her she is a dyer. And	
he and his sister cannot do anything	
except with their mother. And their moth-	
er is in the water which regulates them	[-] … operates
both, the spiritual spirit. And she is the	
one whom the philosophers named «the	sages
wise one», that was never leaving them	sage» who
[the philosophers] in the regulation until	sages … operation
they both [soul and spirit] reach the end	
and the perfection. And she [the mother]	

is their organizer and their nourisher. And peace be upon the one who follows the right way. (85.15)

Comment

This part of the text is atypical. In most alchemical texts, when the couple and the coniunctio appear, the mother disappears, but here she remains as a kind of embracing matrix in which the coniunctio takes place. This reveals that the realization of the coniunctio has remained for the author in a state of projection. This is so for all adepts who tried to bring forth the coniunctio in the retort, and not in their psyche. This, however, is an advantage. Compared to the later Sufi texts, the alchemical mystery is treated as a completely objective event and not pulled into the sphere of subjectivism. In this respect our author is more naive, but through that also more profound than some of the later Sufi masters. It seems to me, as far as I know, that in the later Sufi movement the emphasis glided more and more towards a worshipping of the Father Spirit and away from Mother Nature. In our text, on the contrary, we have a subtle balance between the two aspects of the divinity. 283

Text

(87.1) I have seen people who gave these names and examples to what they had	284
copied of the dirty, impure things. And	adopted
they followed many different ways due to	with respect to
these things, and they said that the	: «The sages
philosophers spoke about what we do not	… cannot be known with words
recognize and what we do not know.	that cannot be understood.»
Therefore I said to some of them: «Ponder and search well and do not make asses out	
of yourselves nor ignorant barbarians,	dumb
having blind eyes and deaf ears.» Then	
they say: «Indeed the philosophers spoke	sages
about what they knew, while we, we do not know.» And they uttered in accordance with their minds, and with those minds some explained the saying of others, who sought the wisdom from those who preceded them.	

Indeed, if you put this in your souls, you	
would make them [the souls] sleep and	kill them [the souls]
you would keep it [the soul] away from	them
following the philosophers and cut off the	reaching the wisdom
curiosity of your mind.	sharpness
Then the hearts get dispersed and the	filled with sadness
mind gets dull and the insights become blind and the intelligence gets hidden and the thinking diminished and hope gets cut off. (87.14)	

Comment

285 Though the Shiʿa did not reject the literalism of the Sunnite confession, they deepened and enlarged it by their symbolic understanding. Now our text warns against a similar problem in alchemy: quite a lot of alchemists understood the older texts literally and, by a concretistic interpretation misunderstood them completely. By a kind of literalism they lost the essence: the actual personal experience of god, to which all the alchemical symbols point. Through that they remained unconscious and unillumined. The other ones, whom the old Greek texts called «the sleepers of Hades», are still waiting for the water of life.

Text

286 (87.14) Yet, were the preceding philosophers among the sons of Adam not just	sages
men and people like you? But they […]	women … had an advantage over you in the peculiarities of their deeds, their thinking, and the principles that they stuck to, not ignoring them.
passed the night awake while you slept	Therefore they
and they searched while you gave up and	
they studied while you refused […].	and they suffered while you
Thus they learned while you remained	took it easy
ignorant. They reached with their efforts the wisdom and whatever else is from the philosophical sciences and what is beyond that, with a truthful and sincere intention and with keeping away from all	the searched-for wisdom

unwanted engagements. The philosophers'	sages'
books were their remedy and their joy,	occupation
and they devoted their mornings and	
evenings to those [books]. (89.10)	

Comment

This part of the text is understandable. The author stresses mainly the passionate perseverance of the search, just as already the Greek texts warn against the spirit of discouragement. 287

Text

(89.11) Therefore their [...] minds	thoughts and	288
became fertilized, their ears listened atten-		
tively, their souls were purified, and that	the fire of their intelligence	
was the fire of their intelligence, and the	was ignited, their mind got	
sharpness of their mind, and the strength	sharpened, and their thinking	
of their thinking. Then their thoughts and	became strong	
what their studies attained fell upon the		
truth, from which those who were before	source of truth	
you obtained their livelihood. Thus the		
one who continued to pursue the right	straight path	
way, until he attained his aim from that,		
will succeed. The one who had not	whose effort fell short of	
enough courage for reaching his aim was		
deprived of it. After the existence of the		
work became evident [...], he fell short	to him	
because of his inability. Therefore he		
abandoned the pursuit of what the		
philosophers of the work prescribed for	sages	
observation, and [they abandoned] the	he	
pursuit of what the philosophers advised	sages	
for study in their books [...].	and pondering over them	
Therefore it became necessary to exclude		
him. And another one pursued the way,	it was sound and proven	
and it proved to him that the work is true,	was	
yet he did not know what it was since he		
did not know the origin [of the work].		
And [this ignorance] is the weakness of	he arbitrarily follows ways in	
the ways, where he acts with all means,	every direction	

and with regulations with different kinds of remedies. (91.11)	every operation

Comment

289 In this part of the text the author becomes more and more explicit that for him the alchemical work is identical with the inner journey in which the mystic is searching for the ultimate inner experience of the divine being.

Text

290 (91.11) Therefore he hopes that he will	
get success with his recklessness in the	through his faults
meantime in what he hopes for […], or in	… and wishes foolishly
a part of that. And he is the one who	
wastes his money and his life […] and	in something useless
dies in agony, because he doesn't know what he is searching for. This is because he loved a description, while he didn't know what is meant by this description. Therefore his body became weak and his	
mind confused in accordance with what	because he loved
he couldn't see and what he didn't know	
what it was, and he didn't know its regu-	operation
lation, because of his excessive confusion.	
And the philosophers said that what is not	sages … the arbitrary seeker
classified [= what is not meant for the work] never gets success in it at all, because the science cannot exist without	
knowing it and aiming for it [the work]	[-]
from one who knew it. And another aims	abolishes it
at it foolishly and ignorantly because he	
has a mental disease. Therefore he relaxed	deficiency of mind
and got rid of the tiresome [work] of the	abandons
reckless one. But the reckless one is for us	arbitrary search
of a higher rank than the one who	
annulled it, because he [the reckless one]	abolishes
has a knowledge with which he knows	[-]
that the work is true. But his insufficiency prevents him, because his understanding was too limited to know the origin. (95.3)	

Comment

The 'reckless one' is a person who has found the initial vision and passionate desire for the goal (for instance in a strong transference to the master), but within himself has not the endurance to carry on with the work. 291

Text

(95.4) Thus the wise seeker, when he searches for the origin of the work, from what it must be, and from where it came, he then finds that it is a gift from the exalted God for his saints, the chosen ones, the	his prophets
pious ones, the possessors of wisdom, the ones who are satisfied with their religion, and who have good principles and who are forsaking the world, from the people	whose religion, right living and detachment from the world finds God's approval
of any religion. The exalted God entrusted it to Adam, the father of mankind, as a substitute for his paradise, from which he had to depart. (95.10)	was expelled

292

Comment

Before Adam left paradise he had the constant unveiled beatific vision of God. The *lapis philosophorum* is the closest approximation mortal man can reach in this life, and the *opus alchemicum* describes the *peripetias* of the long way to this goal. 293

Text

(95.10) If that [origin of the work] has appeared to you, then it had been given to	When it has become clear to him [the wise seeker] that this
the possessor of wisdom and it became true for him that it is a secret from among the secrets of the exalted God. And from Him came a perfect wisdom [...] that does not allow him to adopt dirty things or stinking things, nor can he say that this	which is a sister to prophethood. It is then no longer possible for
wisdom, with its honour and majestic value [...], is either in human excrement, urine, or in rejected dirty hair, or in the rotten stinking eggs, nor in the sperm, or	for the exalted God

294

in blood, or in the gall bladder, or in the brain […], because all of these are dirt that transforms things into a most ugly appearance and a most awful smell. (97.6)	and he does not need the lime of skulls

Comment

295 Here our author comes into the open. He makes it very clear he belongs to the Shiᶜite mystics and, even more, he does not adhere to any chemical operators or alchemy. He openly confesses that the concrete physical elements in man do not belong to the opus. When they are mentioned, the words have a purely symbolic meaning. The opus is a *purely inner* religious experience and has nothing to do with the coarse body and its parts. In this very point the author separates himself from certain other treatises of the Ǧābirean Corpus. He begins openly to engage in the Sufi path, separating himself from chemistry and understanding the opus as a Gnosis, i.e. an inner experience of God.

Text

296 (97.7) How could it be, by the testimony of the Commander of the Faithful, ᶜAlī ibn Abī Ṭālib, may the blessing of God be upon him,	the sister of the prophethood
[…] that, while it is a great secret of God and it is his enigmatic treasure, it is an impure or filthy thing or from something	like … glorified excellent
[…] dirty, stinking and foul? How could it be the wisdom of God which comes out of the bottom of a hen? May the noble wisdom	filthy that the wisdom of God
[…], which gives honour to those who own it, be far from what they assume. No, by God, God does not put his spiritual divine wisdom—which is too delicate to be reached by the minds and by the understanding, in any of these bad, stinking, impure and dirty objects. And the great and exalted God had inspired his prophet	of God claim
Moses to decorate the Bible with gold which the hands of impure people mustn't touch. When Moses knew that, God caused this wisdom to descend upon him.	Torah

So how could this [wisdom] be in an impure or dirty thing, or [how could He] give him [Moses] and the others the order to make that [the work] from human excrement, or urine, or blood? The exalted great God would not occupy his faithful slaves among the people of this wisdom with preparing impure things. And the secret of the exalted God would not be in these things, or in one of them.

his prophets and the righteous

something similar

If he [the seeker] knew the value of this work and did not ignore its merit, and if he knew its great significance, he would know that this secret, as a secret of God, is great and honourable, and that it is wisdom [...], and in what He [God] made up from other honourable sciences there is nothing like it [the wisdom], and He considered that it must be only from the most honourable things, and the highest in value, and best in regard to the elements, and the purest in regard to the body, and the most generous in regard to the soul, and the most subtle in regard to the spirit. Thus when he [the philosopher] realizes this about the greatness of the work, and thus raises it up and makes it eminent, and renders it among the most exalted things, God glorifies him with the work and makes him eminent and raises him up and makes him prepare the most exalted things and the best in regard to smell and the most generous in regard to the elements.

of the exalted God

all other

he would reckon

seeker

he

the noble work honours him

and ennobles him

But when he didn't take the work seriously and made it from the most miserable and most despicable things, like human excrement, blood, arsenics or the burnt sulphurs, which are decayed in smell, and mean things, then the work didn't take him

urine

seriously and despised him and made him prepare the impure, base and abdominal things. Because everyone who believes in a thing must prepare it, and the work puts operate
him where he puts himself. (103.10)

Comment

297 This passage seems clear enough by itself, except that from time to time the author contradicts himself asserting that one should not use despicable materials and then that one should use them. For the initiated this is clear. It is the work upon the inner man who has at the beginning despicable aspects. But it is not a work with outer vile things. In modern language we would say that it is a work on the shadow, but not on outer chemical cheap things, and the continuation of the text most vividly describes how the operator can get lost in shadow projections confusing the outer and the inner world. We must remember here that in Middle Eastern alchemy we are closer to the Orient than to Western thinking. To the Oriental it is more self-evident that the outer world is a kind of *māyā*, a kind of phantasmagoria, which is created by an inner factor in man. If one can influence this inner factor, the outer sequence of events changes too. If therefore I am working in alchemy with some worldly gold in mind, I will be outwardly working with vile materials. The inner goal, however, changes these vile materials, which will no longer be vile, but will synchronistically express another level of being. In the sphere of subtle bodies (*malakuth*) there are no longer vile materials.

Text

298 (103.11) Then he sees the evil of his work and the others see clearly its defects, because the others see in him what he does not see in himself. We ask God out of his generosity that He may grant us the success, and help us in the science in regard to the beloved [stone]. Indeed He is powerful over everything. (105.3)

Comment

299 The beginning of this passage is very meaningful: when the adept operates with shadowy motivations in mind, it all goes wrong. The others see that, but he does not until he wakes up. It is by the grace of God that one is able to wake up and find the right motivation for making the philosophers' stone.

Part III

Ending of Manuscript G, not written by Ibn Umail

1. Introduction by the Editor

The Manuscript *Ǧīm* (G) was obtained from the Āṣafīya Library in Hyderabad, Deccan, India. As stated in the introduction to the text edition of the *Ḥall ar-Rumūz,* CALA I, page XVII, this ending differs completely from the endings of the Mss *Alif* (A) and *Bāʾ* (B) of that text. It must be a late secondary addition to the *Ḥall ar-Rumūz* since it contains a lengthy quotation from the *Ǧāmiʿ al-asrār wa-tarākīb al-anwār* of al-Ḥusain ibn ʿAlī aṭ-Ṭuġrāʾī who died in 515/1121, many generations after Muḥammad ibn Umail. The content of this Part III also shows that the author cannot be Ibn Umail. The text speaks of the creation of the stone out of the four elements in quite a different way to *al-Māʾ al-waraqī* (CALA I, p. 157, lines 17 f., in this book p. 170). For Ibn Umail the fire and the water as opposites unite as smoke and vapour in the air. In the text of the unknown author, the author lets the smoke come out of the dry earth, and he unites it with the vapour of the water in the air. For details I refer to my article 'The Great Vision of Muḥammad Ibn Umail', written in memory of Marie-Louise von Franz.[221]

It is evident from the quotations and content, however, that the author must have been familiar with Ibn Umail's writings. Up till now, no other manuscript of this ending of Ms *Ǧīm* has been found.

221 Th. Abt, 'The Great Vision of Muḥammad Ibn Umail', supplement to *Psychological Perspectives,* Los Angeles 2003.

2. Text and Commentary

First translation, as was at the disposal of M.-L. von Franz	Ameliorated translation of CALA I

Text

(CALA I, p. 143, fol. 21.13) [It is said]	[Know] 300
that the philosophers—may God have	sages
mercy upon them—imitated in their science the action of nature and the creation of the macrocosmos. Therefore they	
searched for a substance which has forces	potencies
and accepts the forms and images by the	shapes
operation. And it must be a complete substance which contains the four elements,	
easily transformable. (143, fol. 21.16)	quickly

Comment

According to the Islamic cosmogony, God's creative action 301
emanates down into all realms of nature and constantly sustains the essence of the being of everything in nature. If the adept finds this secret essence-giving activity of God in nature, he has already the whole thing.

Text

(143, fol. 21.16) Thus they didn't find in	302
the three kingdoms of nature anything	
other except their stone, that they fixed and	on which they insisted
they said: «Without it nothing will be.»	

And when they wanted to work with it and	operate
extract the force which is in it to perform	potency … become active
the action, they did not know another	
way, and they did not find another possi-	
bility to do that except one way, for which	
the philosophers had closed the doors	sages
behind it. And they had locked all the	blocked
ways, and they had made a holy alliance	sworn
on it that they would not make it visible	
except with symbols or signs. And if it	hints
had not been for that, that would be natu-	exactly
rally like other similar substances. And	
that divine work would become like any	art
other work which people do, and it would	art
not be different from any of them. The	
philosophers all agreed to make its inside	sages
like its outside and its outside like its	
inside. (145, fol. 22.5)	

Comment

303 In a modest almost inconspicuous way, our author here expresses a mind-blowing thought: that if a man works on his inner cosmos (what we call the self) the whole outer cosmos falls into harmony with it. The inner God image in man, or the stone, is a centre point, in which the inner and the outer coincide. I do not dare to comment further on this, but I can only testify to our experience in analytical psychology that this seems to be true.

Text

304 (145, fol. 22.5) And likewise the dissolution of	
the stone and the extraction of its soul and making	
the stone subtle and the returning its soul back to	
it again. And that is the first marriage, which has	
nothing before it and nothing after it. And that is	
what they compared to the work of nature, and it	going the same way as
is parallel to it and its requirements. And the mar-	it and following in its
riage comes by mixing the stone with its double	traces … that
from the moisture, which has been prepared for it.	
And the moisture is from where the stone came	
out. And in the moisture the stone was raised, and	
the moisture is its origin. (145, fol. 22.8)	

Comment

In psychological language the dissolution of the stone takes place when we interpret all symbols emerging from within on the subjective level as an inner psychic reality, thus separating it from the material outer world. After this separation we reconnect the inner process with the facts of outer life. That is the first marriage, the first *unificatio* of the outer and inner world. The mediating element our text calls moisture. He means by that the divine water of alchemy which is the absolute reality of the symbolic world. Every dream we dream is a drop of the 'divine water'. 305

Text

(145, fol. 22.9) And the moisture is suit-	306
able for the stone and between them is a	its origin
stable relationship, and it is the pure water	
and it is the key which is not allowed to be	
revealed and absolutely not to be spoken	
about. And it is the water of the people	
[the philosophers] and it is what all the	sages
philosophers are in agreement on. And	sages
between them there hasn't been ever any	
disagreement. (145, fol. 22.11)	

Comment

The flow of inner unconscious fantasies is the very element of our inner and outer life. It is the water of the people, i.e. something very ordinary, but only if we turn to it with honest self-reflection does it become manifest as being the life-sustaining *creatio continua* of God. 307

Text

(145, fol. 22.11) Then one has to put it	308
[the pure water] in the fire and take out its	stone
leftover, and that has to be cooked with	
the tongue of the hot sun and it has to be	flame [rays]
stirred every day three times and its cook-	
ing has to be in the saturation during the	soakings
rotting in the moist dung. And you have to	
employ artful means to stir it. This natural	find a way
operation has to be followed until its	
essence is dissolved and comes out in the	substance … and it makes the

water as the same [soul] moisture of the desired stone. And the dye cannot be seen with the eye. Thereupon resulted in the stone an upper and a lower part. And that is the regulation which the philosophers kept secret and they didn't mention it in any language nor did they speak about it. And they completely refused to mention it. (145, fol. 22.16)

soul of the moisture of the searched-for stone come out in the water

operation … sages

with any tongue

Comment

309 Here the text describes the classical *putrefactio* of the alchemical process. It results from a union of heat (fire) and water, i.e. from turning one's emotional intensity to the inner fantasy process.[222] But it is not violent like our ordinary cooking. It is more a slow fermentation or rotting process, which is supported by the heat of the sun (i.e. Allah). In one's daily working on the inner fantasy processes the former conscious personality is gradually disintegrated and the future inner personality, the self, begins to become visible. This all takes place in the moisture, i.e. in a 'liquid state of mind', where one is completely devoted to the task of understanding what the unconscious wants from us. The *putrefactio* is subjectively a rather depressing phase of the alchemical opus because one cannot hold onto anything 'solid' outside or inside, but has patiently to go on working without knowing where all this leads.

Text

310 (145, fol. 22.16) And the philosopher Galen said: «What is wanted is to know this stone and how to divide it into two halves and to thicken one of the two and to make liquid the other one, and then make subtle the body with the water from which it was created and from which it was formed till it becomes subtle. Then it becomes like the spirit, which it resembles, and it enters quickly into it and mixes with it. Then the regulation with it has to be done repeatedly with the liquid

sage

operation

222 This sentence is based on the first wrong translation that «one has to put the pure water in the fire». It has to be reviewed in the light of the ameliorated translation.

spirit, in order that it [this mixture] takes	the body
its nature and it [the spirit] takes its	its [the spirit's]
[the body's] power. Thus it becomes cor-	
poreal and thickens by its mixing with it	
[the body]. So the liquid of it [the spirit]	
became thick and it [the body] became	
subtle in it [the spirit]. And the aim is	
what is in it from the regulation.» And this	what happens during the oper-
statement contains various works. (147,	ation
fol. 23.4)	

Comment

The separation of the solid from the moist and their reunion refers 311
to the following: the solid is what our ego consciousness believes to be reality and the moist we believe to be the flow of inner fantasy life. They have to be first distinguished. We have to become conscious of what is what, but one day, when we reflect more deeply on it, we will realize that they are aspects of one and the same thing, namely the mysterious (divine) activity of the psyche by which we are carried through life without knowing.

Text

(147, fol. 23.4) They are: The water of the stone	And know that the	312
doesn't come out of it by itself. If it came out from it		
by itself, it would decompose. The extraction of that	be ruined	
water cannot be except with something else, because		
it is strongly connected to its stone and […] strongly	penetrates … is	
mixed with it. Thus treat it skilfully with something		
similar to it, that is the moisture, in order that the	in	
kind is suitable to its kind, and in order to drive away		
the heat of the fire from it [the body], thus it [the	because the fire gets	
body] took the fire from the unmixed moisture more	taken … mixed	
than from the mixed moisture. (147, fol. 23.7)	unmixed	

Comment

Though the union of opposites is a natural process (moisture meets 313
moisture), it cannot take place without the art of the alchemist. The latter must have the right kind of *theoria*, but paradoxically enough the right *theoria* is a gift from God. In alchemical language it comes from the philosophers' stone. So it is the stone itself, which inspires us to make the stone.

Text

314 (147, fol. 23.8) After the encounter with this water two benefits took place: [the first is] the taking of the fire from it [the body] without the water, which is the water of the stone, called the water of life. [The second is][223] the mixing and the fusing of water with something similar to it, thus the moisture of the stone increases after it was in a small amount and its parts get dissolved. So if it [the moisture] conquers its parts, while they are not dissolved, it would be superior to them [the parts]. Thus it made the action on them, which is the action of nature with the fire especially in the gathering of similar things and the separating of dissimilar things. And the stone benefits from the water which is entering into it as a benefit of the moisture which is useful in the dissolution, and that is because its moisture is in itself [the stone]. (147, fol. 23.13)

, because of its similarity to what it got mixed and mingled with

[-] … overpowers

Comment

315 Here the author struggles with the problem of whether the 'making of the stone' is given purely by the stone itself, i.e. by the working of Allah in the human soul, or whether the conscious ethical effort of the alchemist is needed too. This is an age-old insoluble problem. It is a paradox, a yes and a no.

Text

316 (147, fol. 23.13) Then that is the action of the mixing and the intervention. Concerning the intervening of the subtle parts, Galen said in the *Risālat al-Bayān* (Epistle of the Explanation) about making the body subtle with the water, from which it [the body] was created, and from it the stone had come into existence before the pure water, and it got thickened. And from it [the pure water] it [the stone] had been

It performs

penetration

stone

: «It accepted

223 'The first is' and 'The second is' are unreadable in the copy of the manuscript.

created in the past. And with it [the pure water] the preparation has to be done from the beginning to the end. And Ǧābir said in the *Istaqaṣa al-ās* (treatise named «To Follow the Track of the Myrtle»): «The earth needs water ten times its weight that is thus collected from another stone, and let it [the water] fall down on it [the earth]. And what is much used in that nearest way said [unclear] in «The penetration of the pure water». (149, fol. 24.1)	originally operation end.» … *Usṭuqus al-uss* [224] (Elements of the Foundation) in this way is the nearest one.» [Unclear] said «What about the … water?»

Comment

Here the author is still struggling with the problem of whether work or grace achieves the alchemical opus. Does the water, the creative *influx* of God, redeem the earth, i.e. the world of human consciousness, or does the latter attract the water? Does God redeem man or man redeem God? The second alternative is blurred because the author does not dare to express it clearly. The Christian alchemists had the same problem. Jung stresses that the symbols of alchemy in fact represent the drama of the human psyche on the far side of consciousness: «Now, all these mythological pictures represent a drama of the human psyche on the further side of consciousness, showing *man as both the one to be redeemed and the redeemer*. This first formulation is Christian, the second alchemical. In the first case man attributes the need of redemption to himself and leaves the work of redemption, the actual *athlon* or *opus*, to the autonomous divine figure; in the latter case man takes upon himself the duty of carrying out the redeeming opus, and attributes the state of suffering and consequent need of redemption to the *anima mundi* imprisoned in matter. In both cases redemption is a work. In Christianity the life and death of the God-man, as a unique sacrifice, brings about the reconciliation of man, who craves redemption and is sunk in materiality, with God. The mystical effect of the God-man's self-sacrifice extends, broadly speaking, to all men, though it is efficacious only for those who submit through faith or are chosen by divine grace.»[225] Then he continues: «Whereas Catholicism emphasizes the effectual presence of Christ, alchemy is interested in the fate and manifest redemption of the substances, for in them the divine soul lies captive and 317

224 The quotation could not be found in the text of this work edited by E. J. Holmyard, *The Alchemical Works of Geber*, 1928.

225 C. G. Jung, *Psychology and Alchemy* [Coll. Works 12], § 414 f.

awaits the redemption that is granted to it at the moment of release. The captive soul then appears in the form of the 'Son of God'. For the alchemist, the one primarily in need of redemption is not man, but the deity who is lost and sleeping in matter. Only as a secondary consideration does he [man] hope that some benefit may accrue to himself from the transformed substance as the panacea, the *medicina catholica*, just as it may to the imperfect bodies, the base or 'sick' metals, etc. His attention is not directed to his own salvation through God's grace, but to the liberation of God from the darkness of matter. By applying himself to this miraculous work he benefits from its salutary effect, but only incidentally. He may approach the work as one in need of salvation; but he knows that his salvation depends on the success of the work, on whether he can free the divine soul.»[226] For the author the divine grace comes first. It is symbolized by the divine water, but in the opus man has to extract the water and in that way he contributes to the work of redemption.

Text

318 (149, fol. 24.1) He said: «The water existed before the creation of the earth. Then God created the earth. Then God created Adam from the earth. And the earth does not live without water.» And Hermes said: «The secret of everything is the water and the earth, because all things are in the two of them and have to be planted [in them]. And the pure water is the mentioned vessel in the books of the philosophers.» And it is the remote substance which aṭ-Ṭuġrāʾī mentioned in [his treatise] *Tarākīb al-anwār* (Compositions of Lights). (149, fol. 24.5)

get cultivated in the two of them … surnamed … sages

Comment

319 In this passage, by mentioning that the water existed before the earth and is identical with the philosophical vessel, our text clearly states that the water represents the *creatio continua* activity of God Himself. This activity, which as a vessel is a feminine hypostasis of God, was by many mystics identified with Fāṭima, the Creator. The earth has its roots in this water, i.e. our concrete life draws its existence from this creative activity of God.

226 Ibid., § 420, see also p. 94 above, where this quote is also given.

Text

(149, fol. 24.5) He said: «If the remote substance would be explained, the secret would be revealed.» And Hippocrates said: «The stone comes out from the sea, it grows in the sea and it germinates in the sea like the corals and it unites all together. Thus it becomes a stone and it is found on the shore of the sea. Thus you find it there, when the waves and the south wind have calmed down … (149, fol. 24.7) 320

Comment

The sea is the symbol of the unfathomable depth of the uncon- 321
scious, or in mystical language of the depth of the Godhead. When the dark inner world calms down, the emotions of love become quiet, one finds the stone at the shore of the sea. The secret of individuation (the stone) is washed up at the shore of the unconscious, suddenly revealed by the grace of God. This passage reminds one of the Greek saying: «Go to the sources of the Nile; there you will find a stone which contains a spirit.»[227]

Text

(149, fol. 24.7) … because it has light and rays like the sun. Take it with the benevolence of the exalted God and make it into powder with water together with the moisture which is in it. Then extract it and dry it! Do that several times, till you make white your work. That is the hidden secret work and the work stored up […] in the water of wisdom. And it is the key, and it is the dog to which they pointed in their books, and it is the hidden vessel with which the work should start and finish, and it is not outside it [the vessel].» (149, fol. 24.11) 322

Comment

The stone washed up from the sea contains light, the possibility of 323
being illuminated by the grace of God. But one must work on this in order to transform this momentary illumination into a continuous reality. Then, surprisingly, the author calls this a dog and writes a long passage on the exalted mystical qualities of this 'dog'. In reading the following passage

227 Zosimos, *Sur la Vertu*, in: M. Berthelot, *Alch. Grecs*, III, VI, 5.

one must remember that the dog is for the Arabs a despised animal and a word of insult. In Sufism and Sufi poetry the dog plays an important role as a symbol of the *nafs*, the instinctual psyche. On the one hand it is the vile *prima materia* on which the novice has to work, on the other hand this 'low' unknown factor in man contains the divine secret, the impulse towards individuation. According to Sufi tradition the mystic Bisṭāmī had conversations with a dog in which the dog taught Bisṭāmī greater humility and greater submission to God. Among other things the dog says: «I have never put a bone aside for tomorrow, but you have a whole barrel of wheat for the future.» Bisṭāmī exclaims: «I am not even worth being the companion of a dog, how then can I be the companion of the Eternal? Honour to God, who educates the best creatures (man) through the lowest one.»[228]

324 We meet the symbol of the dog first in the alchemical author H̱ālid who is said to have told us: «Hermes said, "My son, take a Corascene dog and an Armenian bitch, join them together, and they will beget a dog of celestial hue, and if ever he is thirsty, give him sea water to drink: for he will guard your friend, and he will guard you from your enemy, and he will help you wherever you may be, always being with you, in this world and in the next." And by dog and bitch, Hermes meant things which preserve bodies from burning and from the heat of the fire. [...] H̱ālid, philosopher and king of Arabia, says in his *Secret*: "Take a Coetanean dog and an Armenian bitch, join them together, and they two will beget you a puppy (*filius canis*) of celestial hue; and that puppy will guard you in your house from the beginning, in this world and in the next."»[229]

Text

325 (149, fol. 24.12) Thus understand this poem:	. Poem
The dog in it is a guard for our souls:	
And the dog pushes away the violence of the fires.	
The dog protects its spirits in its bodies.	their … their
And the dog in it is stable in the basic elements.	
And the dog overcomes, dissolving its breathing	their
like a magnes [magnesia] from the universes.	something like magnesia
And the dog makes appear souls from what it brought together.	contains it [the soul]
And the dog chases away the darkness of the greases.	fats
And the dog purifies them and makes appear their	

228 Translated from F. Meier, 'Die Wandlung des Menschen im mystischen Islam', *Eranos-Jahrbuch* XXIII (1954), p. 131.

229 C. G. Jung, *Mysterium Coniunctionis* [Coll. Works 14], § 174, see also p. 100.

colour, similar to a white stallion, with safety. talcum
And the dog opens any lock that is difficult to open anytime.
And the dog is called the sheikh in their proverbs. examples
And the dog is called the lion in the male. (149, fol. 24.17) their texts

Comment

326 The source of this most positive understanding of the dog symbol probably has its roots in the Persian tradition where the dog was venerated as a soul guide after death. The other source for this belief is probably the Egyptian god Anubis.[230] The leading priest of the embalming procedures wore an Anubis mask. He is the initiator who leads the dead to their transformation and resurrection. The most moving story about the dog symbol is in my opinion to be found at the end of the Hindu *Mahabharata*: When the great king Yudhisthira has finished his task on earth he journeys towards the Himalayas. All his brothers, wives and relatives drop dead on the way. Only a dog, who has joined him follows him right up to the gates of heaven. The great god Indra appears and receives him as the only mortal who will be allowed to enter heaven with his body. But Indra exhorts him to send the dog away because he is an impure creature. Yudhisthira remains firm. He would rather give up heaven than not give protection to this dog, who called for his help. The dog was however no dog, but Yama himself, the god of death and justice. The latter sheds his dog shape and says that Yudhisthira has proved his truly noble attitude so he can enter heaven.[231] Yama, in Hindu mythology, is also the first man, an *anthropos* figure, who became the ruler of the underworld. Just as Anubis is the underworld judge, so is Yama. He personifies man's ultimate inner conscience.[232] Otherwise our text speaks for itself and the most important statement in it: the dog is the sheikh and, I might add, the novice's love for the sheikh.

327 From the psychological perspective the dog symbolizes absolute reliable loyalty, completely faithful eros. The real dog has come over from the wild animal to the side of man. He is more domesticated than any other

230 In a text called *Muṣḥaf aṣ-ṣuwar* (The Book of the Pictures), ascribed to Zosimos (third century), the author states in fol. 229 that the dog is the guardian of the dead body.

231 *Mahabharata*, 17. 3.

232 Already in the *Rig-Veda* (book 10, hymn 14, 10–11) two dogs are mentioned who seem to be the guide of the dead towards destruction and then resurrection. The twoness of the dogs refers to their ambivalent nature. They also have four eyes alluding to totality. I owe this information to the kindness of Dr Barbara Davies.

animal. He therefore symbolizes a union of the opposites of animal instinct and cultural consciousness. That is why in our text he mitigates the violence of fire (driven passion) and makes the colours appear, i.e. the nuances of a more differentiated human feeling. In *Mysterium Coniunctionis* Jung also elaborates on the motif of the dog in Western alchemy.[233] The alchemical infant hermaphrodite suffers in many texts from hydrophobia, having been bitten by a rabid dog. The latter has to be drowned and then becomes transformed into a white spirit. The rabid dog represents the *nigredo*, the psychological state of depression, which sometimes borders on dangerous madness. As Jung has shown, the dog symbol is also specially related to the moon and the chthonic aspect of the feminine principle. Being identical with the lion (which is solar) and the moon goddess the dog unites all opposites, that is why in a certain sense it represents everything. In our text the positive aspect of the dog prevails, but it is later also called a poison, as an allusion to its dangerous aspects. Because the dog represents the eros its dark side is a kind of love-madness. The dog's transformation into a 'white spirit' symbolizes the sublimation of the instinctual unconscious. With these explanations of Jung we can now understand the continuation of our text.

Text

328 (149, fol. 24.17) And the dog is called the sharp one — anger
in their description: thus understand its description.
And the dog is like the poison in the bodies.
And the dog thus is the dog, thus understand their symbol, which they buried in silence.
And the dog is called the motion. The motion is the movement of their poisons.
And like that I got informed with all clarity. — he informed me
And the dog is called the husband at their marriage.
And the dog is an individual with high structure.
And the dog is called the hot one in their symbols.
And the dog thickens her without decreasing her. — them … them
And the dog is called 'the redness', if you understand.
And the dog brings out the water like the great flood.
And the dog is called the vessels, thus understand!

233 C. G. Jung, *Mysterium Coniunctionis* [Coll. Works 14], § 174 ff.

And the dog coagulates it as an ocean of being. them
And the dog is called, O my brother, ammonia, and the dog is found everywhere.
And on the dunghills they may see it [the dog] you will find
thrown away. Thus don't deny it for the sake of God. (151, fol. 25.6)

Comment

The cutting sharpness of the dog refers to the precision with which 329
the god Eros helps us to discriminate situations. It is also called poison. Already in the Comarius text the end result of the opus is described as a poisonous elixir which is all-pervading and can penetrate everything.[234] The experience of the self in a way leads us to realize an ultimate reality which lies behind the world of appearances and thus in a way 'kills' the outer appearances. In other words, the dog represents or leads us to what Jung calls the *unus mundus*.

Our text calls the dog 'motion' because he is the creative activity 330
within the divine principle, the husband at his marriage, when he is generating new life. The dog also brings the great flood because Eros provokes at the beginning of its appearance a powerful coming up of the unconscious, but then our text says it also coagulates the ocean into a sea of being, i.e. it leads to the firm realization of the divine presence of the self.

Text

(151, fol. 25.6) It means that it [the dog] is thrown on 331
the dunghills of the philosophers. And the dunghills sages
of the philosophers are their earth which is in the sages
bottom of the vessel. And the dunghills are also among the names of the ashes which are inside the vessel. Thus you must understand that, and you must
be suspicious. And the philosophers have claimed ponder well … sages
that the dunghills are the dunghills of the cock and the hen, and that it [the dog] is found everywhere, and that no place is devoid of it, and if a place were devoid of it the inhabitants of that place would have died, and every place where it is not found is empty of any living being. (151, fol. 25.10)

234 M. Berthelot, *Alch. Grecs*, IV, XX, 17.

Comment

332 Sigmund Freud stumbled over the symbol of the dog: on the one hand he saw that on the dunghill of repressed contents lay the most important life principle of the psyche, but at the same time he denied its being the power of God by not seeing the divine aspect of love, but calling it only a biological drive. Our author, on the contrary, is fully aware of the paradox of Eros.

333 The symbol of the dog stands for what we reject and throw away because it seems useless. It is also what we take as being banal and self-evident, the naked facts of life so to speak. Within that dung or ashes lies hidden the creative activity of God which constantly sustains our existence. It is through the experience of love that we most frequently discover this hidden miracle of being. It is the same as what Jung calls, in his *Memories, Dreams, Reflections,* being «related to something infinite».[235] If we keep this meaning in mind we can easily understand the continuation of the text:

Text

334 (151, fol. 25.10) Hermes said: I found in the holy books which were revealed unto *Šīṯ* [Seth] that there can't be any dye in a living being that never changes [-] with the passage of the ages and the times and the heat of the fires, nor does it change its dye ever except from the venerated black stone which the kings and others honour. (151, fol. 25.13)

Comment

335 According to Ismāʿīlīyan tradition the secret of alchemy was transmitted from God to Adam and then to his son Seth. Then the text calls the secret «a never-changing dye» (tincture). A person who has experienced the self, i.e. has experienced a numinous encounter with the Godhead, sees everything in a new light: everything is dyed by the colour of eternity. It is as if one would perceive that hand of God or the pattern of eternity behind the veil of banal reality. Then the text identifies the dye with the black stone in the Kaaba, which is for the Arabic alchemist the real philosophers' stone. Then the text goes on concerning the stone:

235 C. G. Jung, *Memories, Dreams, Reflections*, p. 325. The passage reads: «The decisive question for man is: Is he related to something infinite or not? That is the telling question of his life. See also § 52 of this book.»

Text

(151, fol. 25.13) And it is the stone triangular in 336
being, square in quality, and in it are the four natures.
And it [the black stone] is of three angles and it is of
three categories and it is of three colours, in it there kinds
are the blackness, the whiteness and the redness. And
in it there are Sun and Moon and Saturn and Mercury.
And all that comes out from one stone, and nothing
else enters with it; its beginning enters on its end and
its end enters on its beginning. (151, fol. 25.16)

Comment

Here the text turns to the basic problem of alchemy: the problem of 337
three and four. Primarily this refers to the four elements and the three *regimina* (operations): nigredo, albedo, rubedo. C. G. Jung has commented *in extenso* on this problem of alchemy, the wavering between a trinitarian or quaternarian nature of the self. It is a wavering between masculine and feminine, spiritual and material, dynamic and passive, consciousness and the unconscious. For Western man it is the problem of the integration of evil, of the imperfection of nature. In his personal life man encounters this problem in the task of having to integrate his inferior function of consciousness.

Text

(151, fol. 25.16) He who knows that is the wise 338
philosopher. And it [the stone] is the origin of the
benefits from the exalted God, and the philosophers sages
named this stone with innumerable names; from
among them they named it the herb, the egg, the egg
of the philosophers, the egg of Maria, the crown of sages
the king, the crown of the victory and the stone of
androdamus. And they named it the black lead, the
sediments of the bodies, the burnt copper, the burnt
gold, the *ẖaršaqlā*, the magnesia, the *marqašīšā*, the chrysocolla ... mar-
octopus, the coryllium, the black earth, the bodies, casite ... kohl
the iron, the sediment and the magnet. And it has turbid one
more than 10,000 names in the books of the work
and among them some of them are known and some
of them are unknown. (153, fol. 26.5)

Comment

339 The names which our author sums up here point all to one thing.[236] Under the influence of the *tawḥīd*[237] he feels moved to emphasize the oneness of all these designations. Psychologically that is a healing function of monotheism. It emphasizes the oneness of the personality. There has always been, and still goes on, an antagonistic discussion about whether monotheism or polytheism is better. To me this seems ridiculous. If we look closer, all monotheistic religions contain a latent polytheism in the form of angels, hypostases, saints, bodhisattvas, etc. and all polytheistic religions contain a latent monotheism by occasionally stressing that all the many gods are really aspects of the one supreme God. Psychologically, the self (i.e. the God image) is a Multiple Unity or a Unitarian Multiplicity. It embraces the paradox of the One and the Many. There seem to be times where the one or the other aspect needs more to be stressed. The creative period of early Islam stood under the need of inner unification. That is why the author stresses so much the identity of the many aspects of the philosophers' stone.

Text

340 (153, fol. 26.5) What concerns the names of the white
water, the first of its names is the drop, the water of distilled drops
myrrh, the water of the air, the water of the rain, the
water of the clouds, the water of the plants, the water
of the pearls, the water of the eggs and the water of
the hot [= burning the tongue], the water of the sea, acrid
the water of the river, the vinegar of the philosophers, sages
the glory of the philosophers, the urine of the cows, honour … sages
the gall bladders of the cows, the gall bladders of the
goats, the milk of the buffaloes, the urine of the slave
girls, the urine of boys, the water of the root of cop- vein
per, the water of the veins, the raised up urine, the
water of the feather, the water of the lime, the water
of the sulphur, the water of the alkali, the urine of the
dog, the milk of the bitch, the water of the sense of
smelling, the water of the hair, the water of ferula
asafoetida, the water of the soul, the water of life, the

236 This sentence has been shortened by the editor due to the fact that the author of the ending of Ms Ǧīm (G) is not Ibn Umail, as the translators and M.-L. von Franz first thought.

237 This verbal noun means 'to declare something to be one' (Arabic *wāḥid* = one).

water of the sea, the water of heaven, the water of the green sea and the water of every tree, which the exalted God has created. And among the names in the books of the work are the milks, the urines, the pearls, the souls, the water of the hair and the mercury. Thus you must know that they had given that as a simile for this blessed water. (153, fol. 26.14)

Comment

Having first listed all the earth-like names of the alchemical mys- 341
tery the text now lists the water-like names. They all refer to the «silvery water» of the *al-Māʾ al-waraqī*[238] and serve to designate the divine water. In psychological language the *hydor theion* seems to be a word for the living mystery of the human unconscious in its life-giving and illuminating effects. It is the *aqua sapientiae*, the wisdom or Gnosis which we receive if we succeed in understanding the symbolic language of the unconscious. Without the *aqua sapientiae* all spiritual and mental efforts remain 'dry'; they lack the essence of life.

Text

(153, fol. 26.14) And you must know, O my son, that this water, which I mentioned to you, is the base of the work, and you must know, O my son, that this black rock is what is in the earth of the philosophers, and it is their material and their prima materia. 342	sages fundamental and primordial matter
Nobody of the creation of the exalted God continues or reaches its preparation except with the urine of the piebald dog and it is the black zinyūn dog. Thus you must know that, and it is the mercury of the people, and we have explained that with the best possible explanation. And Hermes said that this blessed honoured stone is the result of the urine of the dog, and its preparation is the same as your preparation. Thus you must not dismiss it [the urine], otherwise you are wrong in doing this work. And you must go on in that way which I had advised to you. (155, fol. 27.2)	could remain or reach its operation olive people [sages] : «This operation … operation

238 Our author quotes the *al-Māʾ al-waraqī*, written by Ibn Umail, later in this ending of Ms Ǧīm (G), see p. 172 below. *Al-Māʾ al-waraqī* in Arabic means 'silvery water'.

Comment

343 Whilst the dog represents more the stone, the urine of the dog is equated with the divine water of the alchemist. The two are different aspects of the same thing, but the continuation of the text clarifies the different function of that same thing.

Text

344 (155, fol. 27.2) Then your work will succeed and let
it be done with that. And Hermes said: «The work that.»
will not be accomplished except by the dissolving of
the rock.» And they said: «You [pl.] must dissolve
that black structure with the seeds of the white seed.
And you must introduce into it the secret and the
dye. And you must thicken it [the dissolved rock] by
the eternal thickening. Thus ponder over my words,
O community of philosophers, you can be sure about sages, and
it.» (155, fol. 27.5)

Comment

345 Though the stone and the water are secretly one, the author here stresses that the stone must be dissolved into water and then thickened, i.e. coagulated, again. During that process the stone turns from black to white. In psychological language this means that the self is always existing in us, but in its black form it appears to us to be the self-evident [outer] reality. Dissolving it means to analyse it, and through that we realize that what seems to be self-evident outer reality is really a projection of an inner psychic reality. If we have really understood this, there is only *one* reality, namely the reality of the psyche. This realization is the *albedo*, the whitening of the stone.

Text

346 (155, fol. 27.5) And it is said: «Go to Egypt and he
observe how they make the linen white by heat and
moisture, and learn from them how you make white
your honoured stone in […] 40 days; neither increas- exactly
ing one hour nor decreasing one hour.» And Hermes
said: «Nobody attains the work until the crow turns
white.» The ignorant one thinks that it is the crow
which flies between the sky and the earth. But by the
black crow he meant that you should make white
your black stone. (155, fol. 27.9)

Comment

The washing of dirty linen is a classical alchemical image for producing the *albedo* and implies in psychological terms what we still call «washing dirty linen»: the scrutiny and realization of shadowy elements in our psyche. In that way the crow turns white, the crow being the symbol of a dark feminine element. For instance Coronis, the mother of Asclepius, is a crow und unites with Apollo, the sun god, to conceive Asclepius, the healer. 347

Text

(155, fol. 27.9) It is said: «You are still in fatigue He 348
throughout the night. Then, when it dawns, you will
take your rest from the intensity of the fatigue and
you will dye from it silver [*waraq*], and when the sun
rises up on you [pl.], you will dye from it gold
[*ˁasǧad*].» When the ignorant hear these words they
would think that the work is accomplished in one day
and one night. And they don't know the explanation
of Hermes, and indeed he said: «You will still be in
fatigue as long as your stone is black. Thus when it
turns white, you would then take your rest, and you
will dye pearls and a big pearl. And you [pl.] will eat small and big pearls
and you will obtain, by God, the rest. (155, fol. 27.13)

Comment

There exists a classical alchemical saying that the *opus alchemicum* is a work of *one* day. The author explains that we have to understand this symbolically, not concretely: the *nigredo* with its exhausting work is compared with the night and the *albedo* with the day. The numinous moment, when the new consciousness dawns on the adept, the *aurora consurgens*, is the moment of achievement and rest. Henry Corbin has commented beautifully on this moment *de l'Orient*, the mystical moment, when unconsciousness falls away and a completely new form of consciousness takes possession of us. Into the Western Latin world the same realization entered in a description of Saint Augustine's *cognitio matutina,* which rises after the darkness of the *cognitio vespertina*. As Jung beautifully interpreted, the *cognitio vespertina* is a kind of scientific knowledge by which the ego arrogantly assumes that the ego 'has it'.[239] 349

239 C. G. Jung, *The Spirit Mercurius* [Coll. Works 13], § 299 ff.

The *cognitio matutina* on the contrary is a becoming enlightened with a feeling of awe and reverence. The *cognitio vespertina* results from an effort of our intellect, the *cognitio matutina* on the contrary is given to us by the divine Wisdom. Within the Islamic context, the archangel Gabriel, who led the prophet Muḥammad in his inner voyage, is *l'Ange de l'Orient*, the transmitter of the golden dawn of a new consciousness.

Text

350 (155, fol. 27.13) When your elixir turns red, you
would dye from it gold [*ʿasǧad*], jewels and sap-
phires.» Hermes said: «Whoever knows our water
will not die thirsty.» He also said: «From heaven
descends a blessed water, which revivifies the dead
bodies, God willing. So know, O wise one, that the
secret of the philosophers is in the earth and the water sages
only, because everything has to be sown in it. And the
natures of things are not unfamiliar, but familiar. The strangers [to each
entire work comes from one thing. (155, fol. 27.17) other] but relatives

Comment

351 The gold, the sapphire, the pearl and the jewel all refer to the end product of the opus: the treasure hard to attain, which is, in an Islamic context, union with the inner Godhead. This is simultaneously the moment of resurrection after death, a moment that the mystic can already experience in this life.

Text

352 (155, fol. 27.17) Then it will be two and from the
two will be the three and from the three will be the
four.» And the philosophers said: «Our stone is tri- sages
angular in being and square in its quality.» They
meant by triangularity the single water and the composed water [...]. And they meant by the squareness and the earth
the colours: the whiteness, the greenness, the redness
and the blackness. (157, fol. 28.3)

Comment

353 Here the text returns to the problem of three and four, on which I have commented already above [p. 161]. Then the text continues:

Text

(157, fol. 28.3) Likewise they said: «Our science is in every house.» By house they meant the habitation of the spirit, and it is the dunghill of the divine water, and there can be no dunghill except when there is in it a vapour and the smoke which is seen. And by the vapour they meant that it is the rising morning. (157, fol. 28.5) 354

. And by … and

Comment

The house and the dunghill are the bodily human being from which the opus begins. The rising smoke [and vapour[240]] alludes to the sublimation of the dunghill through which an invisible 'reality of the psyche' is reached. 355

Text

(157, fol. 28.5) Thus when that which is not seen dwells [together] with what is seen and with the peacemaker between the two of them, the wisdom appears with its colours and its meanings. They meant by the peacemaker the earth. […] Know that the exalted God created the earth in the water and he created the sun. Then he threw it [the sun] in the water. Thus from its [the sun's] vapour a smoke rose up, from which He created the sky. (157, fol. 28.8) 356

seen [vapour]
seen [smoke]
[He said]: «
sky.»

Comment

In this part of the text we have three elements: the earth, the water and the sun. The earth is called peacemaker because it reconciles what is visible (material reality) with the water of the unconscious. The sun in an Islamic context symbolizes ʿ*aql*, reason, and more deeper the divine source of cosmic reason. Today we would call it the source of consciousness. When creating the world, Allah has dipped into it the sun of His consciousness. That caused a vapour to rise, which formed the sky. The text reminds one of the famous *Tabula Smaragdina,* a basic text which is already quoted by Ǧābir. This Ǧābir quotation has been published by Holmyard. It runs:[241] 357

240 Added by the editor on the basis of the ameliorated translation.

241 Quoted in J. Ruska, *Tabula Smaragdina*, p. 120. (In the Arabic text No. (5) and (6) are missing.)

«Balinas mentions the engraving of the Table in the hand of Hermes, which says:

(1) Truth! Certainty! That in which there is no doubt!

(2) That which is above is from that which is below and that which is below is from that which is above, working the miracles of one [thing].

(3) As all things were from One …

(4) Its father is the Sun and its mother the Moon. The Earth carried it in her belly, and the Wind nourished it in her belly, as Earth, which shall become Fire. […]

(7) Feed the Earth from that which is subtle, with the greatest power.

(8) It ascends from the Earth to the Heaven and becomes ruler over that which is above and that which is below.»

358 There is, however, a difference in the *Tabula* text. The parents of the stone are sun and moon. In our text only the sun descends into the earth, in order to generate the stone. This latter motif must have different sources.

359 The sun drowning in the muddy water in the beginning of the work appears also in a Buddhist text on which Jung has commented. In the *Tai I Gin Hua Dsung Dschi* Master Lü says: «*The Book of the Successful Contemplation* (Ying Guan Ging) says: «The sun sinks in the great water and magic pictures of trees in rows arise.» The setting of the sun means that in chaos [in the world before phenomena, that is, the intelligible world] a foundation is laid: that is the condition free of opposites (Wu Ging).»[242]

Text

360 (157, fol. 28.8) Thus everything above has been created from the clarity of what is below and everything below has been created from the sediment of what is above. Everything is like that. (157, fol. 28.9)

Comment

361 This is a clear allusion to the *Tabula Smaragdina* which I quoted above, but by adding the word 'clarity' the author shows that he understands the power above as the divine reason, and by the word 'sediment' the power below as matter, which in the Islamic context is the ultimate sediment of the creative emanation of Allah.

242 R. Wilhelm and C. G. Jung, *The Secret of the Golden Flower*, Chapter 6, p. 55 of R. Wilhelm's explanation.

Text

(157, fol. 28.9) And when the heat clashes with the earth and thus burns it, the exalted God created […] water from the sky. Thus the sky rained with it on the thirsty earth. Then it revived and made grow different kinds of flowers, herbs, fruits and minerals. By the heat it [the earth] ripened and became yellow and red. Then […] the rains came down from the sky onto the earth and whatever is on it. Then all that is under the sky and all that is above the earth became alive. And like that our earth is alive by the water of our sky and our water is from a smoke which rises up from it [the earth] and returns to it. And when it has been irrigated with its water, and the heat of the fire has continued on it [the earth], then its flowers and its fruits would appear. (157, fol. 28.14)	clashed it burnt … for it they He made … come our earth. From it [the earth] it rises	362

Comment

It is a well-known adage of Greek alchemy that the making of the stone repeats the divine work of creation. Between the opposites of earth and sky circulates the divine water, the mysterious creativity of the divinity, in order to produce life. 363

Text

(157, fol. 28.14) […] Thus the wisdom of the four natures is that they incline to each other in accordance with the relationship between them. When they become mixed they hold each other and God creates from them every created nature, because the fine one of them is only seen and remains in the thick one, because there is a relationship between them. So know that! The two thick dry ones are the ones which bring into being the beginning of the creation of things. From the smoke … (159, fol. 29.1)	[They said]: « extracts held from which the creation of things begins are from	364

Comment

From uniting above and below through the third element 'water', our text now continues towards the step of the four elements. The 'fine ones' are probably fire and air which become bound with the visible ones, earth and water. 365

Text

366 (159, fol. 29.1) … which rises from the dryness of the earth and from the vapour which comes out from the moisture of the water. Thus from these two, the vapour and the smoke, the air is brought into being, and the substance of everything which moves in the air. This is because the vapour as it is rising up is a nutrition to the air, and the smoke of the earth became nutrition to the fire. From these come into being wondrous things. (159, fol. 29.3)

dry

basis … is

Comment

367 The vapour or smoke symbolizes in psychological parlance the creative fantasies that rise from the depth of the unconscious. It is a creative state of confusion or a kind of pregnancy, in which everything is full of possibilities but has not found its definite form yet. In mythology smoke connects heaven and earth and, especially, carries the sacrifices and prayers up to the gods.

Text

368 (159, fol. 29.3) And the philosopher said: «Nothing can come into being except with the round vessel, which is similar to the sky. And it is the flowing and the rising up of the divine water which belongs to us after the flowing, when that medicine is little. And if it [the medicine] is much it is necessary that there is this vessel because in it the work gets completed. And in it it becomes white, and with it they make solid, and from it it takes the colour and the light, and in it it changes from illness to health, and from death to life, and God knows best.» (159, fol. 29.8)

sage

with it comes into being … decomposition

decomposition. Whether the medicine is little or much

red. And with and from it, it gets dressed in

Comment

369 The 'smoke' of creative fantasies has to be contained. Therefore the author mentions the round vessel of the philosophers, which, as we know from other texts, is the essence of the alchemical mystery and is identical

with the stone. In the *Book of Tetralogies,* ascribed to Aflāṭūn (Plato), the round vessel is described as the human skull because of its similarity with the sky, as Jung has profoundly commented upon and shown.[243] The writer of the *Book of Tetralogies* seems to have understood that the alchemical work is a mysterious transformation of the human mind, and the vessel itself is the human being itself: «Through time and exact definition things are converted into intellect, inasmuch as the parts are assimilated (to one another) in composition and in form. But on account of its proximity to the *anima rationalis* the brain had to be assimilated to the amalgam, and the *anima rationalis* is simple, as we have said.»[244] Altogether in Arabic alchemy as well as in Sabaean magic there were many procedures for working with the human head or skull. They were all based on the idea that this was the thing in which the transformation of the human soul or mind took place. Modern psychiatric pharmacotherapy is still caught in this projection, but the medieval Arabic alchemists were a bit more conscious: they did not believe that the head and the brain *were* the psyche, but that they were only an analogy of the psyche. The transformation of the psyche had priority over the material operation, and meditation had priority over the chemical experimenting. As the *Book of Tetralogies* is quoted by Ǧābir, it must also have been known to the author.

Text

(159, fol. 29.8) Hippocrates was asked about the actualization of the substance. He answered: «O you seeker, it comes out in the small mountain which is in Mount Sinai, near the sea, on the right side of which are two caves and two springs. Thus you must go up on it, because there are in it the remedies for this honoured work, entirely and completely. Then make with it what you want. If you want, the whiteness, and if you want, the redness.» (159, fol. 29.11) 370

accomplishment … matter

Comment

According to Ismāʿīlīyan tradition Moses was one of the prophets before Muḥammad who handed down the Hermetic secret. He transmitted 371

243 *Book of Tetralogies* named in Latin *Liber quartorum,* in: *Theatrum chemicum,* Vol. V, p. 124 f., quoted in C. G. Jung, *Psychology and Alchemy* [Coll. Works 12], § 375 ff.

244 *Liber quartorum,* quoted in C. G. Jung, ibid., § 376.

the voice and will of God to mankind[245] and thus our text makes it indirectly clear that the stone is the bringing into reality of God's will, to make Allah's influence real in earthly life.

Text

372 (159, fol. 29.11) Ǧābir, may God have mercy upon him, said: «The work has two brothers who appear at the end of the time.»[246] And he mentioned in some places that it has a third pious brother, who is the biggest and the most glorious of them, and without whom there would never be any work. And know that Ǧābir, may God have mercy upon him, put himself in the place of the stone and indicated the two brothers, the soul and the spirit … (159, fol. 29.14) eldest

Comment

373 In this passage our text brings in a new idea: the Hermetic master does not only transmit the divine influence to man, he *is*, himself, the manifestation of God, i.e. the stone. We have here an earlier manifestation of what has become official tradition in Sufism, where the sheikh represents for the pupil not just a human being, but the presence of God. This viewpoint coincides strikingly with the Hindu tradition, according to which the guru represents the divine cosmic self. If the disciple worships his guru, he does not worship the human being, but the divine Atman in him. I am inclined to assume that here we have to do with Hindu influences.[247]

Text

374 (159, fol. 29.14) … which are in the stone. They are both from him and he is from them. Thus they are two brothers to him, and he is a brother to them. Between them there is nothing alien. And he said about the third brother that he is the skilful teacher. With him [the brother] he referred to the water that is coming out from the stone and it is the moist spirit.

245 Moses brought the Ten Commandments from Mt Sinai.

246 This is also found in the *al-Māʾ al-waraqī*, in: H. E. Stapleton, *Three Arabic Treatises*, p. 96.6.

247 In the *al-Māʾ al-waraqī* of Ibn Umail, a text our author probably quotes without naming the source, we find on page 96.17 a quote from a Hindu alchemist named Ṭumṭum al-Hindī.

And all the sages glorified it and named it the sage and the Hermes of the Hermeses. And all what you hear from the statements of the sages in praise of the wise one it is Hermes. However, by all of this they meant that [the water], because it is the regulator of the work from its beginning to its end, and without it the work cannot be accomplished. For that, Ǧābir named it the skilful teacher because it [the water] is the one which puts the stone to death, and it is the one which extracts its spirit from it, and it also extracts its soul, and it is the one who makes it [the stone] die, the guardian of it, […] and its regulator, and it is the one which brings it back to its body. And it is the one which revives the body after its death, and that is the water to which we referred that is the noble spirit, and it is from the honourable stone, being its origin. (161, fol. 30.4)

operator

its custodian, …

operator

Comment

The two brothers are the soul (*nafs*) and the spirit (*rūḥ*). They have 375
to be united in the work. Then there is a third brother: the philosophers' stone, whom Ǧābir calls the skilful master, and the continuation of the text praises this skilful master as being the divine water. The divine water is the mystical guiding influence of Allah, which is even above soul and spirit. But these three powers harmonize completely (there is nothing strange between them). In the imam or sheikh they have become one and the same thing. The divine water kills and brings back to life again as the text continues. This clearly hints that it is God Himself who brings about the opus in the alchemist. He brings about the death of the *nigredo* and the resurrection of the glorified body, i.e. the stone.

Text

(161, fol. 30.4) Know that and hide it as 376
much as you can for it is the cold moist key. And a sage said: «Know, O King, that if you mix the water with these three mixed things [yellow, white, red] and then you purify them with it [the water] and regulate them with it, it [the water] would support the white one onto the yellow one.

operate

over

Thus it [the water] whitens them both till it renders them to the whiteness of the white silver [*fiḍḍa*]. Then it supports the yellow onto the white and the red by the regulation and makes them both yellow by the operation and renders them both to the yellowness of the gold. Then it supports the white and the yellow by the regulation and it makes them both red and renders them both to the redness of the sunset over the sea. When you see them both like that, pour that water on it. If the blackness of them both still remains after the redness—if you do that with them—you are missing the way and you spoil everything that you have made up. Then it dies from the pains of the error and from poverty while it is the rich one. Thus know that! And God knows best. (161, fol. 30.12)

over … operation

operation

marinal *aqzal* [gold]

improved

Comment

377 This part of the text seems clear. It describes the *citrinitas* and the *rubedo* which come by themselves. However there is a danger: if there is some blackness left over, that is, if some secret shadow motivation has not been cleared out, then the whole process goes wrong. The danger of power and of vanity increases with the process of individuation, so that even greater humility is required. Otherwise the inner richness turns into the utmost poverty.

Text

378 (161, fol. 30.12) Hermes said: «The secret of everything and its life is in the water.» And this water is receptive for breeding from the people and the others. And in the water is a great secret, because it is that which in the grapes becomes wine, in the wheat, bread, and in the olive, oil, in the terebinth, gum, and in the sesame, oil, and in all of the trees, different kinds of fruits.» (161, fol. 30.15)

lives are

being grown

Comment

The water, the *prima materia*, is the very secret of creation because it symbolizes the hidden, secret, generating and sustaining power of Allah in everything. One of its variations is the human sperm. Thus the text continues with the description of childbirth: 379

Text

(161, fol. 30.15) The beginning of the child is from	newborn child	380
the water, because when the water of the man		
[sperm] falls in the womb of the woman, it clings to		
the womb for seven days, in order that the water	and it is a subtle	
becomes subtle. Then it thickens after seven days in	water	
all the parts of the woman's body, because of its flu-	fineness	
idity and its subtleness. Then it passes on the flesh		
and becomes flesh, and it passes on the bones and it		
becomes bones and it passes on the hair and the		
nerves thus it becomes like them. Then it becomes		
hot on the eighth day. Then it becomes like curd [or		
cheese]. Then it turns red on the 16th day and its		
colour becomes like the colour of the blood. Then on		
the 24th day it begins to manifest its limbs a little like	a little with	
hair. Then on the 32th day it becomes a human being,		
as the exalted God said in the Book. And on the 40th		
day the soul becomes manifest and apparent in it.		
Then, from the 40th day on, blood begins to flow into	appears and flows	
the embryo through its navel and it becomes its		
nutrition. And the soul appears to become strong.		
And it grows up little by little and becomes stronger.		
Know that the water serves the embryo in the womb		
for the first three months. Then the air serves it for		
three months, then the fire cooks it and completes it		
for the third three months.		
When nine months are completed, the blood which		
was feeding it from the navel is cut off. And it [the		
blood] is raised up to the breast of the woman, and		
there it becomes like the snow, and it becomes for him		
food after his emerging from the womb to this middle		
world. All of this is the description of the regulation	operation	
of their stone, and in this way they regulate it. Thus	operate	
understand this regulation and these meanings. And	operation	

the uterus here is the vessel and what is in the vessel. And the closing of its mouth so it happens in the top, and does not find a place to breathe air. Thus it thickens by itself and dissolves by itself, and it regulates in its place.[248] This is what happened to Ǧābir ibn Ḥaiyān, and his question to the Imam Ǧaᶜfar ibn Muḥammad aṣ-Ṣādiq, may God be pleased with him, was: «O truthful [*ṣādiq*] one, in whatever you say, please guide us.» (163, fol. 31.13)

womb
close … mouth
gets operated

Comment

381 The comparison of the philosophers' stone with the formation of a child first appears in Western alchemy in the Comarius treatise, which belongs to the first century after Christ: «But I say to those of you who are well disposed: when you preserve the plants and elements and ores [stones] in their proper place, they seem indeed to be very beautiful, but they are not beautiful when the fire tests them. [Later] when they have taken on the glory of the fire and its shining colour, then you will see how their glory has increased when compared with their former glory, inasmuch as the desired beauty and its fluid nature have been transformed into divinity. Because they [the adepts] nourish them [the plants] in fire, just as an embryo is nourished and grows rapidly within the womb. But when the month of delivery approaches, then it [the embryo] is not prevented from coming forth. Our sacred art [the art of alchemy] proceeds in the same way. The constantly billowing tides and waves wound them [the bodies] in Hades and in the grave in which they lie. But when the grave is opened, then they come forth from Hades, like the child from the womb. When the adepts observe this beauty, like a loving mother observing her child, then they look for ways in which they can nourish the child [the corpse] in their art, [that is,] with water instead of milk. For the art imitates child [birth], since it is also formed like a child, and when it is completed in every way, you will behold the sealed mystery.»[249]

382 The analogy of the lapis with the 'Divine Child' is a symbol which is common to the whole of alchemy. It represents the result of having consciously become aware of the self of the adept. As long as the self operates from the unconscious, but has not been understood by the adept, it is his 'father'. When it becomes conscious in the alchemist it becomes his 'son'

248 The preceding passage is found almost exactly in Ibn Umail's *al-Māʾ al-waraqī*, p. 39.28–40.14. This shows that the author of this ending of Ms Ǧīm (G) knew the writings of Ibn Umail.

249 M. Berthelot, *Alch. Grecs*, IV. XX, 10.

because the alchemist ‘generated’ it. In his paper on the ‘Divine Child,’[250] Jung has amply interpreted the symbol of the mystical child. It represents that inner centre of the human individual which is experienced as eternally alive and unconquerable, completely genuine and the source of all inner renewal. When the self begins to operate in the psyche of the adept it appears as this child. While the symbol of the stone emphasizes the material solidity of the self, the child motif emphasizes the motif of inner rebirth and eternal inner aliveness.

Our text glides smoothly over to the motif of the vessel having to be 383
closed in order that the child or stone coagulates and begins to ‘regulate’ itself by itself (by that it becomes an independent self-sufficient system). Then follows suddenly in our text the long and final passage, which deals on one hand with certain mystical letters, and on the other hand with the description of Ǧābir’s encounter with the Imam Ǧaᶜfar. Ǧābir had gone astray in his research and Ǧaᶜfar puts him right so that Ǧābir now becomes the owner of the alchemical secret as well.

While up till now our author seemed to have followed the Hellenistic 384
Gnostic tradition of alchemy, and while it looked as if he understood the stone in a Gnostic religious way, as did for instance Zosimos, he now suddenly links the whole symbolism of alchemy with the Islamic Qarmaṭo-Ismāᶜīlīyan tradition. He reveals by this last passage that he understood alchemy in a completely new light: for him it was the inner work of purifying one’s own soul through which the alchemist became a secret participant in that secret working of Allah when He installed the imamate.

The Christian tradition of God’s concern with His creation, and 385
especially with man, led to the incarnation of God in Christ, and with the promise of an indwelling of the Holy Ghost in man. In the Islamic doctrine Allah does not become man, but His creative emanation continues in a chain of holy men who have become as close to being God Himself as the Islamic doctrine of the complete otherness of Allah allows (only Ḥallāǧ overstepped that separation). In the Christian tradition God becomes man. In the Shiᶜite view, man approaches the goal of becoming God. The Christian incarnation is a descent of God into matter (the human body). In the Islamic alchemy, probably due to the influence of Neoplatonism, it is more an ascent from matter to the spiritual God. By understanding alchemy in this way, the importance of matter became later gradually lost, and this led to the development of Sufi spiritualism. Matter became only a simile for spiritual inner processes in the mystic. In our text, however, the more ‘alchemical’ harmony between spirit and matter is still preserved.

250 C. G. Jung, *The Psychology of the Child Archetype* [Coll. Works 9/1], § 259 ff.

Text

386 (163, fol. 31.13) [Question of Ǧābir to the Imam Ǧaᶜfar ibn Muḥammad aṣ-Ṣādiq:] «We have been called poor and rich, after the exhausting sacrifice of the worldly things, and the studying of medicine, and the burning of things, our hearts are destroyed from delusion, while you know the medicine and the illness.» Then the Imam Ǧaᶜfar ibn Muḥammad aṣ-Ṣādiq, may God bless him, answered him: «O seeker, who asks us to show him the right way. Listen to a saying that has no attachment:[251]

follows us in true faith, listen to a statement in which there is no misleading

"The secret is in an operated rock / surrounded above with its fire the water. / Its beginning is the letter *qāf*. / Then its origin is in the letter *lām* and the *mīm*, and between the two is the letter *ḥāʾ*. / It [the rock] had formed in a subtle heat, / neither cold nor air enters into it. (165, fol. 32.1)

[with] water above its fire

Comment

387 Here the author alludes to a secret combination of letters which Ǧābir ibn Hayyān received from the Imam Ǧaᶜfar ibn Muḥammad aṣ-Ṣādiq. Henry Corbin has elucidated one of these mysteries in his paper *Le Livre du Glorieux de Jābir ibn Ḥayyān*.[252] In the explanation which follows in our text the letters, however, have a different connotation. Whilst in Ǧābir's text the letters refer to subtle sectarian differences among the Ismāᶜīlīya, the explanation which follows in our text makes them all refer to Allah or to one of his exalted names. This could mean that the author tries to correct the traditions of the Ǧābir school, not in an opposing way, but in the sense of a deepening of the meaning. The whole rest of our treatise must here be quoted as one because it belongs closely together and is stylised as the concluding poem.

251 Fol. 31.16–32.5 are in rhymed prose.

252 H. Corbin, *Le Livre du Glorieux,* p. 47 ff.

Text

(165, fol. 32.1) Then, when its wisdom is completed	388
/ it appears as pearls of the white oysters / And the	
origin of its beginning and cultivation is astonishing	is the marvellous
/ between the two letters of *ḏāl*, O friends. / Two let-	cultivation
ters of *ḏāl* were friendly to our master; / our father of	two human beings
the creation, Adam and Eve. / One of the two is a son	
of a mother in trees, waiting for a voice and in it	
there are sons. / From it to the people of the world	[-]
hopes reach / and in it there is a gift for the benevo-	get hope
lent. / I revealed to you the secret without limit / a	jealousy
root, a verb and a noun are its meaning.	
(fol. 32.5) Then he gave it on a piece of paper to	
Ǧābir and praised him in a good way, and he did not	
hide from him anything except its beginning, the let-	
ter *qāf*. He [Ǧābir] didn't know the meaning of it and	
he was confused. He thought about it, but God did	confused about it
not open the gates to him. Thus he stood up and said:	its meaning
«By God! Nobody resolves the enigma except the	
one who made it up.» Then he pointed to the Imam	
Ǧaᶜfar, thus sought permission and entered. He	
found with him [Ǧaᶜfar] a group of his intimate	
friends and between them a plate and in it the rest of	
the *ḫabīṣ* [a dish made of dates, flower and ghee].	
And they [the group] glorified the making of its cre-	work
ator and the goodness of its sweetness. Thus Ǧaᶜfar,	
may there be peace on him, looked at Ǧābir: «Do	
you believe in what this group says?» And Ǧābir had	
an inspiration, thus he said: «I don't know.»	subtlety
(fol. 32.11) Ǧaᶜfar smiled and said: «The man said	
the truth; it is not allowed that he gives testimony	
except to what he knows.» Then he said to him:	
«Join in their group till you know the truth of their	
statements.» Thus Ǧābir sat down and ate. Thus	
when he had finished eating and the table was lifted	
up Ǧaᶜfar said: «How is the state of the resolvers of	
what is enigmatic for them?» Thus Ǧābir said:	
«O Master, on whomever your lucky star is looking,	
he wins the searched-for thing and for him is solved	

every enigma, and for him is accomplished—O my
Master—the intended thing. My patience and my
thoughts have left me in knowing the secret of the
philosophers and I went very much astray.» sages
Ǧaʿfar said: «Know—may God guide you—that
what you failed to reach is the hidden secret, and
without it our science does not exist. That is the
secret from which there is no way out, and if it were
not secret, this *ẖabīṣ* would not be colourful for us.
(fol. 33.1) Know—may God give you success—that
God has hidden secrets in the letters, but he does not
inform anyone about it, except those from whom He
removes the veil. I will make clear to you something
of the art. The first is the [letter] *alif* and its secret is
the first name of the greatest God, and it is the glory. that it is the first let-
Thus it is the greatest name. People do not name any- ter of the
body with this name except Him. Thus the letter *alif*
points to all the names of the exalted God. To make
a definition with the letters *alif* and *lām* that is
derived from the letter *alif*, they both enter on every
name to define it. Know that the *alif*, which is the
beginning of the glory, points to the divine that
indeed there is no God except Him, and it also points
to the monotheism. It also is the beginning of the
name the One [*al-wāḥid*] and the beginning of the
Unique [*al-aḥad*]. And it is an exalted letter.
And in regard to the *qāf*, it is [also] is an exalted letter. It exists in the names of the exalted God, among
them the Old One [*al-qadīm*] and the Strong one [*al-* Eternal
qawī] and the Conqueror [*al-qāhir*], and the
Everlasting [*al-qāʾim*], and the […] [*al-qābiḍ*], and Steadfast … Grasper
the Provider [*ar-razzāq*], and the Everlasting [*al-*
bāqī] and the Truth [*al-ḥaqq*]. Every one of these
names from the names of the exalted God has an
influence on our science. The existence of the science is opened up only with the existence of the *qāf*.
The beginning of the *qāf* is the eternal divine and
from it comes the *prima materia* similar to its for- matter
mation.»

Then Ǧaᶜfar said: «O skilful seeker, be aware of the pondering of the thoughts over the saying of a truthful man [*rağul ṣādiq*—Ǧaᶜfar aṣ-Ṣādiq]. Indeed, I revealed to you the secret in the clearest words, and I have given to you the most decisive evidence about it and the greatest proof.» At that Ǧābir bowed his head and raised it and said: «By God, my mind became confused and my patience diminished. And if a release from suffering had not come to me from my master, this would have been the last hour of my life.» Then Ǧaᶜfar laughed [so much that] his molar teeth appeared. Then he said: «O Ǧābir, I did not explain to you these names and honoured secrets except to make you understand what God told you from the secret of this work. And I hope from the exalted God that in this our reunion he makes follow words on my lips which may clear up your mind in order that you get removed from the level of the sleepy people.» (169, fol. 34.1) | that you have to ponder

Then he asked for an ink pot and a piece of paper. Then he wrote: «I say—and I ask God for help—the poem of the *qāf*:

In it is the intended and the goal / And the *qāf* is a secret to all what it must be. / The *qāf* was a foot to our master / Adam that led to a war and made necessary a war [with God]. / And the *qāf* is the secret of the descending and it [the secret] didn't stop—He who has intelligence reaches the goal. | must be [-] fall

Then (Ǧaᶜfar) gave the paper to Ǧābir. Ǧābir looked at the paper for a while and then his face beamed with joy. When Ǧaᶜfar set him [Ǧābir] and the secret of his situation right he said: «I think you are happy and I think you have obtained what you are searching for.» Then Ǧābir said to Ǧaᶜfar: «O master, I didn't taste the sweetness of the *ḫabīṣa* except at this very hour.» Then he went on his knees, thanking the exalted God. Then he raised up his head and said: «O my master, may the exalted God guide you to the right way as you were a guide to me after I went the wrong way.» Then he [Ǧaᶜfar] said: [.]O Ǧābir, you | saw that Ǧābir became happy «

have to cut apart the things. | , the secret is in separating the things and parts

[Rhyming prose]
(169, fol. 34.8) Cut every part of the body / Like the cutting apart of the butcher. / Then you must wash the souls and the spirits repeatedly. / And you must follow what they have requested from you like the work of the one who makes ink. / Then gather all like the gathering of the skilful Almighty. / Then watch them till they become like the tar. / Then at this time you must take from them the secrets. / It returns to the body in the better condition due to the *qāf*. | The body returns to [it] in the best … .»
It is alive and old, and it is a proof for the oldness of the science in the kingdom of the exalted God. It is the strong and nothing of the metals and other things shows enmity to him as it is more powerful than they. | eternal … eternity
And from the Omnipotent is a proof that if you make carry one *qīrāṭ* [= 0,195 g] from it on a *qinṭār* [= 100 pound = 44.5 kg] it will carry it. And the *qāf* is not the irresistible except if there has been put one dirham [= 3.12 g] of it onto the iron and the steel. Then it turns them into gold, God willing. | carry | conqueror except if one dirham [=3.12 g] of it is thrown
And praise to God for guiding us to accomplish this copy in the town of Hyderabad Deccan on the first day of the month of Ǧumādā II 1298 [1st May 1881]; Mullā Maḥmūd.

Comment

The description of the encounter of Ǧābir with the great imam Ǧaʿfar
389 is a final *revelation of how the author understood the philosophers' stone: namely as a mystical effect in which the divine secret of Allah's work in man is transmitted from one being to another. When the sheikh transmits the secret the pupil becomes mystically one with the sheikh.* We have that already in the oldest Greek alchemical treatise of *Isis to her son Horus*,[253] where Isis conjures in the name of all the powers of the underworld so that her son may not tell the secret except to his son or closest friend «so that he becomes you and you become him». Here already the sharing of the secret brings forth a *unio mystica* between teacher and disciple. Ǧābir finds a

253 M. Berthelot, *Alch. Grecs,* I. XIII.

group assembled around Ǧaʿfar and on the table the remnants of a meal consisting of *ḫabīṣ* (date-ghee). It seems to me possible that this is an allusion that the group around Ǧaʿfar celebrated a kind of communion or *agape* consisting of *ḫabīṣ*. If that is correct, the existence of secret societies would have to be placed as already existing at the time of Ǧaʿfar and the school of Ǧābir would have to be looked at as a secret community like the later Brethren of Purity (*Iḫwān aṣ-ṣafāʾ*). You would have to see here a direct continuation of the Hellenistic Gnostic sects where many of them celebrated such a communal meal.

The mystical food which brings forth the *unio mystica* of Ǧaʿfar's 390
group is date-ghee. It probably symbolizes, among other things, the sweetness of the loving *unio mystica* of the members. There is a report that the teacher of Qarmaṭ Ḥamdān al-Ahwazī, the teacher of the Qarmaṭī movement in Iraq, was the guardian of date stores.[254] It seems to me probable that this reported fact had a secret symbolic meaning and that dates were looked at as a symbol of the 'secret' of the Qarmaṭian movement. According to a legend, when God created Adam from clay, there was a left-over of that clay, from which Allah created the palm tree.[255] Thus, the palm tree became a kind of feminine equivalent of the divine man Adam, the first imam. As Corbin has shown, the palm tree became a symbol of *Adam's sister* and was also identified with Miriam, the Mother of Jesus and with Fāṭima.[256] Symbolizing the latter, the mystics identified the palm tree with the 'Earth of Sesame' or 'Earth Hurqalyā', that is the dimension of the imaginal, or the reality of the psyche in a Jungian context. Corbin writes: «The tradition of the palm tree created out of Adam's clay is recorded in the great encyclopaedia of Shiʿite tradition, by Muḥammad Bāqir Mağlisī, *Biḥār al-anwār*, XIV, 840 (Safina, II, 581); it figures as a lengthy answer given by the sixth Imam, Ǧaʿfar aṣ-Ṣādiq, to someone who asked him about the origin of the palm tree. The answer includes further details illustrating the significance of the palm tree as a symbol of the celestial Earth. When God banished Adam from Paradise he ordered him to take the palm tree (down) with him. Adam planted it in Mecca. All the palm trees 'directly descended' from it belong to the species *ʿağwa* (the unusually exquisite and substantial Medina dates). All other palm trees, in the Eastern and Western parts of the Earth, came from the pits of these dates.»[257] Corbin therefore states: «The palm tree typifies Gnosis as spiritual food.»[258] Without doubt, in this last

254 Cf. H. Halm, *Kosmologie und Heilslehre der frühen Ismāʿīlīya*, p. 2.

255 H. Corbin, *Spiritual Body and Celestial Earth*, p. 135 ff.

256 Ibid, p. 138, 4 and 5. The Arabic word for palm tree, *naḫla,* is feminine.

257 Quoted from H. Corbin, ibid., footnote 4 on p. 309.

258 Ibid. in footnote 4 on p. 309.

paragraph of our text, the author alludes to these traditions and reveals that in his view Ǧābir did not have the full revelation of Ǧaᶜfar's Gnosis, but was well on the way to understand it.[259]

391 In our text Ǧābir, in as far as he understands the alchemical secret, becomes one with Ǧaᶜfar and also with the whole Qarmaṭic community. Whilst the alchemical opus symbolizing the process of individuation seems to be primarily the lonely preoccupation of the individual, it often also leads to a deeper communion with our fellow men, but in a kind of selective mystical way. Jung has extensively commented on this fact. The encounter of Ǧābir with Ǧaᶜfar illustrates also, as our text says, the self-regulating action in the coagulation of the stone. It is as if Ǧābir was still floating and not inwardly consolidated and therefore also dependent on Ǧaᶜfar. In the moment when he understood what Ǧaᶜfar meant, *he coagulated into being a master himself, independent of Ǧaᶜfar and identical with Ǧaᶜfar simultaneously*. This is alluded to by the letter *qāf*, which is, according to our text, the *rock or stone* and the *ultimate secret*. It is, as the text says, the *secret of the descending* «and it didn't stop». The descending, it seems to me, alludes to Allah's descending again and again towards mankind through the mediation of the imams (and also of the prophets, *nāṭiqs*, etc.), so that there is an everlasting *flow of divine influence from God to man* beginning with Adam till the end of the days.

392 The letter *mīm* (see above passage 163, fol. 31.13–165, fol. 32.1) is common to the names Muḥammad and Adam and therefore alludes to their secret identity. Then the text speaks of the *ḏāl* as the two legs of Adam, the cause of war. Adam and Muḥammad are ultimately both the cosmic gnostic Anthropos who came to earth with one leg in Adam, and with the second leg in Muḥammad. Both times this caused a war: the fall of the angels happened because of Adam, and the war of the Muslims with the infidels has been caused by Muḥammad.[260] This war will find its termination only when the *qāf*, the *qāʾim*, the imam of resurrection will appear. He is the 'Standing One' or the 'Resurrecting One' and brings the real Gnosis, the

259 The following passage has been omitted by the editor, due to the fact that the author of the ending of Ms Ǧīm (G) is not Ibn Umail, as the translators and M.-L. von Franz first thought: «It seems as if Ibn Umail belonged to (or was the founder of ?) a branch of the Shiᶜite movement which understood itself as going back to Ǧābir, but at the same time of having a more complete truth which directly harks back to Ǧaᶜfar. This, to me, explains why the writings of Ibn Umail did not become absorbed into the corpus of Ǧābir.»

260 Concerning the doctrine of the enemies of the imams, see H. Halm, *Kosmologie und Heilslehre der frühen Ismāᶜīlīya*, p. 27 ff.

real religion, in the end of the days, which will dissolve the 'Law' in the only outer teaching of religion. The holy Triad in Ǧābir's letter enigma has been deciphered by Corbin as referring to: *ᶜAlī, Muḥammad, Salmān.* I believe that our letter enigma refers to *Adam, Muḥammad and Qāʾim, or Qarmaṭ.* In his *Book of the Three Words,* H̱ālid ibn Yazīd refers to a secret which was handed down from Adam to the last man, which consists of three words. Apparently, those three names were interpreted differently by the different branches of the Ismāᶜīlīyan sects. But what it really meant is always a triadic appearance of the gnostic Anthropos.

When these Arabic texts reached Christian Europe, the three words 393
were naturally associated to the Trinity as is for instance the case in the *Aurora Consurgens.* The *Aurora* ends with the paraphrase of the Song of Solomon: «He that hath ears to hear, let him hear what the spirit of the doctrine saith to the sons of the discipline concerning the *espousal* of the *lover* to the *beloved.* For he had sowed his seed that there might ripen thereof threefold fruit, which the author of the Three Words saith to be three precious words, wherein is hidden all the science, which is to be given to the pious, that is to the poor, from the first man unto the last.» This *Aurora* text refers to H̱ālid's *Liber trium verborum*: «And these are *three precious words, concealed and open,* to be imparted not to the wicked nor to the impious nor to the unbelievers, but *to the faithful* and to the *poor* from the first man unto the last.» [261]

Our text also mentions the making of ink. Probably this refers to the 394
same process as making tar, namely reducing the prima materia into the nigredo. In Ismāᶜīlīyan tradition the quill and the tablet play a mystical role. The quill symbolizes God's creative action in its masculine creative form (*qadar*). The tablet is the feminine receptive principle (*kūnī*), which makes this creative action materially real.[262] To my knowledge, the texts nowhere mention the ink, but we could conclude that the ink is the psyche of the imam through which Allah transmits (writes) His secret instructions to mankind, flowing on from the first imam, or *nāṭiq*, to the last.

261 See. M.-L. von Franz, *Aurora Consurgens*, ibid., p. 149. The quote is found in *Artis Auriferae quam chemiam vocant* (1610), I, p. 228.

262 See H. Halm, *Kosmologie und Heilslehre*, ibid, p. 63.

Part IV

Apparatus

1. Bibliography

Alchemical treatises in Latin:

Artis auriferae quam chemiam vocant, Basle 1610.
- Calidis liber secretorum, I, p. 208 ff.
- Calidis liber triorum verborum, I, p. 227 ff.
- Practica Mariae Prophetissae in artem alchimicam, I, p. 205 ff.
- Rosinus ad sarratantem episcopum, I, p. 178 ff.

Aurora Consurgens, translated by M.-L. von Franz (see General Literature, von Franz).

Bibliotheca chemica curiosa, edited by J. J. Mangetus, Geneva 1702.
- Artefius Clavis majoris sapientiae I, p. 503 ff.
- Senioris antiquissimi libellus (de chemia), II, p. 216 ff.

IBN SĪNĀ. *Avicenna Latinus–Liber de Anima seu Sextus de Naturalibus IV–V. Edition critique de la traduction latine médiévale*. Simone van Riet and G. Verbeke (eds), Louvain 1986.

MAIER, Michael. *Symbola aureae mensae duodecim nationum*. Frankfurt a. M. 1617.

MAGNUS, Albertus. *De mirabilibus mundi*, Cologne 1485.

Musaeum Hermeticum, Frankfurt a. M. 1678.
- LAMBSPRINCK, *De lapide philosophico*, p. 337 ff.

Tabula Smaragdina, see RUSKA, Julius, in *General Literature* below.

Theatrum Chemicum, edited by L. Zetzner, Argentorati (Strasbourg) 1659–1661.
- Allegoriae sapientum … supra librum Turbae, Vol. V, p. 57 ff.
- Artefius Clavis majoris sapientiae IV, p. 221 ff.
- Platonis liber quartorum, Vol. V, p. 114 ff.
- Senioris Zadith, filii Hamuelis tabula chimica (De Chemia), Vol. V, p. 191 ff.

Turba philosophorum, see RUSKA, Julius, in *General Literature* below.

ZADITH SENIOR (Zadith ben Hamuel). *De Chemia Senioris antiquissimi philosophi libellus*, Strasbourg 1566.

Alchemical treatises in Arabic:

Ibn al-Muḫtār, Abū ᶜAbdullah Muḥammad. *K. Mirʾāt al-ᶜağāʾib*. See M. Ullmann, *Natur- und Geheimwissenschaften*, p. 245.

Ibn Umail, Muḥammad. *Book of the Explanation of the Symbols—Kitāb ḥall ar-rumūz*, edited by Th. ABT, W. MADELUNG and Th. HOFMEIER, translated by S. FUAD and Th. ABT, Corpus Alchemicum Arabicum I (CALA I), Zürich, 2003.

IBN UMAIL, Muḥammad. *Ad-Durra an-naqīya* (to be published), Ms. Āṣafīya II, 1410 et al. (see SEZGIN, *Geschichte des arabischen Schrifttums*, Band IV, p. 287).

- *Al-Qaṣīda al-mīmīya* (to be published), Ms. Beşirağa 505 et al. (see SEZGIN, *Geschichte des arabischen Schrifttums*, Band IV, p. 288).

Three Arabic Treatises on Alchemy by Muḥammad ibn Umail (10th century AD). Edition of the texts by M. TURĀB ʿALĪ, Excursus on the Writings and Date of Ibn Umail with Edition of the Latin Rendering of the *Māʾ al-waraqī* by H.E. STAPLETON and M. HIDĀYAT ḤUSAIN, *Memoirs of the Asiatic Society of Bengal*, Calcutta, Vol. XII (1933) No. 1, p. 117 ff.

ZOSIMOS, *Mafātīḥ aṣ-ṣanʿa*, Ms. Cairo (to be published), Ms. Cairo, Dār al-kutub, 395 kīmiyāʾ 23.

- *Muṣḥaf aṣ-ṣuwar* (The Book of the Pictures), Ms. Istanbul, Arkeoloji Müzesi 1574 (CALA II edition forthcoming).

General Literature:

ABT, Theodor. "The Great Vision of Muḥammad Ibn Umail", supplement to *Psychological Perspectives*, Los Angeles 2003.

ADDAS, Claude. *Ibn ʿArabī ou la quête du soufre rouge*. Paris 1989.

Alch. Grecs, see: BERTHELOT, Marcellin.

ANDREAE, JOHANN VALENTIN. (Christian Rosencreutz, pseud.) *Chymische Hochzeit... Anno 1459.* For translation, see:

- *The Hermetick Romance;* or, *The Chymical Wedding.*Translated by E. Foxcroft. London, 1690.

ANONYMOUS, *Physiologus* (Codex parisianum graecus), Greek-Latin, with the commentaries of Nicolas Caussin, Paris 1618.

ASIN PALACIOS, Miguel. *Islam and the Divine Comedy*, translated and abridged by Harold SUTHERLAND, London 1968.

ʿAṬṬĀR, Farīd ad-Dīn. *The Conference of the Birds (= Manṭiq Uṭ-Ṭair)—* A *Philosophical Religious Poem in Prose*, Rendered into English from the literal and complete French translation of Garcin de Tassy by C. S. NOTT, London 1954.

AURIGEMMA, Luigi. 'Il concetto di sublimazione da Freud a Jung', in: *Prospettive junghiane,* Torino 1989.

BACOT, Jacques, THOMAS, Frederick William and TOUSSAINT, Gustav Charles. *Documents de Touen-Houang relatifs à l'Histoire du Tibet*, Paris 1940–1946.

BERNARD, John Henry (ed.). 'Odes of Solomon', in: *Texts and Studies, contributions to Biblical and Patristic Literature,* Joseph Armytage ROBINSON (ed.*),* Vol. VIII, Cambridge 1912.

BERTHELOT, Marcellin. *Collection des Anciens Alchimistes Grecs*, Paris 1887/88.

- *La Chimie au moyen âge*, Paris 1885.

BONNET, Hans. *Reallexikon der Aegyptischen Religionsgeschichte*, Berlin 1952.

BREHIER, Louis. *L'Eglise et l'Orient au moyen âge–Les Croisades*, Paris 1907.

BUDGE, Ernest Alfred Wallis.

- *Amulets and Superstitions—The Original Texts with Translations and Descriptions of a Long Series of Egyptian, Sumerian, Assyrian, Hebrew, Christian, Gnostic, and Muslim Amulets and Talismans and Magical Figures,* New York 1978 (reprint).

- *From Fetish to God,* Oxford University Press 1934. Reprint New York 1988.

- *The Mummy. A Handbook of Egyptian Funerary Archaeology,* Cambridge 1925.

CARRA DE VAUX, Bernard. *Notes et Textes sur l'Avicennisme aux confins du XI-XIIe siècle*, Bibliothèque Thomiste, Vol. XX, Paris 1939.

CHEVALIER, Jean, and GHEERBRANT, Alain (eds). *Dictionnaire des Symboles*, Editions Robert Laffont et Editions Jupiter, 1969.

COMARIUS. 'Livre de Comarius: Philosophe et Grand-Prêtre enseignant à Cléopatre l'Art Divin et Sacré de la Pierre Philosophale', in: *Collection des Anciens Alchemistes Grecs,* M. BERTHELOT (ed.), Vol. II, p. 278 ff.

CORBIN, Henry. *Creative Imagination in the Sufism of Ibn ᶜArabī*, Bollingen Series XCI, 2, Princeton, New York 1969.

- *Spiritual Body and Celestial Earth—From Mazdean Iran to Shîᶜite Iran*, Bollingen Series XCI, 2, Princeton 1977.

- *L'Homme de Lumière dans le soufisme iranien*, Chambéry 1971.

- 'Le Livre du Glorieux de Jâbir ibn Ḥayyān (alchimie et archétypes)', *Eranos-Jahrbuch*, XVIII/1950, Zürich 1950, p. 47–114.

DENOMY, Alexander Joseph. 'An Inquiry into the Origins of Courtly Love', in: *Mediaeval Studies*, Pontifical Institute of Mediaeval Studies, Toronto, Vol. VI (1944), p.175ff.

DUVAL, Paulette. *La pensée alchimique et le Conte du Graal*, Recherches sur les structures (Gestalten) de la pensée alchimique, leurs correspondances dans le Conte du Graal de Chrétien de Troyes et l'influence de l'Espagne mozarabe de l'Ebre sur la pensée symbolique de l'oeuvre, Paris 1979.

EISLER, Robert. *Weltenmantel und Himmelszelt*, Vol. I, München 1910.

ELIADE, Mircea. *Yoga, Immortality and Freedom*, London 1978.

FESTUGIERE, André Jean. *Hermétisme et Mystique Païenne*, Paris 1967.

von Franz, Marie-Louise. *Aurora Consurgens*, Companion Work to C. G. Jung, *Mysterium Coniunctionis*, Bollingen Series LXXVII, New York 1966.
- *Alchemy: An Introduction to the Symbolism and the Psychology*, Toronto 1980.
- *On Dreams and Death*, Boston, London 1986; Chicago 1998[2].

Ǧābir ibn Ḥaiyān. *Dix traités d'alchimie traduits et commentés par Pierre Lory*, Paris 1983.

Gäng, Peter (ed.). *(see Tantra, das...)*.

Von Grunebaum, Gustave E. *Medieval Islam—A Study in Cultural Orientation*, Chicago 1953.

Gutas, Dimitri. *Greek Thought, Arabic Culture—The Graeco-Arabic Translation Movement in Baghdad and Early ᶜAbbāsid Society (2nd–4th/8th–10th centuries)*, London and New York 1998.

Halm, Heinz. *Kosmologie und Heilslehre der frühen Ismāᶜīlīya – eine Studie zur Islamischen Gnosis*, Wiesbaden 1978.

Hastings, James (ed.). *Encyclopedia of Religion and Ethics*, Vol. 1–13, Edinburgh, New York 1953.

Holmyard, Eric John (ed.). *The Alchemical Works of Geber*, introduction by E. J. Holmyard, reprint of first edition, London 1928.

Hopfner, Theodor. *Griechisch-Aegyptischer Offenbarungszauber: mit einer eingehenden Darstellung des griechisch-synkretistischen Dämonenglaubens und der Voraussetzungen und Mittel des Zaubers überhaupt und der magischen Divination im besonderen*, Mehrteiliges Werk (in Serie), Leipzig 1921.

Ibn Umail, Muḥammad. Text and studies, collected and reprinted by Fuat Sezgin (editor), Frankfurt am Main 2002.

Sīnā, 'A Treatise on Love by Ibn Sina', translated by Emil Fackenheim, in: *Mediaeval Studies,* Toronto, Vol. VII (1945), p. 208–228.

Jacobsohn, Helmuth. 'Das göttliche Wort und der göttliche Stein', *Eranos-Jahrbuch* XXXIX (1970), Gesammelte Schriften, Hildesheim 1992, p. 152 ff.

Jung, Carl Gustav. *Symbols of Transformation, Collected Works,* 5, Princeton 1967.
- *The Archetypes and the Collective Unconscious, Collected Works,* 9/1, Princeton 1968.
- *Aion, Collected Works,* 9/2, Princeton 1968.
- *Psychology and Religion—West and East, Collected Works,* 11, Princeton 1969.
- *Psychology and Alchemy, Collected Works,* 12, Princeton 1968.
- *Alchemical Studies, Collected Works,* 13, Princeton 1967.

- *Mysterium Coniunctionis*, *Collected Works*, 14, Princeton 1974.
- *The Practice of Psychotherapy*, *Collected Works*, 16, Princeton 1970.
- *The Symbolic Life*, *Collected Works*, 18/1 and 18/2, Princeton 1980.
- *Lectures given at the ETH Zürich* 1938/1939, and 1940/1941 (on the 'Process of Individuation'—3: Eastern Texts, 4. Exercitia spiritualia of St Ignatius of Loyola), unpublished private notes, Edition 1960.
- *Letters Vol. I–II*, Gerhard ADLER and Aniela JAFFÉ (eds), translations from the German by R. F. C. Hull, London 1973-1976.
- *Memories, Dreams, Reflections*, New York 1963.
- *The Secret of the Golden Flower* commentary, see WILHELM, Richard, and also *Collected Works*, 13.
- *Seminare—Kinderträume*, Lorenz JUNG and Maria MEYER-GRASS (eds), Olten 1987.
- *Visions, Notes of the Seminar given in 1930–1934*, edited by Claire DOUGLAS, Princeton University Press 1977.

KRAUS, Paul. *Jâbir ibn Ḥayyân—Contribution à l'histoire des idées scientifiques dans l'Islam*, Mémoires de l'Institut d'Egypte, Le Caire 1942, Vol. I et II. Reprint: *Jâbir ibn Ḥayyân – Contribution à l'histoire des idées scientifiques dans l'Islam – Jâbir et la science greques*, Paris 1986.
- *Alchemie, Ketzerei, Apokryphen im frühen Islam, Gesammelte Aufsätze*, Hildesheim 1994.

LEVI DELLA VIDA, Giorgio. 'Something more about Artefius and his *Clavis sapientiae*', in: *Speculum, a Journal of Mediaeval Studies*, Vol. 13, 1938, p. 80ff.
- *Ricerche sulla formazione del piu antico fondo dei manuscritti orientali della Biblioteca Vaticana*, (Studi e Testi, 92), Città del Vaticano 1939.

LEISEGANG, Hans. *Die Gnosis*, Leipzig 1924.

LLULL, Ramon. *Das Buch vom Freunde und Geliebten*, Herausgegeben, eingeleitet und aus dem Altkatalanischen übertragen von Erika LORENZ, Zürich, München, 1988.
- *The Book of the Lover and the Beloved*, an English translation with Latin and Old Catalan versions transcribed from original manuscripts by Mark D. JOHNSTON, foreword by G. PRIDHAM, Warminster 1995.

MADELUNG, Wilferd. *Religious Trends in Early Islamic Iran*, The Persian Heritage Foundation, Columbia Lectures on Iranian Studies, 4, Albany, New York 1988.

Mahabharata, translated into English with Original Sanskrit Text (10 vols). Translation according to M. N. DUTT, Ishwar Chandra SHARMA and O. N. BIMALI (eds), Parimal Sanskrit Series 60, Delhi 2001.

MAHDIHASSAN, Syed. *Indian Alchemy or Rasayana*, New Delhi 1979.

MEIER, Fritz. 'Das Mysterium der Kaaba', *Eranos-Jahrbuch* XI (1944), Zürich 1945, p. 187–214.

- 'The Mystery of the Kaaba—Symbol and Reality in Islamic Mysticism', in Bollingen Series 30, 2 (The Mysteries), *Papers from the Eranos Yearbooks*, 1955, 149–168.

- 'The Problem of Nature in the Esoteric Monism of Islam', in Bollingen Series 30, 1 (Spirit and Nature), *Papers from the Eranos Yearbooks*, 1954, 149–203.

- 'Die Wandlung des Menschen im mystischen Islam', *Eranos-Jahrbuch* XXIII (1954), Zürich 1955, p. 99–139.

MERTENS, Michèle. *Les Alchimistes Grecs*, IV. 1, Zosime de Panapolis, Paris 1995.

MEYERHOF, Max. 'On the Transmission of Greek and Indian Science to the Arabs', in: *Islamic Culture*, Hyderabad, Vol. 11, 1937, p. 17–29.

NASR, Seyyed Hossein. *An Introduction to Islamic Cosmological Doctrines*, Cambridge, Massachusetts 1964.

NEUMANN, Wolfgang. *Der Mensch und sein Doppelgänger – Alter Ego Vorstellungen in Mesoamerika und im Sufismus des Ibn ʿArabī*, Wiesbaden 1981.

NEWMAN, William R. *The Summa Perfectionis of Pseudo-Geber—A Critical Edition, Translation and Study*, Leiden 1991.

Odes of Solomon (see Bernard, J. H.)

PARET, Rudi. 'An-Naẓẓām als Experimentator', in: *Der Islam, Zeitschrift für Geschichte und Kultur des Islamischen Orients,* Berlin, Vol. XXV (1939). p. 228–233.

PARTINGTON, James Riddick. 'Albertus Magnus on Alchemy', in: *Ambix*, London, Vol. 1 (1937–8), p. 3–20.

Physiologus (see ANONYMOUS).

PLESSNER, Martin. 'The Place of the Turba Philosophorum in the Development of Alchemy', in: *Isis—An International Review devoted to the History of Science and Its Cultural Influences,* Quarterly Organ of the History of Science Society and of the International Academy of the History of Science, 45, 1954, p. 331–338.

- *Vorsokratische Philosophie und griechische Alchemie in arabisch-lateinischer Überlieferung – Studien zu Text und Inhalt der Turba philosophorum*, Wiesbaden 1975.

PLINIUS SECUNDUS (MAJOR), Caius. *Historiae naturalis libri XXXVII,* Vol. X, Venezia 1469.

PO-TUANG, Chang. *The Inner Teachings of Taoism*, Commentary by LIU I MING, translated by Th. CLEARY, Shambhala 1986.

PREISENDANZ, Karl (ed.). *Papyri Graecae Magicae – Die griechischen Zauberpapyri*, Berlin, 1928–1931, Vol. II.

PRETZL, Otto. 'Die frühislamische Atomlehre. Ein Beitrag zur Frage über die Beziehungen der frühislamischen Theologie zur griechischen Philosophie', in: *Der Islam, Zeitschrift für Geschichte und Kultur des Islamischen Orients,* Berlin, Vol. XIX, 1931, p. 117–130.

REITZENSTEIN, Richard. *Poimandres,* Leipzig 1904.

- *Die Hellenistischen Mysterienreligionen,* 3rd edition, Leipzig 1927.

Rigveda, The Hymns of the Rigveda. Translated by R. T. H. GRIFFITH, Benares 1896–1897.

ROEDER, Günther. *Urkunden zur Religion des Alten Aegyptens*, Jena 1923.

RUSKA, Julius. *Turba Philosophorum*, Berlin 1931.

- *Tabula Smaragdina*, Heidelberg 1926.

- *Arabische Alchemisten*, Heidelberg 1924.

- 'Studien zu Muḥammad ibn Umail at-Tamîmî's Kitāb al-Māʾ al-Waraqī wa 'l-Ard an-Najmīyah', in: *Isis—An International Review devoted to the History of Science and Civilization*, Quarterly Organ of the History of Science Society and of the International Academy of the History of Science, 24, 1935–1936, p. 310 ff.

SCHIMMEL, Annemarie. *Mystical Dimensions of Islam,* Chapel Hill, 1975.

SERRANO, Miguel. *C. G. Jung and Hermann Hesse—a Record of Two Friendships*, London 1966.

SEZGIN, Fuat. *Geschichte des arabischen Schrifttums*, Vol. I–XII, Leiden 1967–1984, Frankfurt a. Main since 1995.

- *Ibn Umail*, Text and Studies, collected and reprinted by Fuat Sezgin (editor), Frankfurt am Main 2002.

STAPLETON, Harry Ernest, and HIDĀYAT HUSAIN, Muḥammad. *Three Arabic Treatises on Alchemy by Muḥammad ibn Umail (10th Century AD),* Edition of the Texts by M. TURĀB ʿALĪ, *Memoirs of the Asiatic Society of Bengal, Calcutta*, Vol. XII, 1933, No. 1, p. 117 ff.

-'Alchemical Equipment in the Eleventh Century', *Memoirs of the Asiatic Society of Bengal, Calcutta*, Vol. I (1905), No.1, p. 47 ff.

Das Tantra der verborgenen Vereinigung – Guhyasamāja-Tantra, translated from the Sanscrit and edited by Peter GÄNG, München 1988.

TRINICK, John. *The Fire-Tried Stone*, London 1967.

TWEEDIE, Irina. *Daughter of Fire: A Diary of a Spiritual Training with a Sufi Master*, Nevada City, 1986.

ULLMANN, Manfred. 'Kleopatra in einer arabischen Disputation', in:

Wiener Zeitschrift für die Kunde des Morgenlandes, Wien, Vol. 63/64, 1972, p. 158–175.

ULLMANN, Manfred. *Die Natur- und Geheimwissenschaften im Islam*, Handbuch der Orientalistik I, VI.2, Leiden 1972.

VADET, Jean. *L'ésprit courtois en orient,* Paris 1968.

VALERIUS MAXIMUS, *Factorum et dictorum memorabilium*, Libri I–IV, Paris 1535.

WEYER, Jost. 'Einführung in die arabische Chemie und Alchemie', in: *Quellengeschichtliches Lesebuch zur Chemie und Alchemie der Araber im Mittelalter*, K. GARBERS and J. WEYER (eds), Hamburg 1980.

WILHELM, Richard. *The Secret of the Golden Flower*, translated and explained by R. WILHELM, commentary by C. G. JUNG, London 1935.

2. General Index

- A -

abār nuḥās (honoured stone) 65, 68
ᶜAbd ar-Raḥmān ibn Zaid 24
above 39, 63, 68, 99, 104, 110, 166, 168–169, 173, 178, 184
— and the below 110, 168–169
—, lights from 110
Abt, Theodor 10–12, 55, 145
Abū al-Ḥusain ᶜAlī ibn Aḥmad ibn ᶜUmar al-ᶜAdawī 49
Abū al-Qāsim ᶜAbd ar-Raḥmān 49
Abū Ṭāhir 50
acid — ferment 75
— of lemon 126
acrid —, water of the 162
action 44, 104, 147–148, 152, 184–185
activity 18, 36, 39, 74, 147, 151, 154, 159–160
Adam 18–20, 63, 65, 136, 139, 154, 160, 179, 181, 183–185
al-ᶜAdawī; *see* Abū al-Ḥusain
Addas, Claude 101
adept(s); *see also* seeker 17, 21, 36, 66–67, 73, 82, 84, 86, 92–93, 95, 99, 103, 105, 109, 116–117, 120–121, 126–128, 130, 135, 142, 147, 165, 176–177
advantage 135–136
advice, advise (vb) 19, 137, 163
— of the sages 137
affinity 22
Aflāṭūn; *see also* Plato 171
Africa 31
— African 30, 51, 73, 98
ages — passage of the 160
—, Middle 29, 31, 33, 55
agony 97, 138
agreement 149
Aḥmad ibn Abū al-Ḥawārī 24
al-Ahwazī, Ḥamdān 183
aim (n, vb) 37, 52, 73, 137–138, 151
air 18, 68, 115, 124–125, 132, 134, 145, 162, 169–170, 175–176, 178
air — find a place to breathe 176
—, bodily 132
—, eternal 132
—, spirit of the 124
—, water of the 162
airy — water 125
Akhmim (Panopolis) 17
alabaster (nasṭarīs) 69–70, 96–97, 99
Albatenius 34
albedo; *see also* whiteness 69–70, 83–84, 86, 92, 101, 129, 132, 161, 164–165
Albert the Great 35–37, 53
Albertus Magnus; *see* Albert the Great
alchemical 7–8, 11, 16–17, 21–22, 25–26, 35, 38–41, 46, 50, 52–54, 59–60, 62–64, 71, 73–74, 76, 78–79, 88, 92–93, 95, 99–101, 103, 106, 109, 111, 117–118, 124–125, 135–136, 138, 150–151, 153, 156, 158, 163, 165, 170–171, 177, 182, 184
alchemical — opus; *see also* work (alchemical) 25, 51, 63, 69, 71–75, 81, 89, 118, 128, 139–140, 150, 153–154, 159, 165–167, 173, 184
— motifs, *see also* motif 16
— process 7, 17, 46, 52–53, 62, 64, 111, 117, 150
— tradition 26, 50, 52, 71, 106
alchemistic literature 50
alchemist(s) 7, 15–17, 21–22, 25–27, 35, 37–39, 41, 48–50, 53, 59–60, 63–65, 68, 72, 74, 77, 87, 89, 91, 93–95, 101, 104–105, 108, 111, 115, 118, 128, 134, 136, 151–154, 160, 164, 171–173, 176–177
alchemy 7–9, 11, 15–17, 20–23, 25–27, 30–31, 36–39, 45–46, 48, 50–53, 55, 59, 61, 63, 67–71, 73–74, 76–77, 79–80, 85, 87, 89–90, 94, 99, 101, 103–106, 108–109, 111, 117–119, 125, 130, 133, 136, 140, 142, 149, 153, 158, 160–161, 169, 171, 176–177
— a kind of magic 36
— a religion of matter 51
— condemned 38

—, allegorical 15
—, Arabic; *see also* Islamic alchemy 8–9, 11, 26, 31, 35, 60, 69, 160, 171
—, basic/central theme of 17, 20
—, chemical (with chemical content) 25–26, 31, 52–53, 140
—, Gnostic-Hermetic alchemy 11, 26–27, 31, 177
—, Greek 11, 52–53, 68, 72, 74, 79–80, 85, 105, 117, 125, 169
—, Islamic; *see also* Arabic, Sufi — 25–26, 104, 177
—, Latin 7, 11, 35, 54–55, 73, 77, 93, 105, 129
— *Mater Alchimia* 104
—, mystical … of the Arabs 26
—, non-chemical content of 16
—, religious/magico-religious 9, 15, 25–27, 31, 38, 55, 177
—, roots/origin(s) of 15, 17, 20, 50, 79
—, Spanish 37
—, tension of spiritual and chemical 53
—, Sufi 23, 38, 60
—, Taoist 53, 68
—, symbolic content of 15–16
—, Western; *see also* —, Greek; —, Latin 15–17, 21, 31, 36, 38–39, 53, 55, 104–105, 118–119, 158, 176
alembic 78, 109, 124
Alexander (Iskandar) 118–119
—, Romance of 118
Alexandria(n) 51, 66, 108
— Alexandrian school and library 51
Alfarabius (al-Fārābī) 34
Algazel; *see* al-Ġazzālī
ʿAlī ibn Abī Ṭālib, Caliph 140, 185
ʿAlī ibn Aḥmad ibn ʿUmar al-ʿAdawī; *see* Abū al-Ḥusain
alif (first letter) 180
alkali 102, 162
Alkindius 34
Allah; *see also* God 23, 25, 37, 50, 65, 82–83, 88, 91, 93–94, 104, 106, 109, 113–114, 116, 126, 150, 152, 167–168, 172–173, 175, 177–178, 182–185
Allegoriae Sapientum 78
allegory, allegorical 15, 18, 23–25
alliance —, (alchemists) made a holy 148
al-Māʾ al-waraqī see under Māʾ al-waraqī
Alpetragius 34
Alphonso VI 34
Alphonso X (the Wise) 34
alum(s) (ammonium sulfate) 122, 131
—, Egyptian 122
Alvaro of Cordova 33
ammonia(s) 117, 159
ammonium sulfate; *see* alum
amount 15–16, 49, 109, 152
amplification 51, 54, 59–60
amusement 128
analogy (-ies) 77, 113, 127, 171, 176
analyst 43, 131
Andra Pradesh Oriental Manuscript Library and Research Institute (Āṣafīya Library), Hyderabad 8–9, 11, 145
androdamas (*al–andradāmūs*) 120, 161
angel(s), archangel 18, 23, 40, 92, 118, 162, 166, 184
anger 11, 73, 158
angles —, three (of a stone) 99, 161
anima 22–24, 30, 36, 42–44, 48, 86, 101, 130, 153, 171
— *coelestis* 23
— feminine element 23, 30, 44, 101, 165
— fem. element in man 23, 44, 101
— *mundi* 30, 130, 153
animal(s); *see also* ass, beast, bird, bat, bitch, buffaloes, bull, calf, chameleon, cows, dog, dragon, elephant, goat, lion, oysters, puppy, rabbits, scorpion, sheep, snail, snake, stag, unicorn, viper, whale, wolf 46, 69, 75, 93, 105, 107, 109, 119, 126, 156–158
— nature of love 93
— emanation of the … body 126
— milk of all …s 107
—, dung of every 119
—, eye of the 75
—, milk of a pregnant 107
animus 43–44, 46, 48
Antioch 51
anthropos/Anthropos 17–18, 20, 60, 63–64, 77, 92, 118, 157, 184–185

— Gnostic anthropos 17, 20, 63, 184–185
— God-man figure 17, 20
Antimimos, the demon 19
Anubis 157
Apollo 165
Apollonius of Tyana 55
aqua permanens 75, 103
Aquinas, St Thomas 7, 35
aqzal 106, 174
Arab(s) 15, 29, 31, 33–34, 39, 50–52, 72, 74, 79–80, 156
Arabic 7–12, 15, 23, 25–26, 29, 31–35, 37–38, 46, 49, 51–52, 54–55, 60–63, 65–66, 68–70, 72–73, 76–77, 90, 93, 98, 100–101, 110, 112, 121, 123, 160, 162–163, 167, 171–172, 183, 185
— culture 31, 51
— influence 35, 38
— mysticism 35, 76, 101
arcane substance 77, 103
archaic 29–30, 42–43, 51–52
— identity 42–43
archangel Gabriel 92, 166
archetypal — idea 29
— image(s) 16, 23
— models of ideas 23
— motif 17, 78
— roots 80
— themes 21
archetype 41, 60, 67, 177
— of God 41
Archelaos 129
Ares; *see* Ars
Aristotle 33, 34, 64, 97
Ars (Āras) 111, 119, 132
arsenic(s) 91–92, 111–112, 114, 116–117, 141
art(s) 17, 20, 29, 34–35, 103
art (*aṣ-ṣinā*ʿ*a* = alchemy; *see also* work) 19–20, 24, 74, 78, 148, 151, 176, 180
—, the sacred 20, 176
Artefius *Clavis Sapientiae* 54–55
artifex 36
Artis Auriferae 63, 100, 185
artists 29
asafoetida 162
ascend, ascent 18, 31, 95, 113, 168, 177
Asclepius 55, 165
ashes 66, 72, 79, 119, 123, 126, 131, 133, 159–160
— of ashes 65, 72, 119, 123, 131
— of fats 133
— of *sindiyān* trees/holm–oak 133
— potash 131
—, names of the 131, 159
—, water of the 126
Asin Palacios, Miguel 24–25, 31, 34, 38
aspect(s) 15, 23, 25–26, 30, 38–46, 52, 65, 71, 78, 83, 85, 98, 100, 106, 108, 114–115, 121, 125–128, 133, 135, 142, 151, 158, 160, 162, 164
— of alchemy 15, 25–26, 38, 106
— of love/eros 39–45, 52, 100, 160
— of (the) stone 65, 78, 108, 162
—, chemical 26, 106
—, chthonic/earthy 71, 127, 158
—, dangerous/demonic; *see also* danger 41, 78
—, dynamic, active 65, 100
—, feminine 52, 83, 127, 133
—, fourth/four 44–45
—, religious/magical 38, 52
—, mystical 26
—, passive/receptive 65, 83
—, psychic 30
—, sexual 39
—, spiritual 52, 85, 100, 108
ašqūniyā —, gum of 119
ass(es) 107, 124, 126, 135
—, milk of the 107
—, urine of the 124, 126
association(s) 12, 17, 59, 98, 118
Astānis; *see* Ostanes
astrology 20, 33, 36–37, 50–51, 74, 125
—, Chaldean 50
Athenagoras 104
Atman 172
attain (vb) 44, 48, 78, 104, 137, 164, 166
ʿAṭṭār, Farīd ad-Dīn 94, 109
attitude(s) 16, 20, 30, 43, 50–51, 62, 78, 101, 133, 157
—, right 16, 30, 78
Atūtāsiya; *see* Theosebia
Augustine, St 165
Aurigemma, Luigi 41
Aurora Consurgens 7–8, 36–37, 39, 165, 185

author(s) 8, 16–17, 25–26, 30, 35, 37, 46, 48, 50, 55, 59–60, 62–64, 66–67, 73–75, 78–79, 85–87, 91, 93, 96, 98, 102, 106, 109, 111, 113–117, 126, 128–130, 135, 137–138, 140, 142, 145, 148, 152–157, 160, 162–165, 168, 170–172, 176–178, 182, 184–185
Averrhoës (Ibn Rušd) 33–34
ʿasǧad (gold) 165–166
Avicenna; *see* Ibn Sīnā

- B -

bāʾ (letter B) 69, 145
Bacon, Roger 35
Bacot, Jaques 63
bag —, woollen 125
Baghdad 49, 116
Bahrein 50
balance, balanced 30, 67, 98, 135
Bālīnās 55
balsam tree 114
barbarians 135
Barbeliots 118
Bardesanes 118
Baruch (angel) 118
base of the work 163
basis/substance of everything 170
baṭbarīš 69
bat dung 115
battle 23, 53
beast —, gall bladder of every 119
beat (vb) 19, 47
Beatrice 38, 44
beautiful(ly) 24–25, 45–46, 63, 71–72, 165, 176
beauty 24–25, 35, 47, 176
begin (vb) 10, 21–22, 26, 29, 31, 34–37, 39, 41, 62, 104, 106–107, 109, 140, 150, 167, 169, 175, 177
beginning 10, 15, 18–19, 25, 29, 32, 36, 43–44, 51, 61–63, 67, 77, 82, 92, 106–108, 127, 142, 153, 156, 159, 161, 168–169, 173, 175, 178–180, 184
— of the analysis/treatment 106, 127
— of the cooking 107
— of the name the One 180
— of the operation; *see also* of the work 61
— of the qāf 178, 180
— of the work; *see also* of the operation 153, 168, 173
being(s) 18, 20, 22–23, 33, 40–42, 44–48, 51, 54–55, 62–64, 66–68, 71, 74, 77, 80, 82, 87–89, 93, 100–103, 107, 111, 113, 117, 121–122, 124, 127, 131, 133–134, 138, 142, 147, 149, 155–156, 158–161, 165–167, 169–175, 177, 182, 184
— clings/holds on to being 88–89, 111
— enjoys being 88
— is for being 89
—, living 159
—, ocean of 159
belief(s) 51, 81, 157
believe (vb) 16, 30, 36–37, 42, 47–50, 54, 70–71, 142, 151, 171, 179, 185
belly 168
beloved 25, 38, 42, 87, 91–93, 102, 142, 185
— met the beloved 87
—, body of the 102
benefit(s) 84, 94, 119, 152, 154, 161
— two benefits (of the water) 152
— which has many names 119
Bernard, John Henry 108
Bernard, St 40
Berthelot, Marcellin 17, 20, 25, 62, 65, 68, 71, 78, 81, 89, 129, 155, 159, 176, 182
beverage —, every 126
Bible/Torah 140
Bibliotheca Chemica 46, 55, 93
bird; *see also bn.w* bird, chicken, cock, crow, eagle, hen, ostrich, peacock, phoenix, woodpecker 80, 97–98, 112, 124
— birds 75, 94, 109
—, multi-coloured 124
birth; *see also* born 48, 65, 70, 80, 104, 108–109, 112, 127, 133–134, 176
— childbirth 175
— of the self 48
— rebirth 17, 70, 79–80, 118, 132, 177
bitch 99–100, 107, 109, 124, 156, 162
—, milk of 107, 109, 162
—, urine of 124

bitterness 115, 123, 129
Biyā 119
black 9, 51, 60, 64, 66, 72, 77, 84, 96–97, 99, 102–103, 120, 160–161, 163–165
— androdamas 120
— body 84
— crow 164–165
— earth 161
— lead 161
— rock 163
— structure 164
— stone 60, 64, 72, 160–161, 164
—, everything 102
blackness; *see* nigredo
blessed water; *see also* holy water 163, 166
blessing 140
blood 18, 71, 115, 124, 140–141, 175
— bloody 18
— of gazelles 124
blue 9, 61, 69, 100
— dog 100
bn.w bird 80, 112
bodies; *see also* body 18, 66, 68, 79, 85–86, 94, 100, 102, 105–106, 109, 115–116, 125, 142, 154, 156, 158, 161, 166, 176
—, dead 166
—, dry 116
—, four 105
—, fugitive 106
—, master of 102
—, seven 106
—, six 105–106, 125
—, spirits in its/their 156
bodily 18–19, 37, 53, 132, 167
— air 132
body; *see also* bodies 16, 18–19, 21, 23, 25–27, 61–62, 64–67, 71–72, 75–76, 80–81, 84, 86–97, 99–100, 102–103, 105–107, 109–114, 116–122, 124–127, 129-130, 133, 138, 140–141, 150–152, 157, 173, 175, 177, 182–183
— became red 67, 96
— is the vessel 93
— of magnesia 130, 133
— of the beloved 102
—, black 84
— corpse 17, 20, 63, 79, 176
—, dry 90, 114, 116–117
—, every 107
—, fiery 75, 97, 99, 133
—, first 61, 88, 110, 121
—, honoured 102
—, pure … of glass 90
—, second 62, 87–89, 96, 110–111, 129
—, spiritual 23, 26, 65, 71, 120, 133, 183
—, subtle 16, 23, 64–65, 67, 126
—, surface of the 126
—, their (sages') 16, 61, 107, 111, 117, 126
—, water and 90
—, water is the ferment of the 107
—, white 61, 66, 127
bond 18
Bond, James 44
bone(s) 71, 131–132, 175
— bones of the elephant 132
— lime of bones 131
Bonnet, Hans 70
book; *see also* books 7, 9, 16, 19, 38, 42, 54–55, 59, 62, 68, 77–79, 83, 91, 100, 111, 113, 145, 157, 168, 171, 175, 185
Book/Epistle of the Explanation 152
— *of Tetralogies* 77, 171
— *of the Greater Wisdom* 54
— *of the Keys* 10, 54
— *of the Pictures* 10, 157
books; *see also* book 19, 36, 80, 91, 137, 154–155, 160–161, 163
— of the philosophers/sages 80, 137, 154–155
— of the work 161, 163
—, holy ... of Seth 160
born; *see also* birth, newborn 63, 73, 77, 94, 110–111, 114, 118
bottom 95, 110, 123, 140, 159
— of a hen 140
— of the vessel 95, 110, 123, 159
brain 76–77, 79, 115, 140, 171
bread 75, 174
—, wheat turns into 174
breast of the woman 175
breasts 25, 108
breath, breathe (vb) 18, 25, 77, 156, 176
— of Heimarmene 18
Bréhier, Luis 31
Brethren of Purity *see* Iḫwān aṣ-Ṣafāʾ

bridegroom 25
broth 129
brother(s) 19, 22, 43, 134, 157, 159, 172–173
— of the soul 134
— two brothers 172–173
—, third 172–173
bubbles 115, 133
—, froth of 115
Buddhism, Buddhist 21, 68, 168
Budge, Ernest Alfred Wallis 70, 98, 105, 112, 190
buffaloes —, milk of the 162
bull 38, 103, 105
— of Mithras 105
— with six horns 103, 105
bunch of grapes 91
būrnaṭīs; *see* pyrites
burn (vb) 18, 49, 66, 87, 96–97, 100–101, 122, 126–129, 132, 141, 156, 161–162, 169, 178
—t copper 66, 96, 126, 161
—t gold 161
butcher 182
butter 115

- C -

calcification 129
calcified mercury 115
calf 107, 133
—, milk of a female 107
—, milk of a male 107
camphor 93, 127–128
Carra de Vaux, Bernard 35
castor beans —, fat of 115
categories —, three 161
Catholicism 153
caves 47, 171
—, two 171
Chaldean 18, 50
— astrology 50
chameleon 71, 73, 133
chaos 168
chemical(s); *see also* Chymical 15–17, 20, 22, 25–26, 30–31, 36, 52–53, 72–73, 99, 106, 124, 130, 140, 142, 171
— process 17, 20, 30, 130
— terms; *see also* affinity, sublimation 22
chemically 64, 82
chemistry 7–8, 11, 15, 21, 26, 30, 36, 53, 64, 67, 85, 98, 140
—, forerunner/beginning of 7, 15, 67
—, beginning of quantitative 67
—, history of 11, 15
Chevalier, Jean 73
chicken; *see also* cock, hen 45–46
child 22, 70, 109, 175–177
—, Divine 176–177
children 75, 104, 108, 127–128
— i.e. secondary effects 128
— of the Widow 104
Chrétien de Troyes 38
Christ 19, 60, 108, 118, 153, 176–177
—, inner 60
Christendom 33–34
Christian(s) 20, 24, 29, 31–34, 36, 38, 52, 103–104, 108, 153, 177, 185
— civilization 29
— tradition 104, 177
— world 24, 108
Christianity 23, 29, 31, 39, 52, 153
— Christianity/Christian and Islam/Muslim 23, 31–33, 39, 52
chrysocolla (*ḫaršaqlā*) 69, 110, 113, 133, 161
chrysolite, —, green 103–104
chthonic 21, 71, 78, 158
church(es) 32, 38, 47, 55
— *ecclesia spiritualis* 89
Chymical Wedding 48
cinnabar 76, 106–107, 119
—, mercury of/from 106, 119
—, red 76
cinnamon 93, 127–128
circumambulation 59, 73, 128
citrinitas; *see* yellowness
city; *see also* town 34, 89, 94
—, people of one 89
—, our 89
Clare, St 44
clarity 158, 168
clasper 132
claudianus 96
clay 183
Clement of Alexandria 108
Cleopatra 70, 108

cling (vb) 36, 88, 93, 95, 106, 175
clinger 66
close one, —, the … met the … 87–89, 111
cloud(s) 115, 119, 133, 162
—, rain-cloud 115, 133
—, rainy 133
—, water of the 162
coagulate (vb) 102, 109, 159, 164, 177, 184
coagulation 122, 184
coal 92, 95, 102
— of the mountain 102
coarse, -ness 98, 115, 129, 140
— grease 115
cock; *see* chicken, hen 45–46, 93, 115–116, 159
coffee beans 91
cognitio matutina 165–166
cognitio vespertina 165–166
coincide (vb) 37, 39, 55, 81, 148, 172
coins 32
cold 41, 67, 79, 111, 127–129, 173, 178
— coldness 93
— coolness 127
—, water of the sages is hot and … 129
—, hot nor 67
collect (vb) 24, 59, 62, 79–80, 94, 103, 110, 153
collective 16, 30, 41–42, 47, 74, 87
— function 42
— unconscious 16, 30, 41, 47, 87
collectivity 41–42
—, separate from 41
collyrium (kohl) 102, 126, 133, 161
colour; *see also* black, green, purple, red, white, yellow 9, 62, 65, 71, 73, 76, 82–85, 87, 99, 104, 157, 160, 170, 175–176
— coloured 71, 125
— colourful 180
— of silver 82
— of the blood 175
colours 62, 67–68, 70–71, 73–76, 84, 86, 97, 102, 120, 126–127, 132, 158, 161, 166–167
— blackness; *see* nigredo
— greenness 166
— redness; *see* rubedo
— whiteness; *see* albedo
— yellowness; *see* citrinitas
—, many 71, 73–74
—, mother of 132
—, multi-coloured 71, 120, 124
—, multitude of 71, 120
—, (stone) of three 161
—, ten 67–68
Comarius 51, 69, 71, 80–81, 89, 129, 159, 176
commerce (-ial) 31–32, 34
community (-ies) 17, 50, 53, 89, 164, 183–184
companion(s) 24, 107, 156
—, ferment to its 107
—, improves its 107
compensation 42
complete lead-copper 88
completion 68, 121, 129
— of the ten 121
complexio oppositorum 40
composed water 102, 166
composition(s) 25, 102, 154, 171
— *of Lights* (*Tarākīb al-anwār*) 145, 154
compulsion 85, 101
conceal (vb) 77, 99, 131, 185
—, (male) … in her (female) 99
conflict 45, 47
confront (vb), -ation 16, 23, 25–26, 52, 54
confuse (vb); *see also massa confusa* 83, 90, 138, 142, 179, 181
confusion 19, 102, 138, 170
coniunctio; *see also unio mystica*, union, unite 17, 21–23, 27, 35, 39, 45–46, 48, 84, 88–89, 91, 93, 100–101, 105, 111, 116, 130, 134–135
— of conscious and unconscious 22
— of king and queen, sun and moon 22
—, eternal 134
—, highest 93
—, second 88
conquer (vb) 32, 43, 50, 75, 88–89, 152
conquest 31–33
conqueror 34, 180, 182
— (one of God's attributes) 180
conscience(s) 80, 157
conscious 16, 22–23, 43–44, 59, 86, 89, 98, 101,105, 128, 150–152, 171, 176
— consciously 176

consciousness 40, 46, 59, 69, 71,77, 80, 85–86, 101, 104, 118, 127, 151, 153, 158, 161, 165–167
consolidate (vb) 41, 92, 103, 184
contemplation 128, 168
contradict (-s, -ion) 120, 142
contritio 66
control(ler) 66–67, 105, 132, 134
cook (vb) 100, 109, 149, 175
cooking 15, 76, 96, 106–107, 109, 121, 127, 149–150
— cookings 76, 121
—, every 76, 121
—s, nine 121
—s, three 76
copper 9, 61–66, 68–69, 76, 79, 87–88, 90–91, 96, 105, 109, 113, 115, 126, 130, 161–162
— coppery milky water 130
—, burnt 66, 96, 126, 161
—, filings of burnt 66
—, flower of the 113
—, fountains of 61–62, 64–65, 79, 88, 90, 105
—, reddened 90
—, their (the sages') 115
—, water of 109
corals 155
Corbin, Henry 23, 26, 54, 63–65, 71, 92, 96, 104, 120, 126, 134, 165, 178, 183, 185
corporeal 69, 87, 91, 134, 151
— spirit 87
corpus 9–10, 12, 26, 53–55, 67, 95, 140, 184
— Hermeticum 95
— Ğābiricum 26, 54
correct (adj, vb) 9, 44, 61–62, 96, 178, 183
cosmology 36, 50, 95
— cosmological 36–37, 52–53, 113
cosmos 65, 68, 98, 118, 148
—, inner 148
cosmic 17, 48, 63, 68–69, 77, 85, 87, 95, 98, 105, 113, 118, 127, 167, 172, 184
country (-ies) 31, 33, 46, 50, 54, 98, 120, 124
couple 21, 45–46, 48, 135
—, divine 48
—, royal 46, 48
cows 124, 162
—, gall bladders of 162
—, urine of 124, 162
creation 36, 51, 63, 68, 98, 113, 147, 154, 163, 169, 175, 177, 179
— create (vb) 23, 26, 36, 43, 50, 52, 63, 65, 68, 72, 78, 95, 98, 113, 142, 150, 152–154, 163, 167–169, 183
— *creatio continua* 36, 149, 154
— creative 16, 26, 36, 39, 50, 52, 64, 71, 73, 76, 84, 88, 99, 105, 109, 111, 113, 126, 147, 153–154, 159–160, 162, 168, 170, 177, 185
— creative attitude 16
— creativity 36, 42, 105, 169
— creator 40, 87, 113, 154, 179
— of the earth 154
— of the macrocosmos 147
— of things 169
creature(s) 87, 156–157
cross 38, 40, 44–45, 47
crow 164–165
crown(s) 45, 66, 123, 133, 161
— of everything 123, 133
— of the king 123, 161
— of victory 66, 123, 133, 161
— seven crowns 115
crucifixion 47
crusades 31–32
cultivate 42, 154
cultivation —, marvellous 179
culture 7, 24–25, 31, 33–34, 51, 133

- D -

Daēnā (spirit of individual man) 23
ḏāl 179, 184
—, two letters of 179
danger 12, 78, 174
dangerous 41, 51, 77–78, 103,158
Dante 38, 44
dark 21, 38–39, 43, 52, 100, 120, 155, 158, 165
— side of eros 100, 158
darkness 40, 75, 94, 110, 114, 154, 156, 165
— of the greases (fats) 156
date (n, vb) 24, 49–50, 53–54
date (fruit) 179, 183
Davies, Barbara 12, 63, 70, 157

day(s) 19, 25, 100, 121, 128, 149, 151, 164–166, 175, 182, 184–185
—, eighth (8th) 175
—, every 149
—, first … of the month 182
—, fortieth (40th) 175
—, forty (40) 164, 175
—, one … and one night 165
—, seven 121, 175
—, sixteenth (16th) 175
—, twenty-fourth (24th) 175
—, thirty-second (32nd) 175
dead 17, 20, 29, 63–64, 71–73, 80, 90, 112, 132, 157, 166
— dead bodies 166
— dead king 63, 112, 132
death; *see also* die 16–17, 19, 21, 41, 47–48, 71, 73, 78–79, 81, 104, 114, 118, 127, 129, 153, 157, 166, 170, 173
— of the ego 48
—, to put the stone to 173
decompose/be ruined (vb) 87, 151
— decomposition 170
define (vb) 8, 26, 60, 128, 180
— definition 16, 61, 74, 171, 180
degree(s) 43, 74, 126
Democritus (Pseudo-Democritus) 25, 72
demon(s) 53, 77–78
demonic 78, 83
Denomy, Alexander Joseph 35, 37
describe (vb) 7, 20, 30, 45–46, 53, 59, 63, 68, 70–71, 79, 82, 87, 89–90, 93, 96, 100, 103, 108, 110, 118, 127, 129, 139, 142, 150, 159, 171, 174
description(s) 7, 36, 52, 60, 66, 77, 88, 91, 111, 116, 128, 138, 158, 165, 175, 177, 182
— of the operation of their stone 175
desire(s) (n, vb) 20, 37, 40, 44, 47–48, 77–78, 82, 108, 139, 150, 176
detachment — from life/the world 86, 101, 139
develop (vb), development 7, 16, 23, 26–27, 29–30, 35, 39, 43–44, 48, 51–53, 72, 85, 99, 120, 126, 177
— of animus 44
devil 43
devote (vb), devotion 12, 17, 22, 24, 30, 63, 78, 137, 150
die (vb); *see also* dead, death 9, 49, 54, 63, 80, 104, 108, 116, 127, 132, 138, 145, 159, 166, 173–174
dignity 37
Dionysos 71
direction(s) 45, 47, 52, 65, 73, 77, 137
dirham 182
dirt 90, 140
— dirty 135, 139–141, 165
— dirty hair 139
— dirty linen 165
— impure 44, 135, 140–142, 157
— stinking 139–140
disagreement 89, 111, 149
disease 81, 114, 138
— of poverty 81
dissected (dismembered) 17
dissimilar, — things 152
dissolve (vb), dissolvable 17, 63, 70, 76, 97, 100, 106, 117, 121, 123, 125, 132, 149, 152, 156, 164, 176, 185
dissolution 86–87, 126, 148–149, 152
distillation (dripping) 80, 121–122
— distilled drops 162
divided water 106
divine 17, 20, 22, 24–25, 30–31, 38, 43, 46, 48, 52, 63–64, 66, 68–69, 71-72, 75–77, 80, 87–91, 94–95, 98, 101, 106, 108–109, 114–117, 126, 129-130, 132, 138, 140, 148–149, 151, 153–154, 156, 159–160, 163–164, 166–170, 172-173, 176–177, 180, 182–184
— cosmic centre 69
— domain 46
— man; *see also* anthropos 17, 63, 71, 183
— water 75, 80, 88–91, 95, 106, 109, 114–115, 126, 129–130, 149, 154, 163–164, 167, 169–170, 173
— work 148, 169
—, spiritual … wisdom 140
divinity 36, 39–40, 68, 104, 108, 132, 135, 169, 176
dog; *see also* bitch 46, 99–100, 119, 155–160, 162–164
— is a guard for our souls 156
—, blue 100, 156
—, dung of a 119
—, piebald 163

—, urine of the 162–164
—, zinyum 163
Dominican 32
door(s) 130, 148
— of wisdom 130
dragon 62, 74–75, 107, 124, 130, 133
—, head of the 75
—, milk of the 107
—, saliva of the 124
—, tail of the 133
dream 20, 24, 45–48, 59–60, 118, 130, 149
— of bronze clock 47
— of shooting Hitler 45
— of white cock with chickens 45
— with alchemical motif 46
— dreams 7, 15–16, 40, 48, 59, 71, 79, 160
dress — in colour and the light 170
—, woollen 125
dry (adj, vb) 67, 72, 75, 79, 84, 90–91, 114, 116–117, 119, 121, 132–133, 145, 155, 163, 169–170
— body (-ies) 72, 90, 114, 116–117
— desiccated 75
— dryness 116, 127, 170
— firewood 75, 117
— one(s) 116, 169
— origin 117
—, moist nor 67
dung 75, 115, 119, 131, 149, 160
dunghill 159–160, 167
— dunghills of sages 159
— of the divine water 167
ad-Durra an-naqīya 10, 52
dust 66, 131
Duval, Paulette 37
dye 59, 70, 77, 81–85, 88, 107, 110, 115, 119, 125, 130–131, 150, 160, 164–166
— dyed 66–67, 81, 83, 86, 119, 122, 126, 160
— the gold 81–82, 85
—, holder of every 130
—, became one single 107
—, origin for every 70
dyeing 81, 84–87, 107, 119
— elixir 84
— poison 81
— souls 86
— water 87, 119
dyer 66–67, 84–85, 87, 134
dyes 70, 79, 82–84, 86, 90, 103–104, 125–126, 132
—, glass accepts all the 90
—, mother of 70, 132
—, origin of 70

- E -

eagle 63, 72, 99, 112, 114, 119, 132–133
— stone 63, 72, 99, 133
—, falling 114, 132
—, flying 114, 119
—, pure 119
ears 135, 137, 185
earth 7, 18, 23, 26, 61, 63, 65–66, 68–69, 71, 76, 83–84, 92, 95, 102, 104–105, 110–111, 119–120, 131–133, 145 153–154, 157, 159, 161, 163–164, 166–170, 183–184
— and water 154, 166, 169
— does not live without water 154
— hūrqalyā 65, 183
— (named) Biyā 119
— (named) Ṯādāb 119
— (named) Theosebia 119
— of Egypt 132
— of Ethiopia 102, 132
— of gold 61, 131–132
— of metals 132
— of pearls 61, 131–132
— of sesame 183
— of silver/silvery 61, 65, 131–132
—, black 161
—, dried-up 133
—, heaven and 170
—, holy thirsty 61
—, liver of the 131
—, moon of the 132
—, new 65
—, our … is alive 169
—, smoke of the 170
—, snowy 61
—, starry 7, 61
—, their (sages'/philosophers') 83, 105, 119–120, 159, 163
—, they meant by peacemaker the 167
—, thirsty 61, 169
—, vapour of the 132
—, white 61, 66, 69, 95

earthly 19, 29, 48, 68, 172
east, eastern 18, 21, 22, 31–32, 42, 120, 142, 184
— eastern symbol 69
— the East 18, 21–22, 31–32, 120
—, mercury of the 120
ecclesia spiritualis; *see* church
Eden 77
effective poison 120
egg 90, 103, 105, 114–115, 161
— of Maria 161
— of the philosophers/sages 114–115, 161
— shell 103, 105
eggs 45–46, 98, 103, 115, 131, 139, 162
—, fat of 115
—, lime of 131
—, rotten stinking 139
—, water of 115, 162
ego 16, 43, 46, 48, 63–64, 66, 69, 73, 78, 101, 121, 123, 127, 151, 165
— consciousness 69, 78, 151
Egypt 17, 32, 49–50, 73–74, 77, 132, 164
—, earth of 132
Egyptian(s) 16–18, 29–30, 49–52, 68, 70–71, 78–79, 98, 105, 108, 112, 122, 130, 157
— alum 122
— magic 29, 51
— religion 30
eight — eighth day (8th day) 175
Eisler, Robert 103
El Endelesi (the Andalusian), Ebn Amhel 55
element; *see also* female, male element 23, 25, 29–30, 34, 44, 50–51, 85, 88, 101, 123, 149, 153, 165, 169
— *of Foundation* 153
elements 18, 26, 29–30, 34–35, 48, 63, 65, 68, 103, 109, 123, 140–141, 145, 147, 156, 161, 165, 167, 169, 176
—, four 18, 63, 65, 68, 145, 147, 161, 169
elephant 132
Eliade, Mircea 21
elixir 84, 91, 101, 103, 108, 159, 166
— turns red 166
—, dyeing 84
embalming 16–17, 20, 51, 79, 157
— ritual 16, 51
— process 17, 20
embers 97
embrace (vb) 48, 135, 163
embryo 21, 175–176
emerge (vb) 123, 149, 175
emotion (-s, -al) 37, 48, 123, 150, 155
encounter (n, vb) 8, 24, 41, 44, 47–48, 152, 160–161, 177, 182, 184
end (n, vb) 9, 19, 21, 30, 35, 38–40, 46, 60, 62–63, 69, 75, 82–83, 94, 103, 121, 134, 143, 145, 153, 157, 159, 161–163, 166, 172–173, 176, 184–185
— endless 26, 39–40, 128
— of the distillation 121
— of the work 121
—, from the beginning to 153
endeavour 74, 98
endurance 139
enemy 77–78, 100, 124, 156, 184
energy 67
enigma(s) 111, 140, 179–180, 185
— enigmatic 140, 179
Enkidu 78
enter (vb) 33, 36, 45, 62, 73–74, 76, 86–89, 129, 150, 157, 161, 165, 178–180
entering, entrance 62, 75, 99, 121, 152
—, male … into her [female] 99
epistle(s); *see also Explanation, Book of the* 7, 72, 152
Eros, eros 15, 23, 25, 35, 38–41, 45, 47, 64, 67, 100, 157–160
— and love of God 35
— due to Arabic influence 35, 38
— is a cosmogonos 40
— love experience 35
—, Arabic 38
—, dark side of 100, 158
—, destructive aspect of 41
—, religious 23, 25, 39, 45
—, spiritual aspect of 100
escape, -ing 76, 84, 102, 132–133
essence 21, 63–64, 67, 72, 109, 117, 136, 147, 149, 163, 170
eternal 17, 23, 42, 45, 48, 89, 91, 122, 127, 132, 134, 156, 164, 177, 180, 182
— coniunctio 134
— Eternal (one of God's attributes) 156, 180

— eternally 177
— life 89, 91, 127, 177
— Sophia 23
— water 132
eternity 48, 160, 182
etesian stone 71, 120
—, *lithos etesios* 74, 125
ethical — effort 152
Ethiopia —, earth of 102, 132
Euclid 34
euphorbia —, milks of 107
Europe, European 7, 11, 29, 31–36, 39, 48, 53, 60, 89, 185
— European traditions, medieval 39
Eve (Ḥawwāʾ) 18, 44, 179
evening; *see also cognitio vespertina* 137
Everlasting (one of God's attributes) 180
everything 19, 37, 44, 47–48, 62, 74, 76, 80, 92, 94, 97, 102, 109, 113, 119, 123, 133, 142, 147, 154, 158–159, 160, 166, 168, 170, 174–175
— is their stone 123
—, crown of 123, 133
—, magnesia is 92
—, mercury is 92
—, origin of 92
evidence 32, 53, 181
evil 18, 104, 142, 161
example(s) 21, 39, 90, 111, 128, 135, 157
excrement; *see also* dung —, human 75, 131, 139, 141
experience — of the divine 25, 35, 136, 138, 140
—, inner 25, 89, 138, 140
exist (vb) 25, 35, 37, 45, 47–48, 51, 53, 55, 68, 70, 104, 113, 138, 154, 164–165, 180, 183
existence 8, 23, 64, 66, 68, 76, 93, 98, 104, 113, 137, 152, 154, 160, 180, 183
explain (vb) 23–26, 40, 45, 59, 68, 71, 84, 87–88, 99–100, 105–106, 109, 115, 119–121, 135, 155, 163, 165, 181, 184
explanation(s) 8, 17, 26, 42, 62, 65–67, 71, 84, 90, 95, 110–111, 115, 120, 125–126, 152, 158, 163, 165, 168, 178
— *of the Symbols* (book title) 8, 26, 62, 111
— *of the Ten Preparations* (book title) 62
extract, extraction 21, 61, 63, 80, 100, 110, 118–119, 123, 131, 148, 151, 154–155, 169, 173
— from the ashes 123, 131
— of soul 110, 118–119, 148, 173
— of spirit(s) 61, 119, 173
— of the stone 63
— of water 151, 155
eye(s) 25, 68, 75, 102, 133, 135, 150, 157
— eyesight 77
— four eyes alluding to totality 157
— large-eyed 24–25
— of the animal 75

- F -

fāʾ (letter F) 69
face 24, 131, 181
fairy tales 71
Faithful —, Commander of the 140
fantasy; *see also* imagination 15–16, 119, 150–151
—, fantasies 7, 15–16, 22, 118, 149, 170
al-Fārābī, *see* Alfarabius
fascinate, fascination 29, 43, 47
fat(s) 115, 131, 133, 156
— of castor beans 115
— of eggs 115
—, ashes of fats 133
—, every 115
fate 42, 45, 47, 69, 125, 153
father 18, 40, 43, 108, 135, 139, 168, 176, 179
— (Adam) 139, 179
— father-mother (Eros) 40
fatigue 165
Fāṭima 23, 132, 154, 183
Fatimids 50
feather(s) 98, 126, 130, 162
feeling(s) 26–27, 40, 43, 48, 158, 166
female 21, 72, 76, 93–94, 97, 99, 105–107, 115, 120, 124, 127–128, 133
— stone 97
—, every 97, 133
—, male and 72, 93–94, 99, 105–106, 115, 120, 127–128
—, male unites with the 99

—, name of every 133
—, widowed 103–104
feminine 22–23, 30, 44, 52, 83, 85, 100–101, 104, 127, 132–133, 154, 158, 161, 165, 183, 185
— /female principle 100, 104, 106, 132, 158, 185
— earthy aspect 127
— attitude 101, 133
— element 23, 30, 44, 101, 165
—, names for the 94, 133
ferment(s) 75, 79, 106–107, 131
— fermentation 106, 150
— of ferment 131
— of gold 75, 106
— of silver 75
— of the body, water is the 107
— of water 75, 107
— to its companion 107
—, acid 75
ferula asafoetida 162
Festugière, André Jean 95
fiery; *see also* fire 18, 75, 86–87, 92, 97, 99–100, 119, 125, 131, 133
— body 75, 97, 99, 133
— coals 97
— one 119
— poison 119
— spirits 86, 92
— stone 92
— sword 125
— water 119
filings — of burnt copper 66
— of gold 61
— of silver 61, 66
filius philosophorum 104, 108, 110
filth, filthy 116, 139–140
fire(s); *see also* fiery 18, 39, 48, 68, 76–77, 87, 92, 95, 100–101, 107, 115–116, 119, 122– 123, 131, 134, 137, 145, 149–150, 151– 152, 156, 158, 160, 168–170, 175, 176, 178
— and air (fine, invisible elements) 169
— flame (ray) of the hot sun 149
— of love 39, 107
— of passion, emotion 92, 123, 158
— of their intelligence 137
—, by ... they mean the soul 122
—, escape from the 76
—, flower of the 68
—, water and 116, 122–123, 150
firestone 68
firewood 75–76, 117, 125, 133
— of the wool 76
—, dry 117
—, white 75, 133
Firmicus Maternus 104
fixation 94
— fix (vb) 48, 94, 97, 147, 160
flesh 18, 53, 68, 175
flow 31, 50, 65, 91, 97, 106, 117, 149, 151, 170, 175, 184–185
— of love towards God 65
— of the unconscious 106, 149
flower 16, 66–69, 93, 106, 113, 129, 168, 179
— lotus 69–70
— of copper 113
— of gold 67, 106
— of the fire 68
— of the salt 66, 129
—, golden 16, 66, 68, 168
flowers 83–84, 109, 169
— of gold 109
— of grapes 84–85
—, different kinds of 169
foam 95–96, 119
— of the sea 119
followers — of the Greek schools 113
— of St Paul 108
foot 123, 181
foreign —, something 74
forty (40) days 164, 175
foundation 7, 10, 32–33, 153, 168
four (4) 9, 18, 42, 44–45, 63, 65, 67–68, 72, 77, 99–100, 105, 130, 145, 147, 157, 161, 166, 169
— bodies 105
— elements 18, 63, 65, 145, 147, 161, 169
— fourfold marriage 72
— heroes 130
— natures 68, 161, 169
— rotls 130
—, three and four 161, 166
—, wisdom of the ... natures 169
Francis, St 40, 44
Franciscan 32

Franz, Marie-Louise von 7–12, 15–16, 36–37, 49, 53, 61–62, 69, 72, 79, 100, 105, 110, 112, 117, 124, 147, 152, 162, 184–185
Fravarti 23
Frederick, King of Sicily 33
free bull 103, 105
freedom 21, 40, 46
Freud, Sigmund 8, 39, 41, 43, 160
friend(s) 49, 53, 62, 87, 100, 156, 179, 182
— friendship 43, 45
frog 30, 70–71
frontier(s) 31, 45
froth 96, 115, 119
— of bubbles 115
— of every moist 119
— of the moon 96
— of the river 119
— of the sea 119
fruit(s) 64, 169, 174, 185
Fuad, Salwa 8–9, 11–12
fugitive(s) 102–103, 106, 130
— bodies 106
— inner nature 103
— slave 102
—s, (water the holder of) 130
fun 128
fur — of rabbits 126
furnace(s) 19, 75, 93, 133
al-Futūḥāt al-Makkīya (The Meccan Revelations) 63
fusing 152

- G -

Ǧābir ibn Ḥaiyān 26, 49, 53–55, 67, 74, 77, 85, 153, 167, 171–173, 176–179, 181–185
Ǧābirean — Corpus 53, 67, 140
— doctrine 85
— school 121
Ǧaʿfar ibn Muḥammad aṣ-Ṣādiq 54, 176–184
Galen 34, 150, 152
gall bladder 119, 129, 140, 162
— gall bladder of goats 162
— of every beast 119
— of the cows 162
— of the whale 129
Gäng, Peter 21
gather (n, vb) 33, 78, 94, 104, 152, 182
— (mosque gathers) 78–80, 94
gazelles —, blood of 124
al-Ġazzālī (Algazel) 30, 34, 38
Geber; *see also* Ǧābir 54, 153
Gheerbrant, Alain 73
ghoul 76–77
gift(s) 19, 41–42, 139, 151, 179
— for the benevolent 179
— from God 42, 139, 151
al-Ǧildakī, ʿIzz ad-Dīn Aidamir 55, 108
Gilgamesh 78
glass 90, 100–101, 132
—, pure body of 90
glue 70, 106, 119, 131
— of *Asqūntā* 119
— of gold 106
—, water of the 131
gnosis 17, 53, 77, 80, 118, 140, 163, 183–184
— gnostic 11, 17, 20, 26–27, 29–30, 50, 63, 68, 71, 77, 134, 177, 183–185, 190
— Gnostic-Hermetic 11, 17, 26–27, 29–30, 50
— Ismāʿīlīyan Gnosis 80
Gnosticism; *see also* Gnosis 11, 17
goal(s) 19, 25, 44, 48, 51, 62, 66, 68–69, 73, 78, 82, 101, 139, 142, 160, 177, 181
—, to reach the 19, 73, 181
—, ultimate 25
goat 107, 123, 126, 162
—, gall-bladders of goats 162
—, milk of 107, 126
God; *see also* Allah Almighty; Conqueror; divinity; Eternal; Everlasting; Grasper; Omnipotent; One; Provider; Steadfast; Strong; Truth 17–21, 26, 35–43, 45, 48, 51–52, 60–61, 63–65, 67–68, 72–73, 80–85, 87–89, 93–94, 98–99, 101, 105–109, 111–113, 115–116, 118, 123–124, 132–134, 136, 139–142, 147–149, 151, 153–157, 159–163, 165–167, 169–170, 172–185
— concept 41–42
— Godhead 40–41, 64, 73, 76, 84, 106, 133, 155, 160, 166

— -man 20
—, approval of 139
—, name of 40, 115
—, search for 64
—, secret/secrets of 83, 115, 139–141, 147, 156, 182
—, there is no … except Him (God) 180
god; *see also* divine, divinity
— creator 40, 87, 113, 154, 179
— deity 94, 108, 154
— -experience 134
— gods 19, 69, 78, 132, 134, 162, 170
— image 41, 148, 162
— inner Christ 60
— sungod 17, 70, 104
—, mother of gods 69, 132
—, Lord 24, 108
goddess 30, 48, 70, 98, 133, 158
gold; *see also* aqzal 16, 20–21, 25, 36–37, 48, 61–62, 65, 67, 69–70, 75, 81–85, 88, 91, 106, 109, 115, 125, 132, 140, 142, 161, 165–166, 174, 182
— *ʿasǧad* (gold) 165–166
— golden 16, 45, 66–69, 97, 125, 127, 166, 168
— golden flower 16, 66, 68, 168
— into silver 82
— make/dye the ... red 81, 84
— of the people 85
— of the philosophers/sages 82
—, *aurum vulgi* 85
—, burnt 161
—, dye 82
—, earth of 61, 132
—, ferment of 75
—, filings of 61
—, flower(s) of 67, 106, 109
—, glue of 106
—, man of 20, 62, 97
—, mother of 70
—, perfect 65, 88
—, rust of 125
—, yellowness of the 174
gothic 25, 47
Graeco-Roman tradition 97
grail legend 37–38
grapes — of coffee beans 91
— of Hermes 85
—, become wine/turn into wine 174
—, bunch of 91
—, flowers of 84–85
grasps all things 113
Grasper (one of God's attributes) 180
grease(s) 115, 156
greatness — of the work 141
Greek 7, 11, 18–19, 24, 33, 51–53, 66, 68–69, 71–72, 74, 76, 79–80, 83, 96, 101, 105, 113, 117, 125, 130, 136–137, 155, 169, 182
green 9, 103–104, 124, 163
— chrysolite 103–104
— greenish blue 69
— One; *see* Ḫiḍr
— sea, water of the 163
— woodpecker 124
greenness 166
group 24, 46, 53, 86, 179, 183
— of his intimate friends 179
Grunebaum, Gustave Edmund von 49
guardian 157, 173, 183
guide (n, vb) 19, 38, 92, 104, 120, 130, 157, 173, 176, 180–182
guilt 41–42, 44
gum 114, 119, 121, 131, 174
— of ašqūniyā 119
—, all types of 114
—, in the terebinth 174
—, water of the 131
Ǧumādā 182
Gutas, Dimitri 51
gypsum 131

- H -

ḥāʾ (letter Ḥ) 178
ḫabīṣa 179–181
— sweetness of 181
hair 53, 126, 131, 139, 162–163, 175
—, dirty 139
—, lime of 131
—, water of the 162–163
half 33–34, 43, 49
—, two halves (of the stone) 150
Ḫālid ibn Yazīd 82, 93, 100, 156, 185
Ḥallāǧ 116, 177
Halm, Heinz 183–185
Ḥamdān al-Ahwazī 183

Hānā 120
hands 29, 82, 140
—, impure 140
harbours 124
Harīṭis 119
ẖaršaqlā; *see* chrysocolla
Hastings, James 103
head(s) 45, 70, 75, 98, 100, 110, 113, 121, 123, 127, 130, 171, 181
— (upper part) 95
— and tail 121
— dragon with nine heads 130
— of the dragon 75
—, water is the 123
healer 103, 165
healing 76, 115, 131, 162
health 8–9, 170
heart 32, 45, 47–48, 100, 104, 108, 129
— hearts 81, 136, 178
— of the sun 129
heat; *see also* hot 95, 100, 113, 127, 150–151, 156, 160, 164, 169, 178
— and moisture 164
— clashes with the earth 169
— of the fire(s) 100, 151, 156, 160, 169
—, subtle 178
heaven(s); *see also* sky 24, 39, 68, 110, 113, 157, 163, 166, 168, 170
—, coming down/descends down from the 110, 116
—, earth and 110
—, water of 163
—, from the 166
heavenly — soul, upper 134
— sphere(s) 18, 77
Heimarmene 17–19
Heket 70
Helen 44
hellenism — hellenistic 17, 26, 29, 49–50, 54, 60, 64, 68, 70–71, 108, 111, 177, 183
— hellenistic literature 50
— hellenistic traditions 26
help 10–12, 34–36, 43, 46, 52, 82, 100, 124, 142, 156–157, 159, 181
—, ask God for/God's 81, 181
helper 21, 120
hen; *see also* chicken, cock 46, 93, 115–116, 140, 159
—, bottom of a 140
—, cock and 46, 93, 115–116, 159
herb(s) 84, 109, 114, 161, 169
— manifestation of the herbs 84
— with seven leaves 114
hermaphrodite 158
Hermes 18–19, 60, 67, 72, 79, 85, 92, 100, 103, 110, 122, 132, 154, 156, 160, 163–166, 168, 173–174
Hermetic 11, 17, 26–27, 30, 31, 50, 53, 79, 171–172
— mystery 79
—, Pythagorean 53
Hermetism 11, 17, 25, 29
—, gnostic 29
—, hellenistic Ptolemaic 29
Hermetist(s) 27, 50
hero 78
— four heroes 130
Hesiod 18
Hesse, Hermann 48
Hidāyat Ḥusain, Muḥammad 7
hide(s), hid 38, 55, 73, 77, 83, 173, 179
— hidden 12, 48, 55, 63–64, 68–69, 77, 80, 83, 94, 98, 109, 128, 131, 136, 155, 160, 175, 180, 185
Ḫiḍr 104
hierosgamos 46, 48
— mystical wedding 89
Hippocrates (Zubuqrat, Buqrat) 34, 155, 171
history 7–8, 11, 15–16, 25–26, 98
— of chemistry 11, 15, 26
— of depth psychology 16
Hitler 45–46
hold (n, vb) 11, 51, 53, 45, 67–68, 81, 88–89, 111, 113, 115, 134, 150, 169
holder 66, 130, 132
— of every dye 130
— of the fugitives 130
holm oak; *see* oak
Holmyard, Eric John 153, 167
holy 24, 32–33, 47, 61, 102–104, 108, 129–130, 132–133, 148, 160, 177, 185
— alliance 148
— books 160
— Holy Ghost 104, 177
— water 102–103, 129–130

Homer 130
homeostasis *see* balance
honey 66, 107–108, 110
hope(s) 24, 94, 136, 138, 154, 179, 181
Hopfner, Theodor 70
horn(s) 73, 103, 105, 123
— six horns 103, 105
— of a goat 123
horse 24, 102
Horus 70, 103–104, 182
hot; *see also* heat 67, 79, 97, 128–129, 149, 158, 162, 175
— nor cold 67
hour 37, 77, 164, 181
house 70, 101, 113, 156, 167
— the habitation of the spirit 167
houses 34, 70, 124–125, 133
—, salt of 70, 131
human being(s) 20, 41–42, 44–45, 47–48, 62–64, 77, 93, 127, 167, 171–172, 175, 179
humility 156, 174
hungry 102
husband —, dog is called the 158–159
—, murderess of her 119
—, torturer of her 119

- I -

Ibn ʿArabī 23–27, 30, 38, 63–64, 72, 101
Ibn Balʿawān 55
Ibn Ḥaiyān; *see* Ǧābir
Ibn Yazīd; *see* Ḫālid ibn Yazīd
Ibn al-Muḫtār 121
Ibn Umail at-Tamīmī, Muḥammad; *see also* Zadith Senior/ben Hamuel 7–11, 15, 21, 26, 30–31, 35, 38, 46, 49–55, 59, 61–62, 64, 69, 75, 79–80, 83, 85, 90–91, 93, 95, 98, 100, 105, 109, 118, 127, 133, 145, 162–163, 172, 176
— relationship to *Corpus Ǧābiricum* 53
— relationship to *Turba* 52
idea(s) 23, 25, 29–30, 32, 36–38, 53, 63, 65, 67–68, 77, 79, 89, 94, 105, 118, 129, 133, 171–172
— of matter 29
—, archetypal 29
idols 107, 132
—, seven 107
ignorance 137
ignorant 123, 135–136, 164–165
— ignorantly 138
Iḫwān aṣ-Ṣafāʾ (Brethren of Purity) 53, 113, 183
Ikhwan; *see* Iḫwān aṣ-Ṣafāʾ
illness 9, 170, 178
illumination(s) 25, 120, 126, 130, 155
illusion 22, 43
image(s) 16, 20, 23, 26, 41–43, 46–48, 59, 62, 68, 70, 72, 79–80, 95, 100, 103, 111, 121, 133–134, 147–148, 162, 165
—, archetypal 16, 23
imagine 16, 21, 33, 47, 82, 96, 183
imagination 16, 21, 26, 35–36, 64–65, 86, 128
—, active 16, 64–65
—, *imaginatio vera* 21
imam(s) 49–50, 53, 64, 67, 69, 115, 173, 176–179, 182–185
immortality; *see also* eternal 16, 20–21, 89, 91
—, immortalization 17
imprisoned 77, 153
inability (unable/not able) 81, 83, 137
incarnate (-tion) 23, 132–134, 177
incest 22, 101
incorporeal — realm of the 18
increase (vb) 83, 152, 174, 176
— increasing(-ly) 43, 52, 130, 164
individual 20, 23, 40–42, 46, 69, 106, 158, 177, 184
individuation 7, 20, 41–43, 46–48, 73–75, 81–82, 118–119, 155–156, 174, 184
— psychopompos 20
—, process of 7, 20, 41–43, 46, 73, 82, 118–119, 174, 184
infinite 40, 48, 160
initiate (-or, -ion) 35, 38, 71, 142, 157
ink 181–182, 185
— pot 181
inner 7, 16–17, 20, 22–23, 25–27, 30–31, 41–48, 50, 53, 60, 63–65, 68–69, 72–73, 75–76, 86–87, 89, 92, 97, 99, 101–104, 106–107, 109, 118, 120, 123, 126, 134, 138, 140, 142, 148–151, 155,

157, 162, 164, 166, 174, 177
— core/kernel (of psyche/personality) 16, 20
— God-man/Godhead 20, 60, 64, 148, 166
— man 63, 92, 142
— (psychic) process 7, 20, 22, 53, 68, 73, 106, 149, 177
inside 22, 30, 47, 71–72, 77, 97, 99, 148, 150, 159, 176
— like its outer appearance 148
— of stone 72, 99
insufficiency 138
integrate (-ion) 44, 113, 125, 161
intellect 77, 166, 171
intelligence 130, 136–137, 181
— reaches the goal 181
—, fire of their 137
intelligible world 168
intention(s) 78, 106, 136
—, a sincere 137
inter-confessionalism 50
intermingling (Christian and Muslim) 34
interpret (vb) 18, 20, 41, 50, 53, 64, 71, 93, 100–101, 108, 111–112, 117, 126, 149, 165, 177, 185
— symbolically 50
interpretation 8, 10, 40, 47, 51, 53, 59, 91, 136
—, concretistic 52–53, 136
—, essential core of meaning 59
introspection 44
introspective work 44
introverted 8, 52
investigations 31
Ion (priest) 97
Iraq 50, 183
Iran(-ian); *see also* Persia 8, 17, 23, 50, 63
Irenaeus 118
iron 61, 65, 68, 76, 87, 90, 93, 97, 122, 161, 182
— and the steel 182
—, red burning 97
Ishtar 78
Isis 16, 103–104, 182
Islam 15, 23–26, 31–33, 38–39, 45, 49–50, 52–53, 73, 98, 105, 156, 162
— Islamic 23–27, 33–34, 36–39, 42, 50–51, 53–55, 64–65, 71, 80, 88, 91–92, 104–105, 107, 113, 147, 166–168, 177
— Koranic religion 50
Ismāʿīl ibn Ǧaʿfar 49
Ismāʿīlism 53
Ismāʿīlīya 52–53, 115, 178, 183–184
Ismāʿīlīyan 26, 49–50, 52–54, 80, 160, 171, 177, 185
— tradition 160, 171, 177, 185
isolate 86, 125
— isolation 44
Israel, Israelites 74–75

- J -

Jābir; *see* Ǧābir
Jacobsohn, Helmuth 79
jealous 19
— jealousy 47, 179
jewels 166
Job 40
John of the Cross, St 38, 40, 44
joy; *see also* fun 25, 137, 181
— joyful 89
Jung, Carl Gustav 7, 10–11, 15–17, 20–23, 30, 39–48, 52, 59, 63, 67, 71, 73, 77–78, 85, 87, 94, 96, 100–101, 103–104, 117–118, 128, 134, 153, 156, 158–161, 165, 168, 171, 177, 184
Jungian 41, 60, 69, 106, 183
Jupiter 131
justice 98, 157
Justin 118

- K -

Kaaba 24, 60, 63–64, 72–73, 160
key(s) 9, 54–55, 73, 130, 149, 155, 173
—, cold moist 173
kill 19, 78, 81, 97, 100, 120–121, 136, 159, 173
—, killing poison 81, 120
king 17, 22, 33–34, 45–46, 55, 63, 68, 79, 110–112, 119, 123, 132, 156–157, 160–161, 173
—, crown of 123, 161
—, dead 63, 112, 132
kingdoms of nature —, three 147

K. Mir'āt al-ʿaǧā'ib 121
knowledge 31, 34, 49, 51, 64, 78–79, 80, 87, 89, 125, 130, 138, 165, 185
— of the secret of the sages 180
kohl 102, 126, 133, 161
—, talcous 126
Koran 91–92
Kore 95, 130
Kore kosmou 95
Kraus, Paul 26, 50, 54–55, 67–68, 74

- L -

lām (letter L) 178, 180
Lambsprinck 73
language(s) 9, 11, 18, 25, 27, 32–34, 40, 59, 71, 73, 89, 96, 101, 108, 126–127, 142, 149–151, 155, 163–164
— of the people 96
—, alchemical 151
—, modern 71, 127, 142
—, mystical 108, 155
—, our (sages) 89
—, poetic 27
—, psychological 59, 101, 149, 163–164
—, more sober … of antique Hermetists 26
—, symbolic 27, 163
lapis; *see* stone
Latin; *see also* alchemy, Latin 7, 11, 15, 34–35, 54–55, 73, 77, 93, 100, 102, 105, 129, 165, 171
— the Latins 66–67, 70, 76
laughing — slave 120
— youth 105
lead (metal) 9, 61–62, 64–65, 69, 78–79, 88, 90, 99, 102, 105, 116, 122, 161
—, black 161
—, mountain of 99, 102
—, water of the 122
—, white (ceruse)/lead *ibšimīš* 69, 116, 122
lead–copper (abār nuḥās) 9, 61–62, 65, 79, 88, 90, 105
—, complete 88
leaves — of oleander 114
—, seven 114
leg(s) 113, 123, 184
Leisegang, Hans 77
lemon —, acid of 126
—, water of 126
letter 18, 69, 93, 112, 178–180, 184–185
— *alif* (A) 180
— *bā'* (B) 69
— *fā'* (F) 69
— *hā'* (H) 178
— *lām* (L) 178
— *mīm* (M) 178, 184
— *nūn* (N) 112
— *qāf* (Q) 69, 178–179, 184
letters 19, 43, 45, 65, 121, 177–180
— two letters of *dāl* 179
—, God has hidden secrets in the 180
—, nine (9) 121
level(s) 42, 44–45, 47, 86, 142, 149, 181
Levi della Vida, Giorgio 54
libido 42
life (lives); *see also* living 19, 21, 24–25, 30, 34, 39–42, 48–50, 64, 70–73, 75, 78, 86, 89, 91, 97, 99, 101, 103–105, 114, 118, 127, 133, 136, 138–139, 149, 151–154, 159–163, 166, 169–170, 172–174, 181
— life-giving 76, 101, 163
— is in the water 174
—, eternal 89, 91, 127
—, source of 75
—, water of 91, 97, 136, 152, 162
light 16–19, 23, 26, 40, 47, 60, 75, 90, 110, 112–113, 121, 134, 150, 155, 160, 170, 177
— lightning 112
— luminous 69
lights — from above 110
—, *Compositions of* 154
limbs 71, 103–104, 175
lime 75, 129, 131–132, 139–140, 162
— of bones 131
— of eggs 131
— of hair 131
— of Jupiter (planet/metal) 131
— of marble 131
— of Saturn (planet/metal) 131
— of skulls 131, 139–140
— of the moon 131
— of the sun 131
— of wools 131
—, calcium 132
—, every 131

—, water of 129
linen 94–96, 164–165
— rag 94–96
—, make the ... white 164
lion 99–102, 157–158
lips 25, 181
liquid(s) 17, 22, 77, 90, 95, 109, 114, 126, 150–151
— spirit 151
literalism (of Sunnite confession) 136
litharge 99, 131–132
—, whitened 132
liver of the earth 131
living; *see also* life 20, 30, 33, 47, 65, 74, 76, 90, 107, 139, 159–160, 163
Llull, Ramon 38, 53
lock 130, 157,
logos 29, 39, 51, 77
Lory, Pierre 54
lotus 69–70
love; *see also* Eros 21–25, 27, 35–48, 52, 64–65, 67, 71–73, 83, 88, 93, 95–96, 100–101, 107, 109, 155, 157–158, 160
— beloved 25, 38, 42, 87, 91–93, 102, 142, 185
— desire 37
— mysticism 37
— of inner soul image 42
— of God 35, 38–39, 41, 43, 52, 64, 101, 107, 109
—, courtly 23, 39
—, falling in 107
—, four levels of 42
—, goal of 25
—, human 41
—, physical 25
—, sexual aspect of 39
—, transforming effect of 27
—, tree of 107, 109
lover(s) 8, 25, 38, 41–42, 47, 66, 93, 185
loving 30, 42, 88, 113, 176, 183
low 22, 156
—, lower (upper and a … part) 150
Lü, Master 168

- M -

Madelung, Wilferd 9–10, 50
al-Māʾ al-waraqī 7–8, 10, 15, 35, 54–55, 62, 65–66, 68, 72, 75–76, 79, 100, 109, 114, 145, 163, 172, 176
Ma'at 98
macrocosmos —, creation of the 147
mad 78
—, foolish 113
—, foolishly 138
madness 100, 158
Al-Mafātīḥ al-ʿašara 10
Mafātīḥ aṣ-ṣanʿa 62
magic 16, 21, 29–30, 36–37, 51, 108, 124, 168, 171
— black 51
— magical 30, 36, 38, 50–52, 103
— magically 36–37
— magicians 21
— syncretistic magical traditions 50
—, Egyptian 29
magnesia 59, 61, 65, 67–68, 79, 81–83, 90–93, 96, 99, 101, 105, 130, 133–134, 156, 161
— is everything 92
—, body of 92
—, magnesium 87
magnet 93, 119, 161
Magnus, Albertus 37
Mahabharata 157
al-Mahdī, Caliph (Fatimid) 50
Mahdihassan, Syed 16, 21, 90
Mahrārīs 49
maiden 24–25
majestic 139
Malamud, Monika 10
Malamud, René 12
male 72, 85, 92–94, 99–100, 105–107, 109, 115, 120, 127–128, 157
— active principle 85, 106
— and female 72, 93–94, 99–100, 105–106, 115, 120, 127–128
— unites with the female 99
—, masculine element 29, 51
—, names of the/named the 93–94, 99, 105, 127
man 17–24, 27, 29–30, 36, 40–44, 46–48, 51, 60, 62–65, 67, 71–73, 76–78, 86–89, 94, 97, 101, 104–105, 108, 118, 127, 134, 139–140, 142, 148, 153–154, 156–157, 160–161, 172, 175,

177, 179, 181–185
— men 18–19, 23, 33, 35, 40, 44, 113, 118, 136, 153, 177, 184
—, individual 23
—, saying of a truthful 181
—, water of the (sperm) 175
mana 63, 131
Mangetus, J. Jacobi 46, 55, 93
mankind 41–42, 46, 139, 184–185
—, father of 139
Mani 104
manipulate (-ion) 20, 29, 30
marble 62, 70, 79, 96, 131–132
—, lime of 131
marcasite 132, 161
Maria the Hebrew; *see* Maria the Sage
Maria the Prophetess; *see* Maria the Sage
Maria the Sage 59, 89, 109–110, 115, 117, 119, 125–126, 161, 189
Marqūnis 76–77, 97, 100, 110, 131
marriage 24, 34, 71–72, 148–149, 158–159
—, first 148–149
massa confusa 50
master (n, vb) 33–34, 39, 43–44, 55, 72, 78, 102, 125, 135, 139, 168, 172–173, 179–181, 184
— of bodies 102
— of the waters 125
—, our 179, 181
mastery —, given 110
matter (n, vb) 16–17, 19, 21–23, 25, 29–30, 36–38, 48, 51–52, 65, 67–68, 74, 77, 83, 87, 94–96, 98, 104–105, 113, 129, 133, 153–154, 160, 163, 168, 171, 177, 180
— and magic 21
— materia, prima materia (primordial matter) 22, 26, 46, 61–64, 68, 70, 73, 77, 85, 88, 97, 100, 102–106, 125–129, 156, 163, 175, 180, 185
— material (n, adj) 12, 16, 22, 25, 30, 37, 47, 53, 65, 67–68, 79, 84–85, 95, 98, 102, 106, 116, 129, 132, 142, 149, 161, 163, 167, 171, 177
—, animated 29–30
—, divine 30
—, eternal 17
—, fall(en) into 17
—, feminine aspect of; *see also* anima mundi 52
—, goddess of 30
—, great 87
—, idea of 29
—, influence of 30
—, inorganic 30
—, magic effect of 21
—, manipulate 29
—, material world 116
—, primordial 163
—, psychic aspect of 30
—, soul of 30
—, will of the 29
māyā 20, 142
Mazdean tradition 23
mean(s) (n, vb) 9–10, 17, 20, 25, 30, 32, 43–46, 55, 59–61, 64–65, 69, 71–72, 74, 76, 79, 80, 82, 84–86, 88, 90, 92–95, 97, 99, 100–103, 105–107, 110–112, 114–118, 120–124, 127, 130, 134, 137–138, 141, 149, 156, 159, 162–164, 166–168, 173, 178, 185
meaning(s) 9, 24–26, 44, 59–60, 66–68, 70, 72–74, 80, 88–89, 91, 93–94, 96–102, 109, 110–111, 117, 121–122, 126, 132, 140, 160, 167, 175, 178–179, 183
— meaningful 22, 40, 142
— of their (sages) statement/saying 89, 93, 122
—, symbolic 96, 140, 183
meat 108, 113
medicine 95–96, 170, 178
— and the illness 178
—, *medicina catholica* 94, 154
—, studying of 178
medieval; *see* Middle Ages
meditation 16–17, 21, 30, 36, 64, 87, 94, 171
mediator 42, 46
meeting place 80, 94
Meier, Fritz 64, 73, 156
Mercurius; *see also* Hermes 63, 75, 118, 165
mercury 85, 91–92, 106–107, 115, 117, 119–120, 130, 163

— Mercury (planet) 161
— fugitive inner nature 103
— of the East 120
— of the people 163
— of the West 120
— quicksilver 92, 107
—, calcified 115
Mertens, Michèle 17
metal(s) 21, 37–38, 48, 51, 64–65, 83, 91, 94, 114, 132, 154, 182
—, earth of 132
metaphor(s) 27, 30, 51
method 16, 59, 60
Meyerhof, Max 51
microcosm 62
microcosmic space 101
Middle Ages, medieval 21–22, 29, 31, 33, 35, 39, 41, 49, 54–55, 171
midwife 80
milk 53, 107–109, 125–126, 162, 176
— milks 107, 163
— milky water 130
— of a bitch 107, 109, 162
— of a calf (male and female) 107
— of a pregnant animal 107
— of a woman 107, 109
— of all animals 107
— of an immaculate virgin 107
— of asses 107
— of every tree 107
— of rose water 125
— of the buffaloes 162
— of the dragon 107
— of the goat 107
— of the she–asses 107
— of the sheep 126
—s of euphorbia 107
mīm (letter M) 178, 184
mind(s) 18–19, 24–25, 35, 81, 87, 128, 135–138, 140, 142, 148, 150, 160, 171, 181
—, deficiency of 138
— of the people 128
mineral(s) 69, 85, 90, 169
Mithras — bull of 105
mix (vb) 91, 105, 107, 115, 150–152, 169, 173
mixing 102, 148, 151–152
mixture 66–67, 79, 95, 102, 108, 151
moderator 67
moist 67, 71–73, 79, 111, 114, 116–117, 119, 149, 151, 172–173
— dung 149
— nor dry 67
— one 116
— pitch 114
— spirit 172
— vapour 117
moisture 72, 110–112, 116–117, 119, 127, 148–152, 155, 164, 170
— of a gall bladder 119
— of the stone 152
—, benefit of the 152
—, mixed 151
—, unmixed 151
molar teeth 181
molybdochalkos 65
month 73–74, 121, 175–176, 182
— every two months 73
— nine months 121, 175
— three months 175
moon 7, 22, 46, 75, 93, 95–96, 104–105, 118–119, 129, 131–132, 158, 161, 168
— lunar 73, 100, 113
— of the earth 132
—, froth of the 96
—, lime of the 131
—, pupil of the 129
—, spittle of the 119
moral 22, 43
Morienus 59, 63
morning — mornings 137
—, rising 167
mortar 92
Moses 74–75, 130, 140–141, 171–172
Moslem, Muslim 31–34, 36, 53, 113, 184
mosque 50, 78–80, 89, 94
—, congregational 78–79, 94
mother 22, 40, 43, 51, 70, 100–101, 104, 109, 132–135, 165, 168, 176, 179, 183
— of colours 132
— of dyes 69, 132
— of gods 69, 132
— of gold 69
— of natures 69
— of the two vapours/seas 132
motif(s); *see also* image, symbol 16–17, 21–22, 24, 27, 77–78, 98, 120, 127,

134, 158, 168, 177
—, alchemical 16
—, anthropos 17
—, archetypal 17
—, *conjunctio* 21, 27
—, dream 45–47
—, Gnostic 134
—, incest 22
motivation 21, 44, 101, 142, 174
mould 99
mountain(s) 69, 71–72, 75, 77, 99, 102, 128, 171
— Mount Sinai 171–172
—, coal of the 102
mouth 40, 77, 109, 176
— of the alembic 109
Mozarabs 33–34
—, Mozarabic 38
Muḥammad, Prophet 166, 171, 184–185
Muḥammad Bāqir al-Mağlisī 183
Mullā Maḥmūd 182
multi-coloured 71, 120, 124
multiple 59, 162
multiplicatio 48
murderess of her husband 119
Mūsā al-Kāẓim, Imam 49
Musaeum Hermeticum 73
Muṣḥaf aṣ-ṣuwar 10, 157
Muslim; *see* Moslem
myrrh —, water of 162
myrtle 153
Mysterium Coniunctionis 7, 48, 67, 85, 100–101, 103–104, 156, 158
mystery 16–17, 21, 26, 40, 48, 51, 64, 71, 73, 79, 98, 101, 118, 132, 135, 163, 170, 176, 178
mystic 24, 51, 60, 67, 73, 80, 92, 94, 104, 115–116, 138, 156, 166, 177
— mystics 23, 25–26, 38, 41–42, 52, 65, 92, 116, 133, 140, 154, 183
— relationship 51
mystical 11, 17, 25–27, 30, 35, 38– 39, 41, 51–52, 59–60, 63–64, 71, 76, 80, 89, 92, 98, 108–109, 111, 115, 120, 153, 155, 165, 173, 177, 182– 185
— journeys 80
— tradition 60
mysticism 21, 23, 26, 35, 37–39, 41–42, 51, 64–65, 71, 76, 85, 98, 101, 106
—, Arabic 35, 76, 101
—, Islamic 39, 64–65, 71
—, love 21, 37–38
—, Shiʿite 23, 26
—, Sufi 51, 106
mythology 72, 157, 170

- N -

Nağm ad-Dīn Kubrā 104
nafs; *see also* soul 25, 65, 156, 173
Nag Hammadi 11
name (n) 15, 18–20, 22, 33, 40, 53–55, 61, 68–69, 73–74, 82, 84–85, 94, 99, 104, 107, 112, 118, 128, 130, 133, 180, 182
— of every female thing 133
— of God 40
—, single 130
names 8, 26, 40, 61, 69–70, 73, 90–91, 94, 96–97, 102, 105–107, 111, 115–116, 118–121, 124, 128–129, 131, 133–135, 140, 159, 161–163, 178, 180–181, 184–185
— for the feminine/female 94, 105–106, 133
— for the prima materia 97
— of magnesia 133–134
— of the ashes 131, 159
— of the male 94, 105
— of the stone 26, 61, 73
— of the white water 162
— of their divine water 90
— of their dry body 90
— of their land/earth and their sky 105
—, earth–like 163
—, six (6) 131
—, ten (10) 121
—, ten thousand (10,000) 161
—, water–like 163
an-Nasafī, Muḥammad ibn Aḥmad (Qarmaṭian) 50
an-Nasafī (mystic) 73
Nasr, Sayyed Hossein 36–37, 53, 113
Nāṭiq 185
natron 17, 131
nature 15, 17, 22, 30, 36, 41, 52–53, 62, 64, 66, 71, 73–74, 84–85, 88–89, 93,

96– 97, 101, 103–104, 109, 111, 113–115, 133, 135, 147–148, 151–152, 157, 161, 169, 176
— conquers nature 88–89
— enjoys nature 88, 111
— is attracted/holds on to nature 88
— natural operation 149
—, created 169
—, mineral 69, 85
—, three kingdoms of 147
—, way … works 147
natures 68, 70, 92, 127, 161, 166, 169
— of things 166
—, four 68, 161, 169
—, mother of the 70
—, wisdom of the four 169
navel 175
an-Naẓẓām 98
Nebuchadnezzar 118
Neoplatonic 31, 35, 50, 64
Neoplatonism 25, 29, 35, 41, 51, 107, 177
nerves 175
— sympathetic nervous system 87
Neumann, Wolfgang 64
newborn(s); *see also* born 108, 124, 175
Newman, William R. 54
night 24, 38, 45, 136, 165
—, one day and one 165
nigredo (and blackness) 73, 82–83, 96, 102–103, 122, 124, 158, 161, 166, 173–174, 185
— confusion 19, 102, 138, 170
— depression 66, 83, 102, 158
— disorientation 102
Nile 103, 115, 155
nine 19, 121–122, 124, 130, 175
— cookings 121
— letters 121
— months 121
— parts of the water 121
— soakings 124
—ninth (9th) soaking 121
noble 35, 55, 102, 140–141, 157, 173
noun 162, 179
nourish (vb) 91, 108–109, 168, 176
nourisher 135
nourishment 74, 109, 113, 175
nous 17
novice 45, 126, 156–157
number 17, 32, 34–35, 40, 61, 67–68, 86, 113, 121
numen 46
numinous 40, 51, 160, 165
nūn (letter N) 112
Nun 17, 71
nutrition 132, 170, 175

- O -

oak —, evergreen (*Quercus ilex*) 133
—, holm (*Quercus ilex*)/*sindiyān* 133
obelisk 79
object 16
objectivity 48
— objective 16, 30, 48, 101, 135
observer 128
ocean 71, 159
— of being 159
octopus 161
oil 70, 114, 174
— of balsam tree 114
—, fresh 114
—, olive 114, 174
—, sesame 174
Old One (one of God's attributes) 103, 131, 180
oleander —, leaves of 114
olive 114, 163, 174
— oil; *see* oil
Olympiodorus 65, 78
omen —, ill 124
Omnipotent (one of God's attributes) 182
one 8–9, 16, 18–20, 23–24, 26, 29–30, 33, 35, 38–40, 43–44, 46–48, 50, 52–55, 59–60, 63, 66–67, 69, 71–73, 75, 77, 80–81, 86–90, 93–94, 97–99, 101–111, 113–114, 116, 118–124, 126, 128–135, 137–139, 141–142, 148–151, 153–156, 158, 160–162, 164–169, 171, 173–180, 182, 184
One (one of God's attributes) 106, 168, 179–180
— thing 90, 114, 162, 166
— water 90
—, work comes from 166
oneness, unity 48, 51, 75, 98, 106, 113, 116, 128, 162

— completion 68, 121, 129
— of the work 51
— the whole 11–12, 17–18, 20, 22–23, 34, 37–40, 50, 53, 65, 81, 85, 88, 90, 96, 113, 117, 147–148, 174, 176–178, 184
— two-oneness 116
operation; *see also* alchemical process 61, 74, 82–83, 86, 88, 106, 127, 134, 138, 147, 149–151, 153, 163, 171, 174–175
— operations 21, 82, 121, 161
—, beginning of 61
—, every 138
—, first 86
—, natural 149
—, to operate 21, 37, 64, 68, 70, 87–88, 92, 114, 116, 129, 134, 142, 148, 173, 175–178
operator(s) 140, 142, 173
—, water as ... of the work 173
Ophiuchos, the demon 78
opposite(s) 48, 88, 90, 99, 128, 145, 151, 158, 168–169
—, duality 75, 128
—, inner polarity 25
opus; *see* alchemical opus
oracles 108
order (n) 23, 64, 98, 141
—, cosmic 98
Orient 31, 35, 120, 142, 165–166
Oriental(s) 32, 102, 120, 142
— youth 120
origin(s) 15, 17, 35, 50, 66, 70, 92, 105, 116–117, 137–139, 148–149, 161, 173, 178–179, 183
— for every dye 70
— of the art 139
—, dry 117
—, moisture is its 148
original 7, 9–10, 17, 26, 51, 71, 98, 110, 128
Osiris 17, 20, 51, 103–104, 112
Ostanes 77–78, 119
ostrich 30, 97–99
ouroboros; *see also* snake 75, 77
outer 16, 18, 20, 22, 27, 43–44, 47, 71–72, 74, 142, 148–149, 159, 164, 185
— reality 22, 164
— world 43, 142, 149
oxymel (*akšamīl*) 66–67, 123
oysters —, white 179

- P -

palm tree 183
Pandora 18
paper 41, 118, 177–179, 181
— piece of 179, 181
Paracelsus 16, 53
paradise 18, 38, 80, 118, 139, 183
paradox 40, 44, 116, 152, 160, 162
Paret, Rudi 98
part 9, 11, 22, 31, 40–41, 43, 51, 66, 75, 77, 86, 90, 94–96, 98, 114, 116, 121, 125, 127, 129, 133, 135, 137–138, 145, 150, 167, 174, 182
— of alchemy 11
— of the psyche 22
—, divine 77
—, Egyptian ... of the tradition 51
—, every ... of the body 182
—, lower 150
parts 9, 32, 34, 92, 103, 105, 113–115, 121, 125, 130–131, 140, 152, 171, 175, 182, 183
— of the water 114–115, 121
—, all the ... of the woman's body 175
—, all ... of mortar 92
—, nine (9) 121
—, six 103, 105, 125, 130–131
—, subtle 152
participation mystique 16, 42, 44–45
— archaic identity 42–43
Partington, James Riddick. 37
passion(s) 36, 43, 45, 47, 83, 92, 99, 158
path 23, 42, 44, 137, 140
— straight/right 137
patient(-ly) 10, 92, 150
— (under treatment) 39, 43, 59, 106, 131
— patience 180–181
peacemaker 167
peacock 71, 73, 120
pearl 25, 72, 165–166
pearls 61, 132, 162–163, 165, 179
—, earth of 61, 132
—, water of 162
people 15, 33, 35, 40, 43, 45, 51, 79, 80, 82–83, 85, 89, 96, 109, 114, 117, 121, 127–128, 135–136, 139, 140–141,

148–149, 163, 174, 179–181
— any religion 139
— of one city 89
— of wisdom 139
—, egg of the 114
—, gold of the 85
—, mercury of the 163
—, minds of the 128
—, water of the 149
perception 16
perfect 21, 24, 64, 65, 71, 85, 88, 112, 134, 139, 147
— gold 65, 88
— man 134
— thing 88
— wisdom 139
perfection 37, 88, 104, 108, 134
Peripatetics 113
Persia(n); *see also* Iran 19, 23, 77, 85, 105, 157
personality (-ies) 6, 11, 16–17, 20, 53–54, 73, 80, 86, 106–107, 120, 122–123, 125, 130, 150, 162
philosopher; *see also* sage 33, 50, 110, 112, 114, 122–123, 125, 141, 150, 156, 161, 170
—, Galen the; *see* Galen
—, Hermes the; *see* Hermes
—, Maria the; *see* Maria the Sage
philosophers; *see also* sages 20, 22, 33, 35, 48–50, 61–62, 64–67, 72–73, 75, 77, 80, 82–87, 91–92, 100, 110, 114–115, 117–118, 120, 122–123, 127–131, 133–138, 142, 147–151, 154, 159–160, 162–164, 166, 170, 173, 176, 180, 182
—' stone 20, 48–50, 62, 64–65, 67, 72–74, 79–80, 91–92, 100, 118, 120, 122–123, 129, 133, 142, 151, 160, 162, 173, 176, 182
—' soap 122
—, books of the 154
—, community of 164
—, earth of 163
—, egg of the 115, 161
—, egg of the people/philosophers 114
—, gold of the 82
—, human being of the 127
—, secret of the 166, 180
—, statement of the 85–86
—, tree of the; *see also* philosophical tree 78, 118
—, vinegar of the 162
—, water of the 117, 129
philosophical — sciences 136
— tree 78, 118
philosophy 15, 22, 35, 37, 51
phoenix 80, 112
physical 25, 44, 78, 96, 100, 118, 134, 140
physicians 114
picture (n, vb) 22, 44, 46, 48, 70, 117, 125, 153, 157, 168
pilgrims 32
— pilgrimage(s) 32, 132
pious 139, 172, 185
— brother 172
pitch —, moist 114
place(s) 10, 19, 32, 34, 46, 52, 79–80, 82, 94, 118, 120, 159, 172, 176
— to breathe air 176
—, meeting ... of birds 94
—, meeting ... of spirits 80
planet(s); *see also* Jupiter, Mercury, Moon, Saturn, Venus 114, 121–122, 124–125
— seven (7) planets 114, 121–122, 124–125
plant(s); *see also* euphorbia, flower, oak, oleander, olive, palm, tamarisk, terebinth 91, 105, 107, 112, 118, 162, 176
plate 179
Plato (Aflāṭūn); *see also* Neoplatonic, Neoplatonism 18, 77, 79, 171
Platonic 25, 37, 65, 77
— idea 25
Plessner, Martin 52
Plinius Secundus 97
Po-Tuang, Chang 53
poem(s) 7, 49, 156, 178, 181
Poimandres 17
poison(s) 81, 92, 119–121, 124, 133, 158–159
—, dyeing 81, 119
—, effective 120
—, fiery 119
—, killing 81, 120
—, movement of their poisons 158

poisoning 78
polarity 25
—, cosmic oneness of opposites 48
—, inner tension 53
—, Scylla and Charybdis 47
ponder (vb) 135, 137, 159, 164, 181
possession 11, 19, 44, 55, 77, 100–101, 165
pot; *see also* retort 95, 110, 181
—, ink 181
potash —, salt of 131
poverty 81–82, 174
—, disease of 81
power 18–19, 36–37, 43–44, 46, 72, 77–78, 83, 105, 109–110, 113, 151, 160, 168, 174–175
— complex 43
— drive 43–44
— of the above and the below 110
— powerful 102, 142, 159, 182
—, lust for 44
powers 20, 82, 87, 98, 105, 110, 147, 173, 182
prayer(s) 24, 68, 94, 170
pregnancy 121, 170
pregnant animal —, milk of a 107
Preisendanz, Karl 103
Pretzl, Otto 98
priest(s, -ly)) 17–18, 20, 51, 62, 97, 103, 157
prima materia 26, 46, 62–64, 68, 70, 73, 77, 85, 88, 97, 100, 102–106, 125–129, 156, 163, 175, 180, 185
— names for the 97
primordial man; *see also* Adam 118
primordial matter; *see also* prima materia 163
principle 70, 85, 100, 104–106, 132, 158–160, 185
— active 70, 85
— cosmic order 98
— divine 159
— female 100, 104, 106, 132, 158
— male 85, 106
— receptive 85, 185
principles 65, 85, 108, 136, 139
process; *see also* alchemical process, inner process 7, 16–17, 20, 22, 36–37, 39, 41–43, 46, 52–54, 62, 64–66, 68, 72–73, 81–82, 85, 103–106, 111, 117–119, 122, 128–129, 149–151, 164, 174, 184–185
— of individuation 20
— of projection 16
— of transformation 20
—, chemical 17
—, material 16
processes 15–16, 22, 30, 36, 70, 129–130, 150, 177
progress 20, 26, 46
— of mankind 46
project (vb) 22, 43–44, 53, 79, 118, 134
projection 16, 42–43, 92, 135, 164, 171
— into matter 22
— into women 22
— projections 15–16, 42–44, 48, 142
—, process of 16
Prometheus 18
prophet Muḥammad; *see* Muḥammad
prophet Moses; *see* Moses
Provider (one of God's attributes) 180
Pseudo-Democritus; *see* Democritus
psyche; *see also* soul 12, 16, 20, 22, 30, 39, 43, 60, 64, 69, 84–87, 92, 96, 101, 109, 116, 119, 131, 134–135, 151, 153, 156, 160, 164–165, 167, 171, 177, 183, 185
—, human mind 171
—, intellect 77, 166, 171
—, objective 16, 30, 101
—, reality of the 12, 96, 164, 167, 183
psychic 7, 16, 20, 25–27, 30–31, 63, 67, 76, 80, 87, 95, 99, 106, 149, 164
— fact 16
— inner-psychic condition 7, 99
— reality 149, 164
psychological experience 22
psychology 7, 10, 15–17, 22, 39, 42, 46, 77, 85, 94, 99, 101, 104, 107, 117, 148, 153, 171, 177
—, depth 7, 10, 15–16, 39, 85, 99
—, psychological 7–8, 22, 30, 36–37, 44, 53, 59, 66, 73, 75, 81–82, 101, 117, 124, 128–131, 149, 157–158, 163–165, 170
—, psychologically 20, 22, 59–60, 69, 73, 82, 86, 95, 101, 104–106, 123,

128, 162
psychopompos 20
psychosis —, psychotic explosion 78
psychosomatic 16
Ptolemy (-ies) 18, 34
Ptolemaic 29, 50
pupil(s) 53, 55, 98, 103, 108, 129–130, 172, 182
puppy (-ies) 109, 156
pure water 76, 116, 120, 149–150, 152–154
purification 36, 68, 123
purify 37, 60, 65–66, 68, 80, 84, 87, 95, 111, 137, 156, 173
—, purifying 177
—, purity 53, 85, 126, 132, 183
purple(-ness) 69, 121, 127
putrefactio 150
pyramid(s) 79
pyrite (būrnaṭis) 67, 90, 125
—, first 125
—, red/red nūrītis 90
—, second 125

- Q -

qāf (letter Q) 69, 178–182, 184
— is a secret 181
— is an exalted letter 180
— poem of the 181
Qā'im 69, 180, 184–185
Qarmaṭ 49, 183
Qarmaṭ Ḥamdān al-Ahwazī 183
Qarmaṭic community 184
Qarmaṭian(s) 50, 177, 183
al-Qaṣīda al-mīmīya 10
qinṭār (= 44.5 kg) 182
queen 22, 45–46, 109
question 43, 48, 51, 54–55, 64, 94, 160, 176, 178

- R -

rabbits —, fur of 126
rain 115, 124, 162
— rains descend/come down 169
— rainy clouds 133
raincloud; *see also* cloud 115, 133
raise (up) (vb) 33, 112, 116–119, 124, 129–131, 141, 148, 162, 175, 181
raising 105
rank 83, 138
Rasā'il 53, 113
ray; *see also* sun 75, 80, 149, 155
ar-Rāzī, Abū Bakr Muḥammad ibn Zakarīyā (Rhazes) 26, 34, 52–53, 62
Re; *see* sungod
reality 12, 22–23, 30, 45–46, 65, 86, 96, 101–102, 106, 132, 134, 149, 151, 155, 159–160, 164, 167, 172, 183, 193
—, outward 22
reason(s) 8, 45–47, 54–55, 72, 101, 125, 167–168
rebirth 17, 70, 79–80, 118, 132, 177
receive (vb) 8, 15, 41–42, 54, 80, 108, 132, 157, 163, 178
receiver 80
reckless one 138–139
reconcile (-iation) 153, 167
red 18, 47, 67, 69, 71, 75–77, 81–82, 84–86, 90, 93, 96–97, 99–102, 107, 117, 127, 166, 169–170, 173–175
— burning iron 97
— colour 99
— dog is called 'the redness' 158
— red–brown 127
— reddening 69, 71, 84, 125, 171
— reddish 47, 90, 93, 125, 127
— reddish sweet 90
— redness; *see also* rubedo 66, 83, 93, 158, 161, 166, 171, 174
— redness of the sunset over the sea 174
— sulphur 71, 100–101, 107, 117
— yellow reddishness 125
—, everything 102
—, make 86
—, making 69, 71
redemption 94, 153–154
— redeemer (of God) 94, 153
—, redemptrix 104
—, to redeem 17, 63, 153
regeneration; *see also* renewal, rebirth 17
regulate 70, 88, 114, 116, 134, 173, 175–177
— self-regulating action 184
regulation(s); *see also* operation 86, 121,

127, 134, 138, 150–151, 174–175
regulator 66, 173
Reitzenstein, Richard 17, 108
relate (vb) 20, 22, 30, 46, 48, 52, 66, 68, 80, 116–117, 121, 158, 160
relationship(s) 30, 41–44, 47–48, 51–53, 93, 118, 149, 169
—, human 42–43
—, love 47, 93
—, to matter/ to nature 30, 51
relatives 157, 166
relief 103
religion(s) 20, 26, 30, 33, 37, 39, 50–51, 104, 139, 162, 185
— heresy 35, 116
— monotheism 51, 162, 180
— of matter 51
— pantheism 98
— polytheism 162
— people of any 139
— worship(ping) 17, 30, 103, 135, 172
—, Egyptian 30
—, Eros 25
religious 9, 15, 23, 25– 27, 29–32, 36, 38–40, 45, 47, 50–52, 55, 85, 108, 140, 177
— experience 27, 140
— movement 25
remedy (-ies) 91, 137–138, 171
Renaissance 29, 31
renew (-al) 17, 32, 177
rennet 132
resignation 77
result 9, 59, 68–69, 77, 81, 104, 118, 120, 130–131, 150, 159, 163, 166, 176
resurrection 17, 70–72, 76, 79–80, 88–89, 91, 98–99, 104, 112, 118, 129, 157, 166, 173, 184
— body 71, 76, 80, 99, 129
—, to resurrect 17, 20, 51, 112, 184
retort; *see also* pot, vessel 15–16, 22, 95, 100–101, 109–110, 112, 127, 135
reunite, reunion 80, 86, 89, 129, 151, 181
revive, revivify 76, 89, 115, 127, 166, 169, 173
Rhazes; *see* ar-Rāzī
Ribi, Alfred 12
rich one 174
riddle 22, 96
right — living 139
— righteous 141
— rightness 82
Rig-veda 157
Risālat al–bayān 152
Risālat aš-šams ilā al-hilāl 7
rise (vb) 34, 41, 72, 80, 83, 95, 103, 105–106, 110–112, 115–117, 125–126, 128, 134, 165, 167, 169, 170
ritual 16, 51, 71
river 25, 31, 77, 119, 162
rock 70, 132, 163–164, 178, 184
—, black 163
—, operated 178
rock-salt 70, 132
Roeder, Günther 20
Roger II 33
root(s) 7, 16, 20, 80, 154, 157, 162, 179
rose water; *see also* water 125
rotls (weight) —, four 130
—, six 130
rotting, rotten 97, 118, 139, 149–150
round — stone 99
— vessel 170–171
royal couple; *see also* king, queen 46, 48
rūḥ (spirit) 173
rubedo; *see* red/redness 70, 81, 83–86, 161, 174
Ruelle, Ch.-Em. 68
ruler over the above and the below 168
rules (noun) 43
Rūsam; see Zosimos
Ruska, Julius 15, 52, 54, 65, 68, 100, 105, 110, 112, 167
rust 69, 90, 125
— of gold 125
— rusting 69

- S -

sacrifice 153, 170, 178
— of the worldly things 178
—, self–sacrifice 153
—, to sacrifice 43, 62
aṣ-Ṣādiq, Ǧaᶜfar; *see* Ǧaᶜfar aṣ-Ṣādiq
sadness 136
saffron 93, 122, 127
— of the iron 122

sage; *see also* philosopher 72, 87, 92, 110, 112, 114–115, 122–123, 125, 134, 150, 170, 173
—, Galen the; *see* Galen
—, Hermes; *see* Hermes
—, Maria the; *see* Maria
sages; *see also* philosophers 61, 66, 70, 72, 77, 82–86, 88, 114–115, 117, 122, 127–131, 134–138, 147–150, 154, 159, 161–164, 166, 173, 180
— of the art 137
—, advice of the 137
—, books of the 154
—, community of 164
—, earth of 161
—, egg of the 161
—, envious ones of the 66
—, gold of 82
—, human being of 127
—, past 136
—, sea of the 70
—, secret of 166, 180
—, statement of the 85–86
—, vinegar of the 162
—, water of the 117, 129
—' egg of the people 114
—' stone 20, 48–50, 61–62, 64–65, 67, 72–73, 75, 80, 91–92, 100, 118, 120, 122–123, 129, 133, 142, 151, 160, 162, 173, 176, 182
saint(s) (St) 35–36, 38, 40, 44, 108, 139, 162, 165
salt(s) 66–67, 70, 117, 123, 129, 131–132
— of houses 70, 131
— of potash 131
—, durable 132
—, every 123
—, flower of 66, 129
—, other 117
—, rock-salt 70, 132
salvation 94, 154
sand 131
saturate (vb) 35, 83, 86
saturation 86, 149
Saturn 123, 131, 161
saying(s) 18, 24, 65, 82, 93, 110, 115, 117, 122, 135, 155, 165, 178, 181
Schimmel, Annemarie 25
scholastic theologian(s) 49, 98
scholasticism 29
science; *see also* alchemy 21, 27, 33–34, 51, 63, 68, 79, 81, 130, 138, 142, 147, 167, 180, 182, 185
—, Arabic 34
—, Greek 33
—, influence on our 180
—, seekers of this 81, 130
sciences 36, 53, 136, 141
—, natural 27, 36
—, noble 141
—, philosophical 136
scorpion(s) 52, 121
sea 32, 70, 71, 100, 105, 107, 117, 119, 132, 155–156, 159, 162–163, 171, 174
— of the two vapours 70, 117
— of wisdom 70
—, clay/fragrance of the 132
—, foam of the 119
—, redness of the sunset over the 174
—, shore of the 155
—, snails of the 71
—, water of the 162–163
—, water of the green 163
sealed mystery 176
search —, arbitrary 138
searched-for 136, 150, 179
second — body 62, 87–89, 96, 110–111, 129
— būrnaṭīs 125
— coniunctio; *see also* coniunctio 88
— pyrite 125
— stone 61
— time 66, 87
— whiteness 69
secret 16, 22, 37–38, 43, 45, 48–49, 51, 53, 59–60, 68, 83, 89, 99, 102–104, 106, 109, 115–116, 123, 132, 139–141, 147, 150, 154–156, 160, 164, 166, 168, 171, 174–175, 177–185
— enigma(s) 111, 179–180, 185
— of everything 154, 174
— of *qāf* (letter) 181
— of the philosophers/sages 166, 180
— of this work 181
— secretly 19, 123, 164
— secrets 51, 80, 83, 100, 139, 180–182
— work, hidden 155
—(s) of God 140–141

—, eternal secret 45
—, great 83, 140, 174
—(s), hidden 155
sediment(s) 75, 96, 113, 117, 119, 123, 125, 131, 161, 168
seductions 81
seed —s of the white seed 164
seeker(s); *see also* adept 77–78, 81, 130, 132, 138–139, 141, 171, 178, 181
—, wise 139
self 36, 40–45, 48, 54, 60, 64, 69, 72, 76, 78, 80–82, 85, 90, 92, 98, 111, 113, 116, 123, 126, 129, 131, 134, 142, 148–150, 153, 159–162, 164, 172, 176–177, 184
—, *imago Dei* 134
—, inner centre 177
—, self-criticism 129, 131
—, self-reflection 123, 149
—, self-sacrifice 153
semen 104
Senior; *see* Zadith Senior; *see* Ibn Umail
sensuality 44
separation 90, 127, 129, 149, 151, 177
—, cutting apart 182
—, separating 42, 140, 149, 152, 182
Serapeum 18
Serrano, Miguel 48
Seth (Šīṯ) 160
seven 19, 106–107, 114–115, 121–122, 124–125, 175
— bodies 106
— crowns 115
— days 121, 175
— idols 107
— Imams 115
— leaves 114
— parts of water 115
— planets 114, 121–122, 124
— soakings 124
Sezgin, Fuat 10, 15, 22, 29, 49–50, 54–55, 98, 111
sex 44
sexual 21, 39, 45, 47, 70
— erotic 22, 43–44, 64, 71, 105
shadow 47, 52, 78, 123, 142, 174
—, shadowy elements 123, 165
—, shadow(-y) motivations 123, 142, 174
Shakti 48
sharp sword 120
sheep, — milk of the 126
sheikh 67, 72, 92, 107, 157, 172–173, 182
shell 71, 105, 132
shells —, egg; *see* egg
Shiʿa 26, 49, 53, 115, 136
Shiʿite(s) 23, 26, 49–50, 53, 91, 140, 177, 183–184
—' habit of interpreting texts 50
Shiva 48
shore of the sea 155
Suhrawardī 23, 65
sides of the vessel/pot 95
Sidr Būṣīr 49
sight —, love at first sight 43
significance —, great 141
significant 33, 37, 53
sign(s) 8, 37, 104–105, 124, 148
— of the zodiac —, twelve 124–125
silver 61–62, 65–66, 75, 82–84, 131–132, 165, 174
—, colour of 82
—, earth of 61, 132
—, ferment of 75
—, filings of 61, 66
—, gold into 82
—, white 174
silvery — water 7, 72, 76, 98, 163
— earth 65
similarity 152, 171
— similar 16, 31, 40, 42–43, 53, 59, 87, 94, 97, 129, 136, 141, 148, 151–152, 157, 170, 180
simile(s) 72, 93, 97, 111, 163, 177
sincere intention 136
sindiyān; *see* oak
single 8–9, 86, 107, 111, 166
— body 86
sister(s) 22, 43, 71, 86, 134, 139–140, 183
six (6) 36, 68, 86, 103, 105–106, 125, 130–131
— bodies 105–106, 125
— horns 103, 105
— names 131
— parts 103, 105, 125, 130–131
— rotls 130
— saturations/soakings 86
— sixth (6th) 78, 183
sixteenth (16th) day 175

skilful 92, 172–173, 181–182
skilfully 151
skin 133
skull(s) 78–80, 131, 139, 171
—s, lime of 131, 140
sky; *see also* heaven 105–106, 110, 125, 164, 167, 169–171
—, all under the ... becomes alive 169
—, coming down/descends from the sky/heaven 110, 166, 169
—, crow flies between the ... and the earth 164
—, earth and 110, 169
—, rains come down from the 169
—, water of/from 125
slaughtered 105, 127
slave(s) 18–19, 66–67, 107, 120, 141, 162
—, fugitive 102
—, laughing girl 120
—, urine of girls 162
smell —, awful 140
—, best in 141
—, water of the sense of 162
smoke 9, 117, 145, 167, 169–170
— of the earth 170
—, soul is the 117
snail 30, 71–73, 129, 132
— of the mountains 71
— s of the sea 71
—, shell of the 132
snake; *see also* Ouroboros 22, 74–75, 77
— vipers 52, 124
snow 129, 175
—, water of 129
snowy earth 61
soak (vb) 17, 83
soaking(s) 71, 74, 76, 86, 121, 124, 127, 149
—, nine (9) 125
—, ninth (9th) 121
—, seven (7) 124
—, three (3) 76
soap of wisdom 122
solid 22, 72, 91, 102, 105, 132–133, 150–151, 170
— solidification becomes corporeal 87
— solidify (vb) 122
— solidity of the self 177
—, dry and 91
Solomon 108, 185
solution 111, 125
son 17–19, 49, 73–74, 100, 103–104, 108, 110, 125, 134, 154, 156, 160, 163, 176, 179, 182
— of a mother 179
— of God 17–19
— of the Widow (Mani) 104
— of the year 73–74, 125
— sons 136, 179, 185
— sons of Adam 136
Sophia 23, 44, 104, 132
sorrows 81
soul; *see also* psyche, *nafs* 8, 16–20, 23–25, 30, 36–38, 41– 42, 44, 62, 65, 67–68, 72, 80, 86–91, 93–95, 99, 103, 107, 110–112, 115–120, 122–123, 126, 129, 131, 134, 141, 148, 150, 152–154, 156–157, 162, 171–173, 175, 177
— (un)operated 70, 87–88, 111, 176
— and spirit; *see* spirit and soul
— guide 120, 157
— image 42
— is the smoke 117
— moisture 150
— of matter 16, 30, 95
— of the (Sufi) adept 36, 93, 117, 126
— of the alchemist(s) 16, 37, 65, 87, 93
— of the lapis 112
— of the mystic 67, 80, 94, 115
— of their first stone 111
—, brother of the 134
—, corporeal 91
—, divine 68, 94, 153–154
—, heavenly 134
—, human 36–37, 117, 152, 171
—, spiritual 91
—, vessel for the 93
—, water of the 162
souls 17, 25, 32, 79, 81, 86, 91, 95, 113, 136–137, 156, 163, 182
— and the spirits 182
—, dog makes appear 156
—, dyeing 86
—, your 81
source; *see also* spring 9, 40, 47, 68–70, 75, 77, 94–95, 99, 103, 137, 157, 167, 172, 177

— of life 75
— of truth 137
sources 8, 10, 38, 49, 69, 71, 75, 113, 133, 155, 168
—, mountain of the 75
Spain 31–35, 38, 47
—, Andalusia(n) 34, 55, 77–78
speech 25, 109, 111
— and the mouth 109
— of nature 109
—, all their 111
sperm; *see also* water of the man 95, 122, 139, 175
— semen 104
spiral 72–73
spirit 18, 21, 23, 25, 30–31, 38, 61–62, 64, 66, 68, 72, 74, 81, 86–88, 90–91, 94, 96, 107–108, 110–113, 115–117, 119, 122, 124, 127, 129, 132–135, 137, 141, 150–151, 155, 158, 165, 167, 172–173, 177, 185
— and matter 30
— and soul 79, 86–88, 90, 107, 111, 115–117, 119, 122, 129, 134, 141, 172–173, 182
— of God 64
— of the air 124
— of the stone 116
— *spiritus rector* 41
—, corporeal 87
—, divine 66, 68, 87, 94, 116–117
—, habitation of the 167
—, liquid 151
—, moist 172
—, moving 72
—, *spiritus vegetativus* 118
—, subtle 86
—, tincturing 62
spirits 19, 61, 77, 79–80, 85–87, 92–94, 106, 118, 127, 132, 156, 182
— in their bodies 156
—, fiery 86, 92
spiritual 8, 16, 18–21, 23–27, 32, 39, 44–46, 49, 52–53, 65, 71, 80, 85, 87, 89, 91–92, 99–100, 104, 108, 117, 120, 127, 129, 133–134, 140, 161, 163, 177, 183
— body 23, 25, 65, 71, 120, 133, 183
— divine wisdom 140
— realm 27
— spiritualization 51–52
— to spiritualize 29, 51, 66, 85
— spiritually 25, 108
— water of the sages 117
spirituality 25, 47, 69
spiritus rector 41
spittle — of the moon 119
sponge 132
spring; *see also* source — of water 62, 97, 171
— (vb) 22, 43, 64, 96, 118
—s, two 171
staff of Moses 74–75, 130
stag 46
stage(s) 41–42, 44, 62, 69–70, 77, 81, 83, 92, 103–104, 132
Stapleton, Harry Ernest 7, 11, 15, 46, 49, 52, 54–55, 62, 65–66, 68, 72, 93, 100, 172
star(s) 19, 179
— starry earth 7, 61
—, lucky 179
statement 62, 84–86, 88–89, 93, 95–96, 106, 117, 123, 151, 157, 178
statements 8, 10, 82, 173, 179
— of the sages 173
Steadfast (one of God's attributes) 180
steam; *see also* vapour 22
stinking (objects) 139–140
stone 20, 26, 47–50, 59–68, 70–75, 77–83, 86, 90–92, 97, 99–100, 108–109, 111, 114–120, 122–123, 127–129, 133, 142, 147–153, 155, 160–166, 168–169, 171–173, 175–177, 182, 184
— *bnbn* stone 79–80
— hot stones 97
— of the sea 155
—, another 99, 153
—, another … being inside 99
—, balanced 67
—, black 60, 63, 72, 160–161, 164
—, dark side of the 120
—, demonic aspect of 78
—, divide into two halves 150
—, eagle 63, 99
—, etesian 120
—, everything is their 123
—, female 97

—, fiery 92
—, first 111
—, hidden 128
—, honourable/honoured; *see also abār nuḥās* 65, 163–164, 173
—, hostile 78
—, marbly 70
—, moisture of the 152
—, names of the 26, 61, 73
—, philosophers'/their 20, 48–50, 59, 62, 64–65, 67, 72–74, 79–81, 86, 90–92, 97, 99–100, 109, 114–115, 117–118, 120, 122–123, 129, 133, 142, 147, 151, 160, 162, 173, 175–176, 182
—, pyramidal (Ben Ben stone) 79
—, qualities of 76
—, red 90
—, round 99
—, second 61
—, spirit of the 116
—, square 99
—, the beloved 142
—, triangular 99, 161, 166
—, water of the 151–152
—, white 47, 72, 82
store-house 133
— date 182
stranger(s) 46, 132–134, 166
strength 74, 114, 128, 137
—, weakness to 114
strong 23, 35, 69, 103, 108, 137, 139, 175, 180, 182
Strong (one of God's attributes) 180
structure —, black 164
student(s); *see also* seeker, adept 11, 33, 66–67
studying — of medicine 178
— studies 7–8, 35, 54, 77–78, 108, 118, 137, 190–193
sublimation 20, 22, 41, 106, 132, 158, 167
— *sublimatio* 41
— sublimate (vb) 22, 35–36, 41, 64–65, 67, 86, 88–90, 95, 96, 112, 117
submersion 70
substance(s) 8, 16, 22, 37, 75–77, 83, 85, 94, 101–103, 108, 112, 114–116, 120, 126, 129–132, 147–149, 153–155, 170–171
—, central 147
—, remote 154–155
subtle 16, 23, 25, 44, 64–67, 86–87, 99, 111, 126, 129, 135, 141–142, 148, 150–152, 168, 175, 178
— heat 178
— parts 152
— spirit 86
— subtilization 129
— subtleness 175
— subtlety 179
— water 175
—, make (the second body) 150
success 19, 61, 94, 138, 142, 154, 180
—, may God give you 180
suffering 18–19, 66, 68, 153, 181
sufi 23, 29, 38–39, 43, 51, 53, 60, 106, 125–126, 135, 140, 156, 177
— circles 39
— masters 43, 135
— mysticism 51, 106
— sufism 23, 26–27, 29, 35, 64, 99, 101, 156, 172
sulphur (*kibrīt*, masc, *kibrīta*, fem) 59, 75, 84–85, 91, 96, 100–101, 107, 111–112, 114–117, 120, 132, 162
— holds sulphur (masc) 115
— sulphurs 75, 84, 96, 116, 141
—, every 117
—, red 75, 100–101, 107, 117
—, two sulphurs 75, 96, 116
—, white 75, 85, 91, 132
—, whitened 91
sulphury — water 125
sun 7, 22, 46, 62, 68, 72, 74–75, 80, 93, 101, 105, 113, 118, 124, 129, 131, 149–150, 155, 161, 165, 167–168
— rising 79
— tongue/flame (ray) of the hot sun 149
—, God created 167
—, heart of 129
—, hot 149
—, lime of 131
—, rays of 75, 155
sungod 17, 70, 104, 165
sunset 121, 174
Sunnite confession; *see also* Islam 136
surface — of the body 126
— of the water 103, 105
swallow 74, 97, 99

sweet 90
sweetness 108, 179, 181, 183
Swiss 45
Switzerland 45–46
sword 32, 120, 125
—, fiery 125
—, sharp 120
symbol(s) 8–9, 16–17, 21–22, 25–26, 53, 59, 62, 65, 67, 69–71, 73, 75, 78–80, 96, 100, 103–105, 110–111, 121, 124, 126, 128, 130, 132, 136, 148–149, 153, 155–158, 160, 165, 176–177, 183
— mythological pictures 153
— symbolize (vb) 44, 48, 52, 65, 69, 71, 73, 78, 80, 92–93, 105, 118, 154, 157–158, 167, 170, 175, 183–185
—, alchemical symbol(-s, -ism) 16, 22, 39–40, 46, 53, 73, 100, 103, 124, 136
—, *Explanation of the Symbols* 8, 26, 62, 111
—, unconscious 128
symbolic 7, 9, 15–16, 27, 41, 51, 59–60, 62, 72–73, 91, 96, 101, 106, 136, 140, 149, 163, 183
— (alchemical) terms 59–60
— content of Alchemy 16
— language 27, 163
— meaning 96, 140, 183
— symbolically 18, 50, 109, 165
symbolism 7, 9, 15, 21–23, 25, 39–40, 45- 46, 67, 69–70, 98, 100, 103, 113, 118, 121, 125, 177
—, coniunctio 23, 45
sympathy 45
sympathetic nervous system 87
synchronistic 30
syncretistic 50
synopsis (in alchemy) 26

- T -

table 79, 168, 179, 183
Tabula chemica 7
Tabula Smaragdina 110, 167–168
Ṯāḏāb 119
Tai I Gin Hua Dsung Dschi (chinese book) 168
tail 75, 121, 133
talc 103, 105, 132
—, talcous kohl 126
—, white talcum 157
aṭ-Ṭalḥī, ʿAlī 24
tamarisk 111–112, 116–119
Tantra, -ism 21–23, 45, 48, 95
Tantric philosophy 22
Taoism, Taoist 16, 53, 68
tar 114, 182, 185
Tarākīb al-anwār 145, 154
tawḥīd 26, 98, 111, 162
teacher 39, 43, 92–93, 103, 172–173, 182–183
—, skilful 92, 172–173
technology 29
temple 24, 49–50, 62, 75, 78–80, 89, 110
ten 62, 67–68, 121, 124, 153, 172
— names 121
— things 67
— thousand (10,000) names 161
— times 153
— colours 67
—, completion of 121
—, one prevails 121
— tenth (10th) 11, 24, 31–32, 35, 49, 121
terebinth — gum 174
testimony 40, 71, 140, 179
tetractys; *see also* four 68
tetrasomias 65
Theatrum Chemicum 46, 55, 77–78, 93, 171
Theodorus 66
theologian(s) 29, 49, 98, 134
theory (-ies) 35–36, 50
— theoria 151
Theosebeia (Atūtāsiya) 21, 119–120
Theresa of Avila, St 38, 44
thick 151, 169
thicken (vb); *see also* to coagulate 121, 150–152, 158, 164, 175–176
—, thickening 164
thing 22, 37, 46, 48, 59, 63, 66, 74, 88, 90, 92, 97, 102, 113–114, 124, 128, 130, 133, 140–142, 147, 151, 160, 162, 164, 166, 168, 171, 173, 179–180
— name it everything 73, 80, 92
—(s), dirty ... or stinking ... 139
—(s), impure/dirty 135, 139–141, 165
—(s), noble 141
—, every 73

—, filthy 140
—, one 90, 114, 162, 166
—, perfect 88
—, searched-for 179
—, secret of everything 154, 174
things 17–19, 24, 29, 36–37, 39–40, 42, 47, 67, 76, 79, 88, 98, 100, 104, 106, 112–114, 126, 128, 130, 135, 139–142, 152, 154, 156, 166, 168–169, 170–171, 173, 178, 182–183
—, all 17–18, 40, 98, 104, 112–113, 126, 154, 168
—, any of their 128
—, burning of 178
—, creation of 169
—, dissimilar 152
—, elevated 141
—, filthy 140
—, imperfect 88
—, most despicable 141
—, multitude of 130
—, natures of 166
—, other 36–37, 76, 156, 182–183
—, sacrifice of the worldly 178
—, ten (10) 67
—, three mixed (yellow, white, red) 173
think (vb); *see also* thinking, thought 22, 26, 37, 43, 47, 49, 54–55, 59, 64, 91, 162, 164–165, 179, 181, 184
thinking 8, 10–11, 77, 128, 136– 137, 142
thirsty 61, 75, 100, 133, 156, 166, 169
— earth 61, 169
—, holy ... earth 61
Thomas, Frederick William 63
Thomas, St 7, 36, 38
Thot 18
thought(s) (n) 9, 22, 25, 29, 35, 51, 59, 77, 94, 117, 137, 148 180–181
three 15, 46, 49, 54, 62, 65–66, 68, 72, 76, 93, 99–100, 131, 147, 149, 161, 166–167, 173, 175, 185
— become four 166
— angles 99, 161
— categories 161
— colours 161
— cookings 76
— kingdoms of nature 147
— mixed things (yellow, white, red) 173
— months 175
— problem of three and four 161, 166
— soakings 76
— successive uprisings 76
— third (3rd) pious brother 172–173
— times (shaken) 149
—, the two becomes 166
Tibetan tradition 63
time 10–11, 18, 26, 31–38, 40, 45–46, 50–53, 55, 59, 64, 66, 69, 71, 74, 76–77, 80, 82, 84, 87, 96, 101, 107, 109, 110, 119, 129, 133, 142, 160, 171–172, 182–184
— times 17, 31, 39, 69–70, 78, 96, 103, 132, 149, 153, 155, 160, 162, 184
—, end of the 172
—, periods of 82
—, passage of the ages and the times 160
tin 61, 65
Toledo 34
tomb(s) 63, 79–80, 132
tongue 33, 40, 149–150, 162
top(s) 77, 95, 110, 176
Torah 140
torturer of her husband 119
totality 41, 64, 68, 127, 134, 157
Toussaint, Gustave Charles 63
tower 47, 133
town(s); *see also* city 32, 182
traces (n) 53, 83, 98, 148
trade 31–32
transference 39, 41–43, 45–47, 107, 139
—, transference-problem 41
transform 16–17, 23, 27, 41, 48, 51, 94, 96, 99, 114, 140, 154–155, 158, 176
transformation 7, 20, 36–37, 39, 44, 52, 74, 77, 82, 85, 99, 103–104, 107, 116, 118, 131, 157–158, 171
—, magical 36
—, process of 20
translation 8–11, 17, 34, 54–55, 61–62, 64–65, 68, 91, 100, 105, 110, 117, 147, 150, 167
transpersonal 7, 30, 46, 88
treasure(s) 11, 140, 166
—, enigmatic 140
—, excellent 140
tree(s); *see also* balsam, holm oak, olive, terebinth 77–78, 102, 107, 109, 114, 118, 133, 163, 168, 174, 179, 183

— leaves 72, 114, 153
— of love 107, 109
— of the philosophers 118
—, milk of every 107
—, palm 183
—, philosophical 77–78, 118
—, *sindiyān*; *see also* oak 133
—, water of every 163
triangular stone 99, 161, 166
Trinick, John 48
troubadour(s) 24, 33, 35, 42
trouble 43
true — way 81
truth 19, 40, 44, 87, 116, 121, 137, 168, 179, 180, 184
Truth (one of God's attributes) 180
— of their statement 179
—, source of 137
truthful — intention 136
— one 176
— man 181
aṭ-Ṭuġrāʾī, al-Ḥusain ibn ʿAlī 9, 145, 154
Turāb ʿAlī, M. 7
Turba philosophorum 52, 68, 100, 105
—, Ibn Umail's relationship to the 52
turbid 161
Tweedie, Irina 39
twelve —, signs of zodiac 124–125
twenty–fourth (24th) day 175
two (2) caves 171
two; *see also* brothers, caves, letters, half, months, springs, sulphurs, vapours
— becomes three 166
— halves of the stone 150
two-oneness 116

- U -

Ullmann, Manfred 15, 108, 111, 121
ʿUmar, Caliph 51
unconscious 8, 15–16, 20, 22–23, 30, 41–43, 46–47, 69, 76, 87, 101, 103–104, 106, 127–128, 130, 136, 149–150, 155, 158–159, 161, 163, 167, 170, 176
—, collective 16, 30, 41, 47, 87, 192
—, depth of nature 17
—, inner world 41, 44, 47, 142, 149, 155
—, objective psyche 16, 30, 101
—, polarized 41
—, primordial waters 17
understanding 8–9, 44, 78, 106, 123, 136, 138, 140, 150, 157, 163, 177
— understand (vb) 8, 17, 19, 21–22, 35, 39, 41, 45, 48, 59, 68, 71, 78, 89–90, 105–106, 109, 113–114, 116, 120, 125, 127, 130, 135–136, 156, 158–159, 160, 164–165, 168, 171, 175–177, 181–182, 184
underworld 104, 157, 182
unicorn 46
unio mystica 17, 35, 87, 111, 116, 182–183
union 42, 46, 48, 65–66, 87–88, 91, 93, 101, 111, 116–118, 130, 150–151, 158, 166
unite; *see also* coniunctio 21, 23, 26, 48, 68, 93, 99, 103, 118, 122, 145, 155, 158, 165, 173
uniting 169
unity; *see* oneness
universe 17, 41, 47, 77, 113, 156
unknown 22, 40, 59, 68, 80, 125, 145, 156, 161
— known 80
— matter was the ... thing 22
— name the unknown by the unknown 40, 59
unoperated 111
unus mundus 30, 159
uprisings —, three successive 76
urethra 124
urine 124, 126, 139, 141, 162–164
— of asses 124
— of bitch 124
— of boys 124, 162
— of cows 124
— of the dog 162–164
— of the piebald dog 163
— of the slave girls 162
— of the wild ass 126
— of young boys/ newborns 124
Usṭuqus al–uss (*Elements of the Foundation*) 153
ʿUtba al-Ġulām 24
uterus 176

- V -

Vadet, Jean-Claude 35
Valerius Maximus 97
value(s) 26, 84, 139, 141
vanity 174
vapour 9, 111–112, 116–117, 126, 132, 145, 167, 170
— and the smoke 9, 117, 145, 167, 170
— of the earth 132
— of the people 117
— moist 112, 116–117, 170
vapours 70, 117–118, 132
—, mother of the two 132
—, sea of (the) two 70, 117
—, two 70, 117, 132
veil 64, 83, 160, 180
vein(s) 43, 162
Venus 64, 104
verdigris 122
verse(s) 24–25, 35, 82, 113
vessel; *see also* pot 62, 77–79, 93–96, 103–104, 110, 112, 123, 130, 154–155, 159, 170–171, 176–177
—, hidden 155
—, round 170–171
—, sides of the 95
—, womb/uterus is the 176
vessels 32, 63, 129–130, 158
—, dog is called 158
victory 66, 99, 123, 133, 161
—, crown of 66, 123, 133, 161
vinegar 66, 107, 126, 162
—, sour 126
violence 156, 158
— violent lion 102
viper 52, 124
virgin 18, 25, 99–101, 104, 107
—, immaculate 99–100, 107
—, milk of an immaculate 107
vision 20, 63, 97, 118, 139
—, visions 15–16, 20, 38, 62, 71, 75
—, *Visions of Zosimos* 16, 20, 62
vitriol 122
voice 24–25, 45, 172, 179

- W -

war 24, 31, 33, 45, 181, 184
— with God 181
—, World 45
warmth 101
water 7, 26, 29, 59, 62, 67–68, 70, 72, 75–78, 80, 83–84, 86–91, 95, 97–98, 100, 102–103, 105–107, 109–117, 119–126, 129–134, 136, 145, 149–156, 158, 162–164, 166–170, 172–174, 175– 176, 178
— and earth 154, 169
— and fire 123
— and the body 90
— dyes the earth 83
— for the reddening 125
— from the sky/heaven 110, 169
— is receptive 174
— is the ferment of the body 107
— is the head 123
— is the spirit 122
— is wool 125
— juices 126
— liquid(s) 17, 22, 77, 90, 95, 109, 114, 126, 150–151
— moisture 72, 110–111, 116–117, 119, 127, 148–152, 155, 164, 170
— of copper 109
— of eggs 115, 162
— of every tree 163
— of heaven/the sky 125, 163
— of lead 122
— of lemon 126
— of life 91, 97, 136, 152, 162
— of lime 129
— of myrrh 162
— of snow 129
— of the air 162
— of the alkali 162
— of the arsenic 114
— of the ashes 126
— of the clouds 162
— of the feather 162
— of the gum 131
— of the hair 162–163
— of the hot (burning the tongue) 162
— of the man (sperm) 175
— of the Nile 103, 115
— of the pearls 162
— of the philosophers 117, 129
— of the plants 162
— of the rain 162
— of the river 162

— of the sea 162–163
— of the sense of smelling 162
— of the soul 162
— of the stone 151–152
— of the sulfate of iron/vitriol 122
— of the sulphur 114–115, 120, 162
— of the tree of love 107
— of wisdom 155
— which regulates/operates 134
—, airy 125
—, blessed 163, 166
—, composed 102, 166
—, coppery milky 130
—, divided 106
—, divine 75, 80, 88–91, 95, 106, 109, 114–115, 126, 129–130, 149, 154, 163–164, 167, 169–170, 173
—, dyeing 87, 119
—, earth needs 153
—, eternal 132
—, ferment of the 75, 107
—, flowing 97
—, flying 97
—, holy 102–103, 129
—, life is in the 174
—, milk of rose 125
—, moisture of the 170
—, mother is in the 134
—, names of the 105
—, names of the white 162
—, nine parts of the 121
—, one 90
—, our 109, 166, 169
—, pure 75, 116, 120, 149, 150, 152–154
—, rained 169
—, rose 125
—, silvery 71–72, 75, 98, 163
—, solid 132
—, subtle 175
—, sulphury 125
—, surface of 103, 105
—, their (philosophers/sages) 72, 83, 91, 105, 107, 111–112, 114–115, 119, 122, 124–126, 129
—, wash 122, 165, 182
waters —, master of 125
waves 107, 155, 176
way 7–8, 16–17, 21–22, 25, 29–30, 34, 36, 38–39, 41–43, 45–48, 53, 68, 70–72, 78, 81, 90, 94–95, 97, 106, 109, 111, 114, 116, 130, 134–135, 137, 139, 145, 148–149, 153–154, 157, 159, 163, 165, 174–182, 184
— ways 7, 19, 135, 137, 148, 176
—, good 179
—, right 130, 137, 178, 181
—, true 81
weakness 114, 137
— weak 138
wealth 16, 133
weight 46, 153
well-known 46, 72, 74, 77, 80, 105, 112, 169
West —, mercury of the 120
Western thinking 142
wet 67
Weyer, Jost 15
whale — gall bladder of the 129
wheat 156, 174
white 45, 47, 61, 65–67, 69, 72, 75, 77, 79, 82, 84–85, 91–92, 95–97, 99, 101–102, 109, 116, 122, 127, 131–133, 155, 157–158, 162, 164–165, 170, 173–174, 179
— arsenic 91
— body 61, 66, 127
— colour 99
— earth 61, 66, 69, 95
— firewood 75, 133
— lead (ceruse) 69, 116, 122
— oysters 179
— silver 174
— stone 47, 72, 82
— sulphur 75, 85, 91, 132
— talcum 157
—, everything 102
—, names of the ... water 162
whiten 86, 91, 132, 174
— whitened litharge 132
— whitened sulphur 91
—, making white 82, 84
—, whitening 84, 164
whiteness; *see also* albedo 66, 69, 72, 82–83, 90, 93, 122, 161, 166, 171, 174
—, second 69
whole 11–12, 17–18, 20, 22, 24, 26, 30, 34–35, 37–40, 42, 47, 50, 53, 65, 73, 75, 78, 81, 85–86, 88, 90, 96, 113,

117, 121, 125, 147–148, 156, 174, 176–178, 184
widow 103–104
Wilhelm, Richard 68, 168
will (n) 29, 43, 101, 172
—, conscious 101
wind 125, 155, 168
—, south 155
wine 85, 108, 174
wisdom 25, 40, 44, 54–55, 64, 67–68, 70, 84, 118, 122, 130, 135–136, 139–141, 155, 163, 166–167, 169, 179
— of God 68, 140
— of the four natures 169
— wise 34, 44, 63–64, 72, 92, 134, 139, 161, 166, 173
—, doors of 130
—, owner of 139
—, people of 139
—, perfect 139
—, sea of 70
—, searched-for 179
—, soap of 122
—, spiritual divine 140
—, water of 155
wish (n, vb) 8, 25, 40, 43, 47, 101, 138
wolf 46
woman; *see also* women 17, 22–25, 39, 42–48, 100, 104, 107, 109, 124, 131, 175
—'s body, all the parts of the 175
— scaring the enemy 124
—, breast of the 175
—, milk of a 107, 109
womb 17, 175–176
women; *see also* woman 21–22, 25, 44, 102, 136
—, men and … , *see also* male and female 136
wondrous things 170
wood 75–76, 118, 125, 133
—, firewood 75–76, 117, 125, 133
woodpecker —, green 124
wool 76, 125–126, 131
—, fleece of 125
—, lime of 131
woollen bag, dress 125
word 11, 17–18, 20, 22, 37, 40, 44– 45, 50, 61, 66–67, 72–73, 79–80, 90, 94, 98, 101, 105, 108, 112–113, 156, 163, 168, 183
words 9, 15, 18, 25, 30, 34, 40, 59, 63, 64, 68–70, 86, 92, 109, 116, 118, 123, 131–133, 135, 140, 159, 164–165, 181, 185
work (alchemical); *see also* alchemical opus, art 27, 35, 51, 53, 62, 65–66, 68, 70, 77–78, 86, 94, 101–103, 107, 121–122, 137–139, 141–142, 148, 153–154, 161, 163–166, 168–169, 170–173, 181–182
— making of the rust 69
— of nature 148
—, base of the 163
—, books of the 161, 163
—, comes from a single one 111
—, divine 148, 169
—, finishing of 121
—, first 121
—, hidden secret 155
—, secret (of this) 155, 181
—, tiresome 138
—, water as operator of 173
working 21, 43, 46, 112, 115, 123, 142, 150, 152, 168, 171, 177
world 11, 19, 21, 23–24, 26–27, 30–31, 36, 38, 41, 43–47, 55, 65, 67–69, 85, 100–102, 104, 108, 113, 116, 118, 126, 139, 142, 149, 153, 155–156, 159, 165, 167–168, 175, 179
— of appearances 159
— of human consciousness 153
—, Christian 23, 108
—, detachment from the 101, 139
—, end of the 19, 69
—, Hermetic–Gnostic 30
—, inner 41, 44, 47, 142, 149, 155
—, Islamic 26
—, new 11, 47
—, outer 43, 142, 149
—, symbolic 149
—, this middle 175
—, unitary (*unus mundus*) 30, 159
—, Western 31
worshipping 135
— worship (n, vb) 17, 30, 103, 172

- Y -

Yama 157
yang and yin 85
year —, every 73
—, son of the 73–74, 125
— years 8, 10, 32, 38, 51, 55, 75
yellow 93, 125, 127, 132, 169, 173–174
— marcasite 132
— one 173
yellowness 174
yoga 15–16, 21–23, 36, 39, 64, 69, 95
—, Indian 16
—, Tantra 21–23, 95
—, Taoist 16, 69
yogi 21
youth —, laughing 105
—, Oriental 120
—, ploughing 120
Yudhisthira 157

- Z -

Zadith ben Hamuel; *see* Ibn Umail
Zadith Senior; *see also* Ibn Umail 7, 11, 15, 38–39, 46
Zaida 34
zandarīǧ 91, 117
Zarathustra 118
Zetzner 55
Zeus 18–19
zinc 61, 65–66, 132–133
— ore 66, 133
—, marinal white 132
zodiac 74, 105, 124–125
— zodiacal symbolism 125
—, twelve houses of the 125
Zosimos of Panopolis 10, 16–17, 20–22, 51, 53, 59–60, 62–65, 68, 71, 75, 79, 97, 119, 127, 155, 157, 177

3. Glossary

albedo	Latin alchemical term for making the arcane substance white.
anima	Personification of the feminine nature of a man's unconscious. The anima manifests most typically in personified form as figures in dreams and fantasies ('dream girl'), or in the irrationalities of a man's feelings.
animus	Personification of the masculine nature of a woman's unconscious. The animus manifests most typically in personified form as figures in dreams and fantasies ('dream lover'), or in the irrationalities of woman's thinking.
aqua divina	Latin term for the divine water.
aqua permanens	Latin term for the eternal water.
aqua sapientiae	Latin term for the water of wisdom, a name of the divine water.
aurora	Latin term for the dawning of the sun.
citrinitas	Latin alchemical term for making the arcane substance yellow.
cognitio matutina	Morning knowledge
cognitio vespertina	Evening knowledge
coniunctio oppositorum	Latin term for the union of the opposites.
creatio continua	Latin term for 'continuing creation'; it expresses the idea that creation is an ongoing process, and that it continues even today.

hierosgamos	Holy wedding
lavatio	Latin alchemical term standing for a process of purification.
nigredo	Latin alchemical term for making the arcane substance black. Psychological term for confusion, disorientation or depression.
opus	Latin term for work, standing for the alchemical work.
prima materia	Latin alchemical term for the first substance, the original arcane substance.
rubedo	Latin alchemical term for making the arcane substance red.
self	Term used by C. G. Jung, standing for the central archetype. It is supraordinate to the conscious ego. It embraces not only the conscious but also the unconscious psyche. It is the centre of this totality, just as the ego is the centre of consciousness.
separatio	Latin alchemical term for separating.
unus mundus	Latin alchemical term used by the alchemist Dorneus (16th century) for the unity of the psycho-material reality.

4. Diacritical Signs: Pronunciation

ʾ	glottal stop
ā	long a
ṯ	th, unvoiced, as in ‘thing’
ğ	voiced g, as in ‘gentleman’
ḥ	aspirated h, pronounced in the back of the throat
ḫ	fricative h, as in Scottish ‘loch’
ḏ	voiced th, as in ‘there’
š	sh, unvoiced, as in ‘sheep’
ṣ	dark s
ḍ	dark d
ṭ	dark t
ẓ	dark z
ʿ	very deep a, pronounced in the throat
ġ	gutteral r
ū	long u
ī	long i